ACPL ITEM
DISCARDED

SO-EEK-566

Mailing list services on
your home-based PC

Mailing List Your Home-

Windcrest® / McGraw-Hill

New York   San Francisco   Washington, D.C.   Auckland   Bogotá
Caracas   Lisbon   London   Madrid   Mexico City   Milan
Montreal   New Delhi   San Juan   Singapore
Sidney   Tokyo   Toronto

Services on Based PC

Linda Rohrbough

FIRST EDITION
FIRST PRINTING

©1994 by **Windcrest.**
Published by Windcrest , an imprint of McGraw-Hill, Inc.
The name "Windcrest" is a registered trademark of McGraw-Hill, Inc.

Library of Congress Cataloging-in-Publication Data
Rohrbough, Linda
    Mailing list sevices on your home-based PC/ by Linda Rohrbough.
       p.   cm.
    Includes index
ISBN 0-8306-4473-3 (H)   ISBN 0-8306-4474-1 (P)
    1. Mailing list services industry—United states. 2. New business
enterprises—United States. 3. Microcomputers—United States
I. Title.
HF5863.R64   1993   93-29458
65.13'3 —dc 20   CIP

Acquisitions editor: Brad J. Schepp
Editorial team: Sandra J. Bottomley, Book Editor
                Joanne M. Slike, Excutive Editor
                Joann Woy, Indexer
Production team: Katherine G. Brown, Director
                Susan E. Hansford, Coding
                Patsy D. Harne, Layout
                Tara Ernst, Proofreading
Design team: Jaclyn J. Boone, Designer
                Brian Allison, Associate Designer
Cover design: Lori E. Schlosser   EPC1
Marble paper border courtesy of Douglas M. Parks, Blue Ridge Summit, Pa.   4439

To Mark

Contents

3 Getting started   54

4 Tools of the trade   82

Introduction

Have you been approached about a great business opportunity lately? Work your own hours, be your own boss, small investment, unlimited income potential, ground floor opportunity—just sign here.

I'm embarrassed to admit I've fallen for those schemes where the only one who benefits is the guy who got me signed up. He hooked me because I really want all those things, but what I didn't want was to impose myself on my friends, relatives, and acquaintances. I want to do something. . . well. . . something "real." Of course, the "real" things that everyone knows are successful require you to be successful to get into them. A McDonald's restaurant franchise has never failed, but if you had that kind of money, you wouldn't be here, looking over this book.

The problem with new opportunities is they don't look like much. Anyone with 20-20 hindsight can look back and say, "Yep, if I had bought IBM stock in 1961, I'd be a rich man now." But the time to catch a wave is before it reaches its crest, not after everyone on the beach can tell it's a big wave. That's what this book is about.

A revolution in business is sweeping the United States. Growth in home-based businesses has been occurring since 1987 and up to 31 million people were estimated to be working at home by the end of 1992. The personal computer is a big part of the revolution, making it possible for a new breed of entrepreneur. You might be one of this new breed even if you're one of the casualties of the recession, someone looking to get out of the corporate rat-race, a young person who doesn't want to pursue college, or even someone who has a business now and is looking for a profitable "back room" operation.

The mailing list service business could be your ticket. The income potential is six figures, according to the mailing pioneers who are out there beginning to ride the wave. The business itself requires the smallest investment of almost any computer business, some know-how, and determination.

While the investment and the determination will have to be yours, the know-how is here in seven chapters.

Chapter 1 explains how two forces, the United States Government and the recession, are creating the need for mailing list service businesses. The United States Postal Service (USPS) is creating a wave of demand expected to rise sharply in the next two to three years. The year 1995 is when the USPS has said it plans to require mail to conform to its automated systems.

However, the wave is also being created by businesses themselves who are facing the need to get more customers, yet cut costs. One of the major ways to do so is to offer better service and promotion via, you got it, mailing lists.

Chapter 2 is devoted to explaining what mailing list services do and ways to give your business that first critical push, then keep it going. Topics include: finding customers in everyday places, building marketable lists, competitive pricing, and protecting your investment from mail list thieves.

Working with the United States Postal Service is the focus of chapter 3. All the information you'd expect about mailing is offered including: how the current system works, how you can prepare mail to get discounts, the standards for preparing mail pieces for postal automation, and insider tips on working with the post office. But more importantly, you will find contact information, as well as special programs offered by the United States Postal Service to help you.

Once you've gotten customers, chapter 4 will help you with the tips and tricks of direct marketing to make your customer's mailing successful. And, of course, the more successful your customers are, the more business you'll earn for yourself.

The fifth chapter is about the tools you need to get the business going, including getting a computer or perhaps using one you already have, as well as an explanation of the type of computer programs that are needed.

Chapter 6 offers critical information for setting up the mail list information itself in a general format called a *database*. Included are illustrations and information on how to set up a database to prevent getting "boxed in" as well as how to get around the "boxes" your clients might have built in their information.

Chapter 7 outlines ways to leverage your investment by offering other, related services to your customers.

Finally, the appendices are full of additional resources and help on the subject of mail and direct marketing, including toll-free numbers, information that will help you with mailing, information to help you add value to your mailing lists, USPS resources, publications, conference information, vendors, and other aids.

So here's something "real," the crest of a breaking wave of opportunity. The stories, from personal interviews, of those who are already out in the surf are offered here as well. And they really do tell you their secrets.

Here's to you, in the hope you'll catch the wave.

1 The opportunity

"There is one thing stronger than all the armies in the world, and that is an idea whose time has come."

— Victor Hugo

The mailing list service is a business opportunity almost anyone can learn. It is a perfect business to operate from home, and the variety of services that can be offered can be tailored both to the individual running the business and to the community the business serves. The business of doing all or even some aspects of the task of sending critical materials through a delivery system like the United States Postal Service might not sound like a particularly lucrative endeavor. But even an individual who can use a computer can process, correct, and speed up the mail, and do so much cheaper than it can be done by hand. If that weren't enough, the income potential for performing these services can put an individual into the upper 20 percent of income earners in the United States.

Two forces are driving the need for mailing list services. One is the work force cuts coupled with automation at the United States Post Office and the other is recession-driven businesses who are looking for less expensive alternatives to mailing or want to expand their customer base.

The need for mail list services

The United States Postal Service (USPS), the most efficiently run mail delivery organization in the world, is in crisis. Increases in the amount of mail, increased expenses, and competition from other delivery sources has forced the USPS to take advantage of modern technology. In a sense, the USPS's move into modern technology is forcing everyone else into the same technology as well.

The need to reduce costs

The volume of mail the USPS has been handling has increased significantly every year since 1970 to an all time high of 166.3 billion pieces in 1990 (FIG. 1-1). The recession and the increase in postage are being blamed for the cutback in the total volume of mail processed in 1991 to 165.9 billion pieces, but this was the first slowdown in 15 years. Estimates are the 1991 flow of mail was reduced by 450 million pieces, a 0.3 percent drop. But compared to the last recessionary drop in mail of 832 million pieces of mail, driven by the oil crisis in 1975, this reduction is a minor one as shown in the comparison in FIG. 1-2.

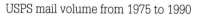

USPS mail volume from 1975 to 1990

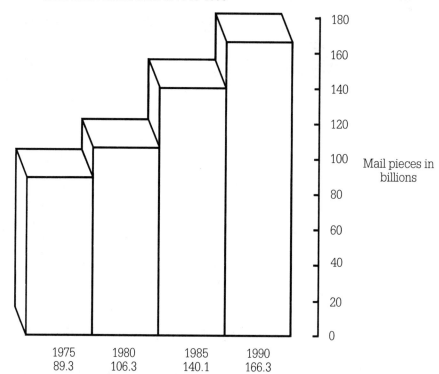

Mail pieces in billions

	1975	1980	1985	1990
	89.3	106.3	140.1	166.3

1-1

The volume of mail the USPS has been handling has increased significantly every year since 1970 to an all-time high of 166.3 billion pieces in 1990.

The real crisis for the USPS is the sudden burden of having to carry an additional $2.4 billion of additional costs for retiree health and cost-of-living (COLA) benefits. This is due to the Omnibus Budget Reconciliation Act of 1990 (OBRA) enacted by Congress. The USPS says it might have to pick up the tab on an additional $9 billion in similar costs through 1995 from OBRAs passed in 1985, 1987, 1989, and 1990.

The USPS is facing hard times by implementing cost-cutting measures which include automation. More mail can be processed with fewer personnel when machines are doing the work.

Comparison change in total mail volume
in recession years

1975 compared to 1991

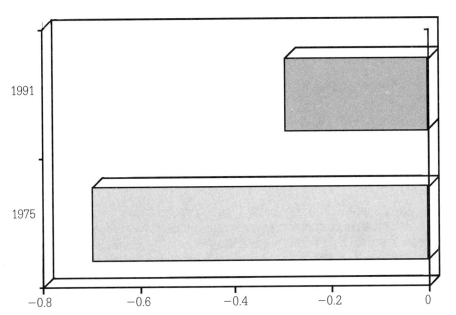

1-2
The recession driven drop in mail volume in 1991 of 3 percent compared to the recessionary drop in mail volume of 7 percent in 1975 due to the oil crisis.

The savings from automation are dramatic, according to Senior Assistant Postmaster General Richard Strasser, who said sorting and distributing 1000 letters by hand costs the Postal Service over $42, but processing the same 1000 letters with automated equipment can cost as little as $3. Those USPS cost-cutting measures can put money in your pocket if you are in the business of offering mailing list services.

The least expensive piece of automation equipment is a barcode reader. A barcode is a translation of numbers into coded lines that a computer can read with speed and accuracy. The post office has come up with a numbering system that gives each delivery point a unique 11 digit numeric code. That code, when translated into a barcode, allows machines to handle the mail. However, for a postal machine to process mail, it has to have a barcode printed on it. If the senders of the mail can't or won't prebarcode the mail, the mail processing facility has to do it.

The stated goal of the USPS is to have 40 percent of all mail barcoded by the sender by 1995, a process that requires a computer. To motivate the effort, any help the USPS gets, it rewards financially. As Norma Pace, the chairman of the U.S. Postal Service's board of governors put it: "If you do a little bit more, we'll charge you a little bit less."

A little bit less may not seem like much, but multiplied times the billions of pieces of mail the USPS processes, it is a sizable amount. Right now the post office offers discounts of as much as 10 percent on mail that is prepared to save it processing time. Ten percent of each first-class mail piece is $.029 or almost $.03.

Even though each piece of mail is not sent first-class, let's say mailing list services saved $.03 on each piece of the 166.3 billion pieces of mail processed in 1990. That adds up to a savings of $4,980,000,000. If you make that savings just $.01 each, the total is still a staggering $1,663,000,000.

As proof of the profitability of the postal incentives, the USPS was awarded the "Innovator of the Year" in 1991 from Xplor International for its automation technology. Xplor said it and its member firms estimate a savings of $1 billion annually—up to 21 percent of their postage costs—because of the implementation of the postal discounts for automation. What this means is, in many cases, businesses can afford to pay a mailing list service to help them with mail processing and still come out money ahead.

Only an estimated 20 percent of the mail is hand addressed. The vast majority of mail is business or advertising mail that could probably have been sent for less with help from a mailing list service. Now the USPS wants to get small- and medium-volume businesses mailers, defined as those who do less than $100,000 a year in postal revenue, to start preparing their mail for automation.

The need to increase revenues

But the push for efficiency on the part of the USPS isn't the only force increasing the demand for mailing list services. The recession is forcing businesses to provide more and better service. Common advice for business survival is to build a mailing list of customers in order to offer them incentives to come back.

Businesses are also discovering their best source for potential new business is customers who have already used their services. *Adweek's Marketing Week*, the May 11, 1992, edition illustrated this point with a case study of a bank, Corestates Financial Corporation of Philadelphia. The bank did a mass mailing in 1989 offering home equity loans to 100,000 homeowners whose names were bought from a direct-mail list broker. The response rate was 2 percent or 2000 responses, which is a good response rate for a purchased list. However, in 1990, the bank made the same offer by mail to only 20,000 of its own customers who own homes and received 2200 applications—an 11 percent response.

Direct mailers have known for some time that mailings to an existing customer base are more effective than mailings to a new customer base. But who has time to do these mailings and run a business?

Stan Golomb has built a successful mailing list service business in which he leverages his knowledge of the dry-cleaning business gained from his former job of selling advertising space in dry cleaning trade journals. *Direct Marketing* reported in its March 1992 issue in an article entitled "The Man With The Plan" that Golomb got the idea from an article about how a supermarket built its business by compiling a direct mail list gathered from customer's checks.

Golomb calls his tactics in mailing a "battering ram" that will break down the resistance of any customer. He mails millions of advertising pieces for dry cleaners around the US every year, and his clients are enthusiastic about his work. The owner of Bel-Aire Cleaners in Fremont, Ohio, says Golomb's mailings have quadrupled the company's sales over the last ten years. The Willowbrook Athletic Club in Willowbrook, Illinois, wrote him this testimonial: "Your direct mail attracts 10 times the number of people as all other means of external advertising combined. I originally thought direct mail was too expensive, but it is the only promotional plan that more than pays for itself each and every time we mail. It is unquestionably the best use of my advertising dollar."

Stan Golomb
Golomb Group Productions, Willowbrook, Illinois

Profile

Stan Golomb used to sell advertising in the back of trade journals before he hit on the idea of combining his wide range of knowledge and experience with mailing services. After 13 years, he now mails millions of advertising pieces for dry cleaners around the US every year and loves doing it. His customers love it, too.

He went out on his own by offering a weekly newsletter to small independent dry cleaners on how to grow their business. Stan said he wrote a promotional letter, included his picture, and asked, "Would you hire this man for $10 per week?" He sent the letter to 500 prospects and got back 40 subscriptions for $100 each. His newsletter was launched.

Stan didn't stop there. Instead of just telling dry cleaners how to increase their business, he decided he would start a service to do it for them. He printed an inexpensive brochure designed to sell dry cleaners on his idea, which he calls "Stan's Plan." To encourage businesses to sign up, Stan describes his plan like this:

Say you have a market of 2000 homes in your immediate area. Perhaps you do business with 500 customers. This means your market share is 25 percent. It also means you're not doing business with 75 percent of the residents.

Stan's Plan is designed to break down the resistance of the 75 percent noncustomers. This relentless, constant battering will increase your share of the marketplace. A 10 percent increase in market share equates to 200 additional customers and over a 40 percent increase in annual sales.

He also explains that one-fifth of the population in their area moves every year, so there's an opportunity to attract that 20 percent as well.

Stan offers to do everything: supplying the names, printing, addressing, mailing, maintaining, and cleaning the list which he guarantees is accurate and up-to-date. He also submits the mailing piece to the dry cleaner for approval.

When a dry cleaner signs up, Stan goes into action to determine the size of the market and where the traffic is coming from. He first purchases demographic information about the residences within two to three miles of the dry cleaner. (If a dry cleaner signs up in an area where Stan already has a client, Stan turns it down. He says he doesn't pit cleaners against each other.)

Stan knows, the more affluent the area, the more the average household spends on dry cleaning. The range of potential weekly business can be anywhere from $0.10 per household to $6 per household depending on the demographics of the neighborhood. For example, white collar-workers, who wear dress clothes to work, tend to spend more on cleaning than blue collar- workers. If the demographics reveal there are 10,000 homes in the area and the potential is $3 per household, then that's a $30,000-a-week market potential. That means a cleaner in that area doing $3000 a week only has 10 percent of the potential market.

The second part of the research is to determine the direction of the traffic, or where people are coming from. This is done by placing a map on the counter divided into four sections and having each customer place an "X" in the section they live in. Stan says the majority of traffic usually comes from one of the four sections and that's where he concentrates his mailing efforts.

The mailing is ongoing. At the end of each three-month cycle an automatic repeat of coverage is in effect. Some customers have been using this program since its inception in 1986. If the client is backing up the product or service they are selling, they will eventually dominate their market. They also automatically pick up the lion's share of the newcomer business, because these new residents are being contacted within months of their arrival.

All mailings are addressed to occupant due to an estimated 20 percent turnover of residents. The entire job is done in full-color, specially designed 4-by-6" postcards using first-class presort rates.

Stan has expanded his mailing programs to include supermarkets, dentists, health clubs, and restaurants. His work has been so successful that one particular health club with fifty locations in the US does half a million dollars worth of business with Stan each year. In addition, he's just published a book, *How To Find, Capture, and Keep Customers* (Raphel Publishing 1993).

Mailing is also being advocated in order to attract new customers. The January 1992 issue of *Nation's Business* said while the business outlook is grim, small businesses can survive in part by building a mailing list, and then using mail to offer special bargains to attract customers.

Just attracting new customers to come into established businesses isn't the only outlet for direct mail. A growing number of people are shopping by mail. The Direct Marketing Association says 52.6 percent, or more than half the adult population in the United States, ordered merchandise by phone or mail in 1991. These people spent an estimated $25 to $35 billion on catalog purchases alone. And where did they find out about the goods and services available to them? Many received the information by mail, of course.

Even accountants are getting into direct mail. In an article from the September 21, 1992 issue of *Accounting Today* entitled "Healthcare Rules Open Marketing Opportunities," author Brenda Geist says accountants should be educating themselves in specifics about the healthcare industry and then making their skills known to potential healthcare clients via direct mailings, seminars, brochures, and newsletters.

Much of the advice to businesses is to hold back on hiring, but market more aggressively. While direct mail is effective, many businesses just don't have the time or the expertise to keep up. That's another opportunity for mailing list service businesses. A.G. Pitsilos, Bethlehem, Pennsylvania-based owner of mailing list service TechImages, Inc., said: "I allow my customers to concentrate on doing the business of their business."

What they are mailing

A quick look in your own mailbox will tell you some of the things being mailed. However, the study of what is being mailed and by whom is a complete topic in itself. In fact, an entire publication, *Who's Mailing What*, is dedicated to the topic and published by the editor of *Target Marketing* magazine. What is being mailed is studied by the magazine who has people all over the country sending in their mail.

Not everything being mailed has to do with advertising. Informational materials are being mailed to people expecting the information. Nonprofit groups are mailing information to members, informational newsletters that focus on specific subjects are mailed, software is updated via disks sent through the mail, magazines are mailed, and companies are mailing information to employees in the field. In addition, there's the entire field of bills being sent through the mail for services, and not just by large companies but by small ones as well. Answering services, cellular phone services, beeper and pager services, housekeeping services, gardeners, pool maintenance, and a myriad of other services often bill once a month by mail. Mailing list services handle much of this material in the form of letters, postcards, envelopes of varying sizes, disk mailers, folded materials such as newsletters and flyers, and promotional materials in containers of varying sizes and shapes.

Benefits of the mail list business

There's certainly a need for mailing list services, but what's in it for you? Can you really make a living doing this? Will it cost a lot to get started?

High income potential

The income potential is as high as six figures, according to those operating mailing list services. Many of the smaller, home-based services were bringing in $40,000 annually, some of the more successful ones were doing $70,000 to $80,000 a year, and some are bringing in six-figure net incomes. Some of the larger operations have moved out of their homes, but several of the services have simply turned the garage into the business space and continue to do everything from home.

In fact, the business is so lucrative, some mailing list services I was referred to did not want to contribute to this book when they discovered it was to be a "how-to" book. Many of the business owners were quite frank and simply said they just didn't want any competition.

In general, most of the mailing list services thought $20,000 is a reasonable gross income estimate working full-time in the first year. The second year, that figure can double and depending on how hard you work and how many customers you can keep, it can keep doubling each year. One estimate was an established mailing list service should be able to gross $125,000 to $150,000 per person. However, all the services said it was important to have some other means of support if you're starting from scratch. Working for a direct mail operation is also helpful in starting your own mailing list service and has the advantage that you get paid while you learn.

It's home based

Of course, the advantages to starting a business out of your home are substantial. The biggest advantage is avoiding extra expenses. You have to live somewhere, so making that extra bedroom or turning the breakfast nook into an office for the business doesn't cause you to incur any additional fixed expenses. Avoiding fixed expenses, such as additional rent, can give you the edge it takes to get your business going.

Also, if an entire room is dedicated to the business, that portion of the total expense of the housing, including rent or house payment, utilities, insurance, and so on may be deducted as a business expense. (Check with an accountant to be sure the expenses you deduct are within the guidelines of the Internal Revenue Service rules.)

Even without deductions, for many, the savings gained from not incurring gasoline, automobile maintenance, clothes, child care, and eating out expenses associated with working elsewhere allows them to justify a lower income to get started. I've seen several families with one spouse working a regular job, begin a home-based business together to earn extra income and avoid the expenses associated with working outside the home.

Also, an added factor is that businesses started out of an individual's home have a higher probability of succeeding. Without the monstrous debt load and pressures business owners face who borrow start-up money in the form of business loans, your home-based business has more time to become established and offers you more time to learn the nuances of your particular niche.

The downside is your business is difficult to get away from. Working from home often means you don't leave the office, and you might work more hours just because the work is there. Time management and family issues become more of a concern when working from home. One way to handle this problem is to simply establish office hours and get an answering machine to take the calls at odd hours. This also looks more professional.

As for investment, this is the business with the lowest investment of any I know of, and my research bears that out. Realistically, if you don't have a computer already, you'll need $2500 to $6000 to buy the equipment and software you need to start. While there are always more items you can purchase, the more expensive equipment and software can be purchased out of the profits once your business has grown enough to justify the expense. A more detailed breakdown of the costs is provided throughout the book.

Only requires a small investment

I interviewed people who approached the mailing list service business in many ways, each using their individual strengths to their advantage and making the business fit their particular interests and lifestyle. In the strictest sense the mailing list service, sometimes called a service bureau, is the computer end of mailing. The work that requires knowledge of the computer, including processing addresses and maintaining the mailing lists, falls into the service bureau category. The manual labor end is termed *letter shop*. This includes folding mailing pieces, collating and inserting into the envelopes, addressing the envelope, affixing postage, sorting, and delivery to the post office.

Many flavors to choose from

These services overlap, especially in the smaller mailing list service, because the operator can often produce the labels in the order necessary for sorting, so no further sorting is needed. A similar service can be offered for the printing of envelopes. Also, letter shop work may involve receiving the mailing list on disk, and using a computer to sort and print the list with barcodes before any manual labor is done.

Some mailing list services have customers who want to keep the list but allow the service to produce the labels, others who bring the labels already generated, and still others who want the mailing list service to keep all the information, including keying in new or changed information as it comes in. Some mailing list services only take lists in an electronic format, and they limit their services to what they can do with the computer alone.

Mailing list services also have the flexibility to work when it is convenient for them, as long as they get the job done. One grandmother likes to take late afternoons off to spend with her grandchildren, while another young man who works alone says there just aren't enough hours in the day to do all he wants to accomplish.

Several mailing list service businesses said one of the biggest selling points for them was they could offer the services the customer wanted and give more personal attention to each customer's mailing. Shirley Grose of West Hills, California-based Totally Automated Service does a good deal of collating mailing pieces for her customers as well as preparing labels. She customizes her services to do exactly what her customers need, and her attention to detail for each client has kept her business growing for several years. Each business said some of their customers preferred to maintain their own lists, while other customers wanted the mailing service to do the work of maintaining the lists, and some wanted services somewhere in between.

Cleaning large lists can be profitable for companies who do very large mailings of several thousand to a million or more. Many large firms turn their lists and lists they purchase over to a mailing service who checks for duplicates and corrects errors.

Other mailing list services are brokers for people with mailing lists. They have access to unusual, hard-to-get lists, or specific niche lists and get a commission each time the list is rented. List rental is a profitable business, and some companies make several million dollars a year simply from the reuse of their own customer lists.

Still other mailing list services have built their own lists by taking information available to everyone, such as the "Doing Business As" or DBA statements of new or changing businesses published in the local newspaper. What makes their lists more valuable is they add information to the list by cross-referencing it with another list, adding the phone numbers or fax numbers, and making calls to ask for additional information.

Millions of businesses need help

An estimated 7.5 million small-to-medium firms are currently doing volume mailings and are targeted by the USPS as in need of help to increase the efficiency of their mail for automation. That doesn't count the firms that would start mailing if they could see how it would benefit them to do so.

Even large corporations will use mailing list services as they move from expensive mainframe computers to smaller workstation and personal computers. Many companies are strangling in their own bureaucracy. The Management Information Systems (MIS) department that runs the computer system in large companies is traditionally viewed as expensive, slow, and unresponsive.

Most corporate employees will tell you getting a single report out of the MIS department often takes months and thousands of dollars. Corporations, in allocating costs, require each department be charged for internal services provided by other departments, just as though they went outside the corporation to get the work done. The purpose of this is to accurately track costs to see what's profitable and what isn't. This has sparked a new trend called *outsourcing* in which departments in corporations are sending work out to various types of smaller companies, including mailing list services, who are quicker, cost less, and are more responsive than the company's internal resources. Outsourcing is an especially attractive option in the cases where the information needs to be processed quickly, such as sales leads that come in from advertising or order fulfillment.

For example, a large insurance company might use a mailing list service to speedily move leads from advertising to their agents in the field. The mailing list service receives the leads as they come in, puts them into the computer, and then faxes a daily lead list to the company's agents in the field. That same procedure might take literally weeks for the insurance company's MIS department who is overloaded with tasks required by upper management, but can now be done in a day or less. It is not hard to see how sitting on leads for agents could cost the company money and why a company such as the one in our example, would outsource the work.

A profitable addition to an existing business

A mailing list service business can also be an opportunity for established businesses to increase their income base or offer more services. Katie Allegato, owner of Allegato and Associates in Kissimmee, Florida, uses her mailing list service business as a springboard to get clients for her desktop publishing services. Especially if there's already a computer in the back room, a mailing list service business makes for an excellent addition to a desktop publishing operation, a bookkeeping business, a print shop, or other types of businesses where the customers might have a list of clients to communicate with.

Profile

Katie Allegato
Allegato and Associates, Kissimmee, Florida

Katie says she was working for a company that did a lot of marketing when she saw an opportunity to serve smaller businesses with mailing lists. She noted that the large company she worked for could afford to buy thousands of names at a time, but smaller companies were unable to find the lists of 500 to 2500 they needed.

To start the mailing list service, Katie approached small hotels and offered to maintain their lists of travel agents. After checking prices with other firms doing similar work, she bid a little below the competition and offered more. For example, while others charged for changes and deletions, Katie offered those services at no charge.

She also watched her advertising mail, and one day got a very good lead from a hand-addressed coupon. A call to the company revealed the coupon was part of a 10,000-piece mailing, all done by hand. Katie offered her services and was hired.

Allegato and Associates also builds and sells lists, both business and residential, for a three-county area. Katie checks her lists against directories from the phone company, such as the reverse phone book, which offers residential and business listings by address. One selling point for her residential lists is the occupant's name is offered instead of "resident." To target specific areas, Katie has developed a coding system so she knows what street and what area the listing is in. In this way, she can target an area right down to a specific street for businesses, such as a newly opened video store, who only want to mail to potential customers in their immediate area.

Business lists are constantly changing in her fast-growing area and Katie says she has to literally drive around to get the new businesses opening up and closing. In addition, she gets local new business license listings by going down to the county courthouse. She pays for the listings and in some counties can even get phone numbers, which she can also sell as a hard copy listing. The hard copy listing allows clients to do follow-up phone calls after a mailing goes out. The drawback to county lists where Katie lives is the business identification codes used by the county are different from the SIC codes used by the U.S. Department of Commerce. Because the county codes serve the same function as the SIC codes, Katie says it's not really a problem for her.

Gathering more information about the businesses on the lists makes the lists more valuable. Even small distinctions, such as restaurants with lounges or restaurants without lounges, make a difference, Katie maintains. "Customers want specific information in the lists they're buying."

Fast service is important. Katie can usually deliver labels to a customer from lists she maintains in 24 hours. She also offers the ability to sort the list by any of the items entered. This means the program used needs to be flexible. After working with a mail list program, Katie had to switch to a database program and recommends new users start with a database because it offers more flexibility.

Yellow Pages advertising is important, and Katie gets about a call a week from her ad under "Mail Lists." However, those calls bring referrals, which turn into more business as well.

As far as selling customers, Katie relies heavily on her experience in marketing and feels she can be pretty convincing. However, she doesn't try to sell her service if she feels it wouldn't be "cost justified" for the business in question. The way she judges if her services will be beneficial is by looking at the volume of mail possible and the workload of the current staff. If she feels they can do better themselves, she says so.

In addition to mailing, Allegato and Associates offer other services. For example, Katie mentioned doing inventory lists for a gift shop where she inputs and maintains the items, the cost, the retail price, and the number on hand to generate a monthly report. Other services Katie offers include training courses in the use of the software she uses as well as selling the software herself. She also offers consulting services on a one-on-one basis. Also, Katie uses her mailing list service as a springboard for her desktop publishing services.

Starting from home was a real advantage in the beginning, Katie asserts. She cautions newcomers to the mailing list service that it is easy to grow too fast and overlook your own limitations. Prompt, accurate service can be sacrificed if the mailing list service doesn't try to grow deliberately, instead of overnight. "You have to keep in mind, you're not only building a mailing list service, but you're building a reputation for this service."

The main benefit

The most important opportunity is mailing list services are based on information about people and people are always changing. People get married, divorced, find different interests, age, move, have children, grandchildren, join clubs, and so on. Estimates are that just the people living in a given physical area may change by as much as 20 percent or more a year.

Also businesses face change. They start, expand, partner with other business, change their product lines, offer new phone numbers, are sold, move, grow, and so on. The USPS recognizes variation in this arena is constant and so the largest and most lucrative mail discounts currently are for mailings which have been recently updated and are generated by computer.

What change means for mailing list services is a constant flow of work and an opportunity that increases with each passing year. So dig in. You're on your way to your own financial independence.

References

Gibbons, Kent. "Lessons for tough times—and better times." January 1992. *Nation's Business*, v80 (n1): p16.

Geist, Brenda. "Healthcare Rules Open Marketing Opportunities." September 21, 1992. *Accounting Today*, v6 (n18): p18(2).

Raphel, Murray. "The man with the plan: direct mail programs of Stan Golomb." March 1992. *Direct Marketing*, v54 (n11): p38(2).

Berry, Jon. "The rich and the worthy: America's banks are taking direct marketing one step further." May 11, 1992. *Adweek's Marketing Week*, v33 (n19): p14(4).

US Department of Commerce. 1992. *Statistical Abstract of the United States*. Washington, DC: US Government Printing Office.

2 The postal system & mailing list services

"Our goal is the lowest combined mailer and Postal Service costs in preparing and delivering mail. To achieve this goal, we plan to have a barcode on all letter mail and all non-carrier route presort flat mail by the end of 1995—either by you (with rate incentives) or by us."

— Anthony M. Frank, Postmaster General
September 26, 1988

Our country has the most efficient mail service of any country in the world. The USPS processes more mail per employee workyear than any other country, including Japan, yet has the lowest postage rates of any country. A massive operation, over 47 billion stamps were printed in 1991 and sold in some 40,000 post offices, stations, and branches nationwide.

While the USPS is a world leader now, it didn't start out that way. Our present mail system has its roots in Europe, but mail delivery is a time-honored practice that only relatively recently in history became available to everyone. We'll take a look at the history of the post office, discuss the current postal system, then take a look at how you can prepare mail to get discounts, and offer you insider tips used by professional mailers. You'll also find out about the special services available to you, including reference materials, videotapes, and special programs offered by the USPS to help you.

The history of the post office

Mail delivery has been around for centuries. The Mesopotamians had a mail delivery system, and the Bible talks about delivery of written notices sealed with the king's seal. In centuries past, only the ruling class, such as kings and government officials, had the convenience of mail delivery.

The roots of the present system

The roots of our present system in the United States go back to Great Britain. Thomas Witherings, Chief Postmaster in the 1600s in England is called a "great British postal reformer" and is credited with getting the proclamation of 1637 implemented, which banned the carriage of letters by anyone other than employees of the King's Postmaster-General. That ruling is still being upheld in the United States today, as the United States Postal Service has a legally imposed monopoly on the delivery of private mail.

In 1660, the first post office, known as the General Letter Office, was said to have started and mail was hardly addressed with the precision it is today. According to *Stamps, Posts and Postmarks* by Ian Angus, letters were commonly addressed like the following: "To the right worll. [worshipful] Nicholas ffuller Phelder Esquire at his house called Chamberhouse give these."

Problems cropped up right off the bat and by 1661 the General Letter Office issued an announcement that a Post Mark, known by collectors as the "Bishop Mark," would be applied to mail when it was received. The announcement, made in the April 1661 issue of Mercurius Publicus was, "And to prevent any neglect of the Letter-Caryers in the speedy delivery of Letters, from the said Office; Its notifyed that the days of the recept of every letter at the Office is printed upon the Letter and the Letter-Carryers ought to deliver them the same day in the Summer, and the next morning at farthest in the Winter and if any fayler be complayned of at the post office, it shall be redressed."

I don't have any proof, but I'm guessing the introduction of the Post Mark was preceded by the introduction of that time honored phrase, "The check is in the mail." Timely delivery was just as much an issue then as it is today.

Franking, the practice of sending correspondence without postage, was the only method used in the beginning, as all mail was exclusively used by government officials. It was later decided the general public could be allowed to use mail service but were to be charged for the use of it. At that time it became necessary to distinguish between mail sent by individuals and government mail.

Sending mail was not cheap. In the 1830s, it cost 14 pence to send a letter between 400 and 500 miles, such as from London to Glasgow. In the light of the fact that many workers only earned a few pence a week, the cost of sending mail was high indeed.

Rowland Hill, a school teacher, was one of the strongest advocates of postal reform. He is credited with the introduction of the postage stamp. Hill said in 1832 it was not the distance the mail traveled but the cumbersome method of mail handling that made mail expensive and a single rate based on weight should be established. Prepayment was recommended by Hill in the form of a postage stamp, described as "a piece of paper just large enough to bear the stamp, and covered at the back with a glutinous wash, which the bringer might, by applying a little moisture, attach to the back of the letter." Hill was knighted because of this idea, and the first postage stamp was introduced in 1847.

Of course, once there were stamps, the post office had to come up with a way to indicate the stamp had no value once used to mail a letter. Canceling was introduced and was performed by hand.

Efforts to use machines to speed up postal processes go back to 1857. In that year Pearson Hill, son of Roland Hill, invented a machine that could postmark letters at the rate of 118 per minute. The machine had problems at first, but the idea caught on and the post office has been trying to further automate its mail handling processes ever since.

In the American colonies in the 1700s, Benjamin Franklin was appointed the first Postmaster General. One of the early users of direct mail for his publications and pamphlets, Franklin is credited for making the postal system take root in the young United States.

Use of the postal system has been increasing since its introduction. This is evident in postal revenues which increased rapidly in the United States after the War for Independence from $37,935 in 1790 to $1,707,000 in 1829. The post office has been continually offering improvements, such as free collection using mail boxes, free delivery in cities, and rural free delivery. Rural free delivery is said to be the candle that sparked the introduction of catalog sales pioneers such as Montgomery Ward and Sears, Roebuck.

Full mechanization took root in the U.S. Postal System in the 1950s but machine handling reached its peak efficiency in the 1970s. As mail volumes increased, mechanization wasn't enough and the Postal Service began looking into ways to automate using computer technology.

Postal reform continued with the Postal Reorganization Act of 1970 which made the post office a government-owned corporation called the United States Postal Service. The Postal Reorganization Act also prevents Congress from establishing postal tariffs or controlling employee's salaries, permitted the post office to raise capital to modernize its equipment and buildings, and made the post office subject to competition from private companies in certain areas, which helped in the introduction of one of the first overnight delivery services; Federal Express started in 1973.

Competition

The post office has faced competition from private sources since the 1680s when William Dockwra introduced the Penny Post in London. Dockwra outperformed the British Postal system with his private delivery system, which the *1984 Encyclopaedia Britannica Macropaedia* (Volume 14) described as so efficient that deliveries were made almost hourly.

The British government prosecuted Dockwra for infringing on the state monopoly and his service was shut down, only to be reopened by the government. A similar situation occurred with another entrepreneur in France, but the French government purchased the operation rather than shutting it down.

Today, the United States Postal Service (USPS), is facing pressure from competition. Besides obvious competition from overnight and parcel delivery services, the post office is faced with losing some of its lucrative catalog delivery market to private delivery firms who operate much like newspaper delivery operations.

According to the USPS Household Diary Survey (1989) the average American household receives 1.5 catalogs per week. The Direct Marketing Association estimates overall catalog volume in 1991 to be 13.4 billion, with the overall number of catalogs rising steadily from the 8.7 billion in 1985. This is despite the fact that postage for sending catalogs has increased nearly 70 percent. In spite of the outcry from the direct marketing industry, in 1991, postage rates for catalogs were hiked more than 40 percent.

Automation

The USPS was attempting to cut costs in the largest area of expenditure it currently has, personnel. Figure 2-1 illustrates that over 62 percent of the expenses incurred by the USPS in 1991 were employee compensation and approximately 20 percent more went for personnel benefits. By introducing automated equipment the post office has been able to eliminate 39,000 positions since May of 1989, at an estimated 1991 savings of $1.1 billion. A reduction of 45,000 more employees has been completed as part of the reorganization implemented by the current Postmaster General, Marvin Runyon.

Former Postmaster General Anthony Frank said in his 1991 annual report that 20 percent of the automation equipment planned is in place and the USPS plans to improve its productivity by at least 4.8 percent by 1995.

The receiver's address

Everyone knows how to address a letter. You can send a letter with just the name, address, city, and state, and it will eventually arrive. However, to operate a mail list business you must understand how the USPS designates its delivery areas. Some of the USPS designations will be familiar to you, but others are not familiar to the general public.

Zip (zoning improvement plan) code

Originally introduced in 1963, a five-digit numeric postal code, called the zoning improvement plan (ZIP) code, is used by the USPS to subdivide geographical areas for the purpose of automating the mail process. When it was introduced, mailers thought the new code would cost them a good deal more work and would scare off customers. But the zip code turned out to be an easy way to subdivide geographic areas for mailers, too. The zip code is

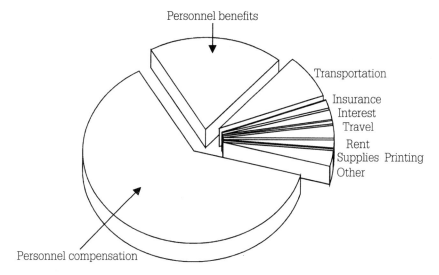

USPS analysis of expenses, fiscal year 1991*

2-1
The actual breakdown of expenditures by the USPS as reported for 1991. Notice costs associated with personnel make up over 80 percent of the pie.

$62.69 Personnel compensation
$19.75 Personnel benefits
$07.58 Transportation
$02.54 Other services
$00.25 Insurance claims and idemnities
$01.38 Interest on notes, mortgages,
        and bonds

$00.68 Depreciation and writes-offs
$00.38 Travel
$02.23 Rent, communications, and utilities
$01.31 Supplies and materials
$00.21 Printing

*Annual report of the Postmaster General 1991

often used by mailers to target certain groups of people, it helps move the mail faster, and customers never did seem to mind adapting to it.

Fully implemented in 1967, the zip code is that series of numbers at the end of an address. The five-digit zip code designates large geographical areas and information concerning those areas is easily obtained.

As illustrated in FIG. 2-2, the zip code has expanded from the five-digit code introduced originally to include four additional digits, or the +4 (pronounced "plus four"). The +4 further subdivides each area, but the USPS doesn't publish +4 maps and the +4 areas change frequently. The +4 appears to be a way for the USPS to eventually sidestep the complex and confusing subdivisions called carrier route and saturation walk sequence discussed later in this chapter.

Zip+4

Zoning improvement plan (ZIP) code

President Bill Clinton
1600 Pennsylvania Ave NW
Washington, DC 20006-9900

Delivery point

+4 (plus four)

Delivery point

By adding two more digits the zip+4 code has been further expanded to point precisely to one of the 115 million individual points in the US where the USPS delivers mail. Hence, the eleven-digit zip code is also called the *delivery point* or *delivery point code*. The two additional digits usually come from the last two digits of the numerical portion of the street address, but not always. For example, large firms in an office building who receive a lot of mail may have a separate two digits from the remainder of firms in the same building.

The POSTNET barcode

The least expensive way to make mail readable by machine is to barcode the mail. A barcode is a series of vertical lines which can be translated into numeric values by a special computerized light source called an optical scanner. Much like the Universal Product Code (UPC) barcodes on retail products, the USPS has implemented its own barcoding system called the POSTNET barcode. When correctly barcoded with its eleven-digit delivery point, a piece of mail such as the one in FIG. 2-3, can be machine sorted mail right down to the way your mail carrier walks his or her delivery route. Figure 2-4 illustrates the conversion between decimal numbers and the POSTNET barcode.

2-3
The POSTNET delivery point barcode is at the bottom right of this envelope, and is a machine-readable representation of the unique address illustrated in Fig. 2-2.

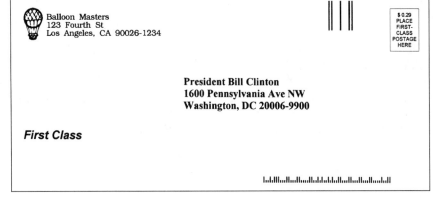

Balloon Masters
123 Fourth St
Los Angeles, CA 90026-1234

$0.29
PLACE
FIRST-
CLASS
POSTAGE
HERE

President Bill Clinton
1600 Pennsylvania Ave NW
Washington, DC 20006-9900

First Class

Numeric value	Binary 74210	Barcode 74210
1	00011	ııı‖
2	00101	ıı‖ı
3	00110	ıı‖ıı
4	01001	ı‖ıı
5	01010	ı‖ı‖ı
6	01100	ı‖‖ıı
7	10001	‖ıı‖
8	10010	‖ıı‖ı
9	10100	‖ı‖ıı
0	11000	‖‖ııı

2-4
The conversion from decimal numbers to the POSTNET barcode is represented.

Each number is represented by five lines; short lines equal 0, long lines equal 1. From left to right the positions are weighted 7,4,2,1. A number is represented by adding up the equivalents of the positions with long bars.

For example, the number 5 is represented by 01010, with a long bar in the four and one positions. The sum of 4 and 1 is 5. However, the 0 combination of 11000 actually adds up to 11, but has been assigned a value of 0.

When the unique eleven-digit delivery point code is represented by a barcode, the result is called the *delivery point barcode*. Figure 2-5 shows specifically how various portions of the delivery point barcode, using POSTNET code, represent the zip, the +4, and the last two digits in the street address. When the mail is barcoded by someone other than the USPS, it is said to be *prebarcoded mail*.

Barcodes bring mail processing costs down radically from $42 per 1000 pieces sorted by hand to a low $3 per 1000 pieces when sorted by machine. A delivery barcode sorter (DBCS) is shown sorting mail in FIG. 2-6.

Sample Address:

JOE AND JANE CUSTOMER
101 MAIN ST
ANYTOWN US   12345-6789

Delivery point number is 1 2 3 4 5 6 7 8 9 <u>0</u> <u>1</u> <u>4</u>

01 = the last two numbers of the primary street address

4 is the correction character

2-5

A sample barcoded address shows where the numbers in the address are represented in POSTNET barcode.

The correction character is determined by taking the sum of the digits in the delivery point barcode, then adding a number that will bring the total to a multiple of 10.

$$1+2+3+4+5+6+7+8+9+0+1= 46$$
$$\underline{+4}$$
$$50$$

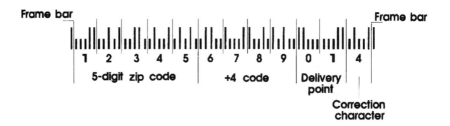

Frame bar   Frame bar

1   2   3   4   5   6   7   8   9   0   1   4

5-digit zip code   +4 code   Delivery point

Correction character

2-6

USPS mail processor Mary Sampson operates a delivery barcode sorter (DBCS).

The postal system & mailing list services

The USPS isn't counting on everyone prebarcoding, but has also implemented optical character reader (OCR) machines, such as the one in FIG. 2-7, that use light to read characters, then spray on a barcode. While the savings in OCR or "mechanized" processing isn't as great as that offered by prebarcoding, it is still less than half of sorting by hand at $19 per 1000.

2-7
Optical character readers such as this one can process up to 30,000 letters per hour.

The problem with OCR processing is it can't read everything, especially when the contrast between the paper and the printing on the paper isn't high enough. That's why some post offices have put out special colored mail boxes on holidays such as Christmas and Valentine's Day. Colored envelopes, such as red, pink, orange, and green don't offer a high enough contrast with the characters printed on them for OCR readers and will produce what is known in the post office as *loop mail*. Loop mail is mail that might receive a barcode for the return address instead of the delivery address and is therefore sent to a destination for which it is not addressed.

The USPS OCR machines like all capital or uppercase characters, no punctuation except the dash in the zip+4 code, and standardized abbreviations. The standardized two-character state abbreviations and the other abbreviations, used such as ST for Street, are listed in appendix F. Unfortunately, standardizing mail makes it look a lot less personal and unique, which is the appearance direct mailers like to avoid, but you can use almost any font you want to if you have the correct barcode on the mail. If you don't barcode, you need to have fonts the optical character reader (OCR) machines can read in order to get discounted rates.

The OCR machines also prefer certain typefaces and sizes of letters, known as fonts and listed in FIG. 2-8. The general rules are the fonts need to be non-proportional, with no kerning, and preferably sans-serif. Non-proportional

Tested and verified	Similar styles	Tested and verified	Similar styles
Centry Light Schoolbook	Century	Megaron Bold	Hamilton
Elite		Megaron Medium	Newton
Fritz Quadrata		News Gothic	Alpha Gothic
Futura Medium	Airport Alphatura Contempra Future Photura Sparta Stylon Techica Techno Tempo Twentieth Century Vogue	Trade Gothic	Classified News
		Newtext Regular Condensed	
		OCR B	
		Optima	Athena Chelmsford Musica October Omega Optimist Oracle Roma Theme Zenith
Helios	Akzidenz-Grotesk Buch		
Helios Light	Aristocrat		
Helvetica Helvetica Light Helvetica Regular	Claro Europa Grotesk Geneva	Pica	
		Standard Typewriter	
Honeywell H200		Stymie Medium	Alexandria Beton Cairo Karnak Memphis Pyramid Rockwell
IBM 1403 IBM 1428			
Koronna Regular	Aquarius Corona Crown Koronna News No. 3 News No. 5 News No. 6 Nimbus Royal		
		Triumvirate Triumvirate Bold Triumvirate Regular	Sonoman Sanserif Spectra Vega
Manifold 72		Univers Univers 5 Univers Medium	Alphavers Eterna Galaxy Kosmos Versatile
		Universal	

2-8 *The USPS list of acceptable type styles, both those that have been tested and verified and others that are similar.*

The postal system & mailing list services

means each character takes up the same amount of room. Kerning is moving individual characters closer together to improve the appearance of a word. Sans-serif are type styles that do not have the small curves at the ends of the letters. Figure 2-9 illustrates the differences.

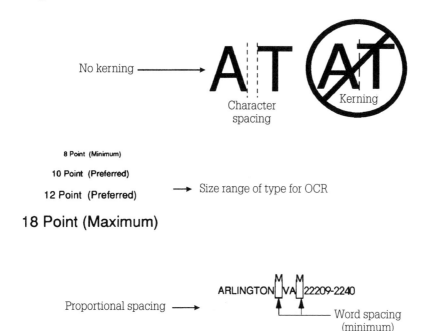

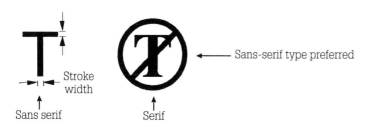

2-9
The difference between proportional and non-proportional spacing, kerning and no kerning, and serif and sans-serif fonts is illustrated here. The USPS wants non-proportional sans-serif fonts and no kerning for its OCR machines to read.

You can produce attractive and professional looking mailing pieces that meet the typeface and size guidelines. If you do, you'll find the mail you process moves much faster through the system. Of course, the right typeface and size won't mean much with smudged ink or limited contrast between the ink and the paper. Neatness and readability are important factors as well.

The mail process

Mail is picked up by mail carriers and postal vehicles and brought from other post offices to a *Sectional Center Facility* (SCF) where it is processed for delivery. It could also be dropped off by customers using *bulk business mail* (BBM) at the *business mail entry unit* (BMEU). SCFs handle the distribution of mail for the geographical area designated by the first three digits of the zip code. The last two digits of the five-digit zip code designate a delivery area covered individually by units of the post office called a branch, station, or associate post office and from which individual mail carriers pick up mail for delivery.

Mail, when it comes into a SCF, is sorted by hand and by size and non-machinable pieces are removed in a process called "culling," as shown in FIG. 2-10. The mail then has to be faced, meaning it has to be placed face up with the stamp at the upper right so the stamp can be canceled. Cleverly, the post office discovered a machine could face the mail if phosphorus was put on stamps and into the ink used in postage meters. Figure 2-11 shows an advanced facer canceler machine. The machine uses an ultraviolet light, senses the phosphorus, and faces the mail.

2-10
Non-machineable pieces are culled by hand out of the mail entering the mail stream. This is one of the first steps in the processing procedure.

United States Postal Service

Once the mail is faced it is sent to computerized optical character recognition (OCR) machines, such as the one in FIG. 2-12, that attempt to read the handwriting or printing on the letter. The machine reads from the bottom line of the address, upward until it recognizes an address. After reading the address, the OCR will print the appropriate POSTNET Barcode, representing the zip code or zip+4 code, in the lower right hand corner of the envelope.

If a piece cannot be read by the OCR equipment, it is taken to machines where specially trained postal employees look at the piece and key in the address for barcoding, as the postal employee in FIG. 2-13 is doing. This is a

United States Postal Service

2-11
An advanced facer canceler (AFC) operated by Eddie Teran, AFC operator.

United States Postal Service

2-12
Mail processor Cleofe Partido makes sure faced mail is correctly entering an optical character reader (OCR) machine.

much slower process as it can only be done at the rate of 50 to 60 pieces per minute.

Once the mail is faced and barcoded it goes to the *barcode sorter* (BCS), like the one in FIG. 2-14, where it is sorted. Barcoded mail moves faster because it can be machine sorted, travel to the SCF of the city where it is going, and be machine sorted there right down to the mail carrier.

2-13
A letter sorting machine (LSM) operator sorts letters that cannot be read by automated equipment. This machine is eventually being phased out as the remote barcoding system comes on-line.

United States Postal Service

2-14
A barcode sorter (BCS) being fed mail by Elaine Rutledge in the foreground. Sorted mail is removed by mail processor Debra Brewster.

United States Postal Service

Mail that can't go through the mechanization process because of its size and isn't barcoded is handled up to 50 times before it reaches its destination like the mail handled in FIG. 2-15. On the other hand, if the mail is of a standard size, metered (or precanceled stamps are used), flexible enough to move around large wheels and between belts, and barcoded it is handled only 10 times, which means it can arrive at its destination much faster.

United States Postal Service

2-15
Non-machineable mail can be handled as many as 50 times. Here, postal employee Ernest Loera is manually distributing parcel post mail at a bulk mail center (BMC).

The post office will tell you to plan on a week for local third-class bulk mail delivery and 10 to 14 days on bulk mail to other states. But some bulk mailers claim their metered, barcoded third-class mail, which is processed last by any postal facility, has traveled as far as from New York to delivery in California in an unheard-of three days.

To stay in business, the post office needs mail, and third-class mail generates mail volume. As FIG. 2-16 illustrates, estimates are every response to a piece of third-class mail generates as many as two fourth-class shipments in the form of packages, thirteen pieces of first-class (such as letters, bills, or inquiries) and between twenty and twenty-five more pieces of third-class mail.

Mailing discounts

The USPS calls its discounted mail preparation programs *worksharing*, which helps eliminate the kind of hand-sorting illustrated in FIG. 2-17. The first discounts for worksharing were introduced in 1978 when presort reductions were offered for third-class mail. When discounts were introduced, the volume of third-class mail began to rise steadily until the last two rate increases by the USPS. The vast majority of third-class mail, 83 percent, is presorted to take advantage of the highest discounts.

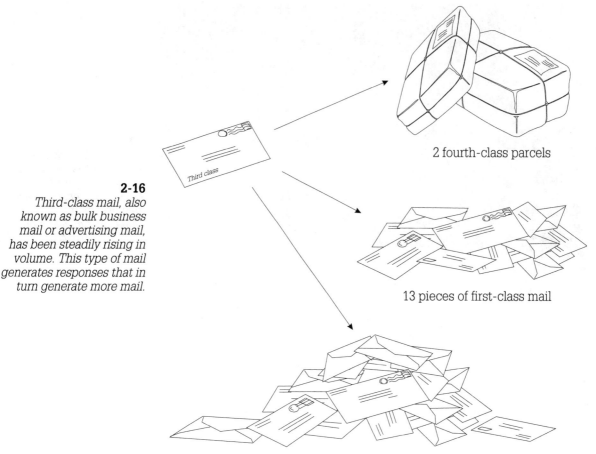

2-16
*Third-class mail, also
known as bulk business
mail or advertising mail,
has been steadily rising in
volume. This type of mail
generates responses that in
turn generate more mail.*

2 fourth-class parcels

13 pieces of first-class mail

20 to 25 pieces of third-class mail

The discount programs offered by the post office are both complex and
constantly changing. Asking what discount you can get for a mailing is like
asking what taxes you'll pay—it depends. Many of the mailers I spoke with
said they depend heavily on the mailing software they use in order to know
what discounts their mailing qualifies for. In addition, you might often find
confusion on the part of postal employees as to the requirements. Jim
McCartney of LCS Direct Mail Advertising & Printing said he takes a
questionable piece of mail down to the post office and asks if it will qualify for
certain discounts. When he gets the answer, he has the postal employee
round stamp the piece using the special stamp that identifies the employee.
Then, when he brings the mailing back in, if the postal worker on the dock
won't accept the mailing for the discount, McCartney gets out the round
stamped piece. This turns the discussion into an internal matter among the
postal employees, and even if they end up fighting about the requirements,
McCartney gets his mail through.

2-17
A postal employee is, by hand, loading mail onto a small parcel/bundle sorter (SPBS).

One of the software vendors who offers a mailing program said the company spends a good portion of its day on the phone with postal employees educating them regarding the USPS requirements. This usually occurs because a mailer using the company's software ran into a postal employee who maintains the software is incorrect in the way it sorted and discounted the mail.

However, don't be discouraged. What this means for you is more business because many companies cannot stay on top of the changing postal requirements.

Even though there are too many different discounts offered by the USPS to identify each one here, a few underlying guidelines are followed in the discount programs. Mailing discounts are based on the class of mail, the size of the mail, how "automation compatible" the individual mailing piece is, how many of the same mailing piece are going to the same area, where the mailer delivers the mailing, and how it is sorted. A look at the form used for third-class regular rate mail shown in FIG. 2-18 will give you an idea of the prioritization the USPS makes in the categories of discounts and the many combinations of criteria for the discounted rates. Also, you'll see discounts range from 5 to nearly 40 percent.

Form 3602-R — Third-Class Regular Rate — Permit Imprint

Postage Computation — Bulk Rates

Entry Discount (If Any)	Presort/Automation Discounts	Net Rate	Count (Pcs/Lbs)	Charge
Automation-Compatible Letter (DMM 520)				
None	Saturation W/S	.124 ×	_____ pcs. = $ _____	
	Carrier Route	.131 ×	_____ pcs. = $ _____	
	5-Digit Barcoded	.146 ×	_____ pcs. = $ _____	
	3-Digit Barcoded	.154 ×	_____ pcs. = $ _____	
	3/5-Digit ZIP + 4	.161 ×	_____ pcs. = $ _____	
	3/5-Digit Presort	.165 ×	_____ pcs. = $ _____	
	Basic ZIP + 4 Barcoded	.179 ×	_____ pcs. = $ _____	
	Basic ZIP + 4	.189 ×	_____ pcs. = $ _____	
	Basic	.198 ×	_____ pcs. = $ _____	
BMC Entry	Saturation W/S	.112 ×	_____ pcs. = $ _____	
	Carrier Route	.119 ×	_____ pcs. = $ _____	
	5-Digit Barcoded	.134 ×	_____ pcs. = $ _____	
	3-Digit Barcoded	.142 ×	_____ pcs. = $ _____	
	3/5-Digit ZIP + 4	.149 ×	_____ pcs. = $ _____	
	3/5-Digit Presort	.153 ×	_____ pcs. = $ _____	
	Basic ZIP + 4 Barcoded	.167 ×	_____ pcs. = $ _____	
	Basic ZIP + 4	.177 ×	_____ pcs. = $ _____	
	Basic	.186 ×	_____ pcs. = $ _____	
SCF Entry	Saturation W/S	.107 ×	_____ pcs. = $ _____	
	Carrier Route	.114 ×	_____ pcs. = $ _____	
	5-Digit Barcoded	.129 ×	_____ pcs. = $ _____	
	3-Digit Barcoded	.137 ×	_____ pcs. = $ _____	
	3/5-Digit ZIP + 4	.144 ×	_____ pcs. = $ _____	
	3/5-Digit Presort	.148 ×	_____ pcs. = $ _____	
	Basic ZIP + 4 Barcoded	.162 ×	_____ pcs. = $ _____	
	Basic ZIP + 4	.172 ×	_____ pcs. = $ _____	
	Basic	.181 ×	_____ pcs. = $ _____	
DDU Entry	Saturation W/S	.102 ×	_____ pcs. = $ _____	
	Carrier Route	.109 ×	_____ pcs. = $ _____	

Total – Part A (Carry to front of form) $ _____

Check one: ☐ Automation-Compatible Flat (DMM 522) ☐ Other Nonletter – .2067 lb. (3.3067 oz.) or less

Entry Discount	Presort/Automation	Net Rate	Count	Charge
None	Saturation W/S	.127 ×	_____ pcs. = $ _____	
	125-pc. W/S	.137 ×	_____ pcs. = $ _____	
	Carrier Route	.142 ×	_____ pcs. = $ _____	
	3/5-Digit ZIP + 4 Barcoded*	.170 ×	_____ pcs. = $ _____	
	3/5-Digit Presort	.187 ×	_____ pcs. = $ _____	
	Basic ZIP + 4 Barcoded*	.208 ×	_____ pcs. = $ _____	
	Basic	.233 ×	_____ pcs. = $ _____	
BMC Entry	Saturation W/S	.115 ×	_____ pcs. = $ _____	
	125-pc. W/S	.125 ×	_____ pcs. = $ _____	
	Carrier Route	.130 ×	_____ pcs. = $ _____	
	3/5-Digit ZIP + 4 Barcoded*	.158 ×	_____ pcs. = $ _____	
	3/5-Digit Presort	.175 ×	_____ pcs. = $ _____	
	Basic ZIP + 4 Barcoded*	.196 ×	_____ pcs. = $ _____	
	Basic	.221 ×	_____ pcs. = $ _____	
SCF Entry	Saturation W/S	.110 ×	_____ pcs. = $ _____	
	125-pc. W/S	.120 ×	_____ pcs. = $ _____	
	Carrier Route	.125 ×	_____ pcs. = $ _____	
	3/5-Digit ZIP + 4 Barcoded*	.153 ×	_____ pcs. = $ _____	
	3/5-Digit Presort	.170 ×	_____ pcs. = $ _____	
	Basic ZIP + 4 Barcoded*	.191 ×	_____ pcs. = $ _____	
	Basic	.216 ×	_____ pcs. = $ _____	
DDU Entry	Saturation W/S	.105 ×	_____ pcs. = $ _____	
	125-pc. W/S	.115 ×	_____ pcs. = $ _____	
	Carrier Route	.120 ×	_____ pcs. = $ _____	

*Available only for Automation-Compatible Flats (DMM 522)

Total – Part C (Carry to front of form) $ _____

Entry Discount (If Any)	Presort/Automation Discounts	Net Rate	Count (Pcs/Lbs)	Charge
Non-Automation-Compatible Letter .2067 lb. (3.3067 oz.) or less				
None	Saturation W/S	.124 ×	_____ pcs. = $ _____	
	Carrier Route	.131 ×	_____ pcs. = $ _____	
	3/5-Digit Presort	.165 ×	_____ pcs. = $ _____	
	Basic	.198 ×	_____ pcs. = $ _____	
BMC Entry	Saturation W/S	.112 ×	_____ pcs. = $ _____	
	Carrier Route	.119 ×	_____ pcs. = $ _____	
	3/5-Digit Presort	.153 ×	_____ pcs. = $ _____	
	Basic	.186 ×	_____ pcs. = $ _____	
SCF Entry	Saturation W/S	.107 ×	_____ pcs. = $ _____	
	Carrier Route	.114 ×	_____ pcs. = $ _____	
	3/5-Digit Presort	.148 ×	_____ pcs. = $ _____	
	Basic	.181 ×	_____ pcs. = $ _____	
DDU Entry	Saturation W/S	.102 ×	_____ pcs. = $ _____	
	Carrier Route	.109 ×	_____ pcs. = $ _____	

Total – Part B (Carry to front of form) $ _____

Check one: ☐ Letter** ☐ Automation-Compatible Flat (DMM 522) ☐ Other Nonletter – More than .2067 lb. (3.3067 oz.) But less than 1.0 lb. (16.0 oz.)

Entry Discount	Presort/Automation	Net Rate	Count	Charge
None	Saturation W/S	.003 ×	_____ pcs. = $ _____	
	plus	.600 ×	_____ lbs. = $ _____	
	125-pc. W/S	.013 ×	_____ pcs. = $ _____	
	plus	.600 ×	_____ lbs. = $ _____	
	Carrier Route	.018 ×	_____ pcs. = $ _____	
	plus	.600 ×	_____ lbs. = $ _____	
	3/5-Digit ZIP + 4 Barcoded*	.046 ×	_____ pcs. = $ _____	
	plus	.600 ×	_____ lbs. = $ _____	
	3/5-Digit Presort	.063 ×	_____ pcs. = $ _____	
	plus	.600 ×	_____ lbs. = $ _____	
	Basic ZIP + 4 Barcoded*	.084 ×	_____ pcs. = $ _____	
	plus	.600 ×	_____ lbs. = $ _____	
	Basic	.109 ×	_____ pcs. = $ _____	
	plus	.600 ×	_____ lbs. = $ _____	
BMC Entry	Saturation W/S	.003 ×	_____ pcs. = $ _____	
	plus	.542 ×	_____ lbs. = $ _____	
	125-pc. W/S	.013 ×	_____ pcs. = $ _____	
	plus	.542 ×	_____ lbs. = $ _____	
	Carrier Route	.018 ×	_____ pcs. = $ _____	
	plus	.542 ×	_____ lbs. = $ _____	
	3/5-Digit ZIP + 4 Barcoded*	.046 ×	_____ pcs. = $ _____	
	plus	.542 ×	_____ lbs. = $ _____	
	3/5-Digit Presort	.063 ×	_____ pcs. = $ _____	
	plus	.542 ×	_____ lbs. = $ _____	
	Basic ZIP + 4 Barcoded*	.084 ×	_____ pcs. = $ _____	
	plus	.542 ×	_____ lbs. = $ _____	
	Basic	.109 ×	_____ pcs. = $ _____	
	plus	.542 ×	_____ lbs. = $ _____	
SCF Entry	Saturation W/S	.003 ×	_____ pcs. = $ _____	
	plus	.519 ×	_____ lbs. = $ _____	
	125-pc. W/S	.013 ×	_____ pcs. = $ _____	
	plus	.519 ×	_____ lbs. = $ _____	
	Carrier Route	.018 ×	_____ pcs. = $ _____	
	plus	.519 ×	_____ lbs. = $ _____	
	3/5-Digit ZIP + 4 Barcoded*	.046 ×	_____ pcs. = $ _____	
	plus	.519 ×	_____ lbs. = $ _____	
	3/5-Digit Presort	.063 ×	_____ pcs. = $ _____	
	plus	.519 ×	_____ lbs. = $ _____	
	Basic ZIP + Barcoded*	.084 ×	_____ pcs. = $ _____	
	plus	.519 ×	_____ lbs. = $ _____	
	Basic	.109 ×	_____ pcs. = $ _____	
	plus	.519 ×	_____ lbs. = $ _____	
DDU Entry	Saturation W/S	.003 ×	_____ pcs. = $ _____	
	plus	.496 ×	_____ lbs. = $ _____	
	125-pc. W/S	.013 ×	_____ pcs. = $ _____	
	plus	.496 ×	_____ lbs. = $ _____	
	Carrier Route	.018 ×	_____ pcs. = $ _____	
	plus	.496 ×	_____ lbs. = $ _____	

*Available only for Automation-Compatible Flats (DMM 522)
**Letter-size pieces cannot be claimed at the 125-piece W/S rate

Total – Part D (Carry to front of form) $ _____

PS Form **3602-R**, June 1992 (Reverse)   *U.S. GPO: 1992-312-805/62486

2-18 *The discount postage rates at the time of this writing are shown. Note the prioritization the USPS makes in its discount categories. Also, note how many of the rates are broken down to hundredths of a cent.*

The four types of mail are first-, second-, third-, and fourth-class mail. *First-class mail* is for mail that needs to be delivered quickly or is private such as personal correspondence, checks, and money orders. *Second-class mail* is for material of a timely nature such as magazines, periodicals and is not as expensive as first-class mail. *Third-class mail* or *bulk business mail* (BBM) is lower in handling priority and in price for delivery than first- or second-class mail and is used heavily by advertisers, hence it is sometimes called *advertising mail* or *direct mail. Fourth-class mail* is a special rate used for books, educational materials, and catalogs and is sometimes called *library-rate mail*. The only classes of mail we are interested in are first-class and third-class, because those are the only two classes receiving the worksharing discounts.

Mail classification

One of the first places to start saving money on mailing is in the design of the mailing piece itself. Mailers tell me if they get opposition, it is from their own marketing people who don't think standardization will get the attention the piece needs. But nonstandardization is expensive and there are ways to get attention without sacrificing the attractive discounts available. USPS Publication 25, "Designing Business Letter Mail," is a very good and very specific publication, free to those who ask for it, about designing mail to meet mechanization and automation requirements for discounts.

Mail design

When you look at a mailing, one of the things you're looking for is how the piece fits the postal size and automation requirements. The closer to letter size, the better. If the piece is too high, too long or too thick, it is going to be charged a $.10 surcharge, above the $.29 rate. If a piece of mail meets the thickness guidelines, but is longer or wider than the requirements, it is no longer a letter but is called instead a *flat*.

While a piece may fall in the guidelines for a letter, how it is addressed also may determine whether it is considered a letter or a flat. If it is addressed so that the long side becomes the height, it is a flat. Simply moving the address so it is parallel to the longest side, as illustrated in FIG. 2-19, can mean a savings of as much as $52 per thousand, even if the piece is prepared for automation and is barcoded. Anytime you can make a mailing piece qualify for a letter rate instead of being designated as a flat, you save money.

The post office offers several templates against which you can simply lay a piece of mail to check if it meets the letter requirements. One of the best is the Letter-Size Mail Dimensional Standards Template (Notice 3A), which is printed on thick plastic and even has a properly-sized ¼-inch-thick slot cut in it. A reproduction of both sides of Notice 3A is shown in FIG. 2-20 and FIG. 2-21. This is the acid test, because if you can't slide the piece through the slot, you know it doesn't meet the letter standard.

Further help for the ins and outs of mail design for automation is available in the form of a self-study design course that even includes videocassettes. The

Mailing piece C
Considered a "flat" by USPS

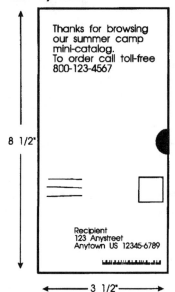

Thanks for browsing
our summer camp
mini-catalog.
To order call toll-free
800-123-4567

8 1/2"

Recipient
123 Anystreet
Anytown US 12345-6789

3 1/2"

2-19
Simply putting the address information on a mailing piece a different way offers savings in postal costs.

Mailing piece D
Same piece as piece C, but now considered a letter by the USPS

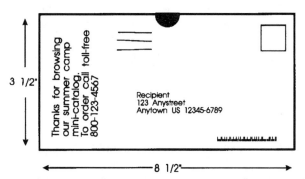

3 1/2"

Thanks for browsing
our summer camp
mini-catalog.
To order call toll-free
800-123-4567

Recipient
123 Anystreet
Anytown US 12345-6789

8 1/2"

By turning the brochure sideways and addressing it the long way, as much as $52 per 1000 can be saved.

USPS puts out the course, called the *Mail Piece Quality Control (MPQC) Training Program* and an initial two-year subscription is $150. The initial order includes an "Administrator's Guide," the "Self-Study Workbook," a video entitled "Designing for Delivery," a current issue of the *Domestic Mail Manual,* and other reference materials. After the initial two-year subscription, subscription prices for two years at a time are $75. The program offers information on how to meet the USPS requirements and minimize postage costs and is kept up as the postal regulations change.

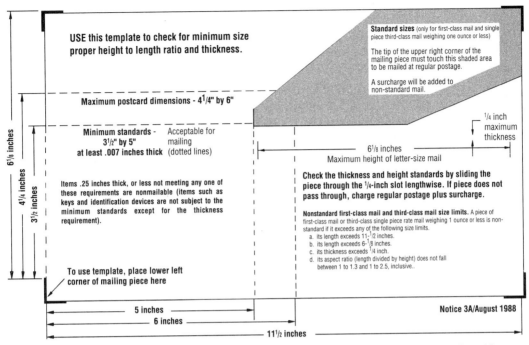

2-20 *A reduced reproduction of the front of Notice 3A. Available free from the post office, Notice 3A is made of durable plastic and large enough to actually place mailing pieces against for comparison.*

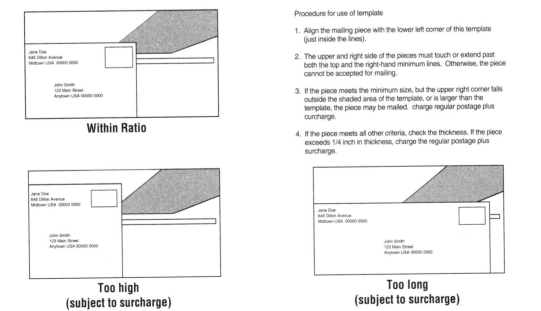

2-21 *The back of Notice 3A. The front is shown in Fig. 2-20.*

To subscribe, send check or money order made payable to "US Postal Service" to MPQC Training Program, National Address Information Center, US Postal Service, 6060 Primacy Parkway Suite 101, Memphis, TN 38188-0001, or call (800) 331-5746 extension 640.

Automation requirements

Mail that will work in the post office automation equipment has to be uniform. Most of the business world has standardized on basic sizes for letters, and those standard sizes are what the post office is geared toward. Larger pieces, such as manila envelopes or flat regular-sized paper, are called flats. They can also be handled by machine, such as the machines in FIG. 2-22 and FIG. 2-23, but flats have size limitations as well. Anything larger or thicker doesn't qualify for a discount and will be charged at the regular first-class rate.

2-22
A multi-position flats sorting machine.

United States Postal Service

Also, anything that might stop high-speed machine processing, such as thickly stuffed envelopes, staples, or paper clips are forbidden. So are items inside such as keys or pencils. Mail cannot be open and loose like a newsletter folded in half because it flaps when moving along at high rates of speed. It's not that you can't mail these types of materials, but you cannot get a discount if you do.

2-23
A side view of the multi-position flats sorting machine.

Mail sorted for discounts must be delivered to the Bulk Mail Unit of the post office where you hold your permit. You can garner additional discounts for delivering your mail to more specific mail processing facilities once you've checked in where you hold your permit, as long as the delivery is done the same day. For example, permit holders anywhere in the greater Los Angeles area can get an additional discount per piece on bulk business mailings if they deliver the mail to the Bulk Mail Center (BMC) in downtown Los Angeles. The discount does require they check in at the post office where they hold their permit and then transport the mail to the downtown BMC and would probably be too much trouble unless you already have an entire truckload of bulk mail.

Delivering mail

Sorting has been basically the same for some time. However, the USPS's move to automation is forcing changes in the way mail is sorted. A general explanation is offered in this section to help you understand what the post office wants, but it is no substitute for the free instructional classes the post office holds. The easiest way to proceed is to read this over first to get the terminology, then attend the bulk mail class at the post office. You can call your nearest post office and ask when and where the bulk mail classes are held.

Sorting mail for discounts

Saturation walk sequence   The greatest discounts are for *saturation walk sequence* (w/s). In order to get this discount, a mail piece has to be delivered to each address in a particular carrier route and sorted in the sequence the mail carrier walks the route. This is often the mail you see addressed to "resident" or "occupant." Saturation walk sequence is used heavily by mailers who want to penetrate an area, such as local businesses who depend on customers in the neighborhood to stay in business.

Carrier route   If you are not delivering to every address in a carrier route, but deliver to more than 10, you are eligible for the *carrier route discounts*. The system for dividing down geographical areas into the routes each individual mail carrier delivers is designated by a number called the *carrier route number*. Mail sorted in the way the mail carrier delivers it and labeled with the carrier route number is called *carrier route mail*. The only way to be sure of carrier routes is by running your mailing list through software that has been tested and certified by the USPS.

Automated walk sequence or delivery point barcode (DPBC)   Mail carriers can spend as long as four hours hand sorting mail into the walk sequence (FIG. 2-24). To encourage mailers doing large mailings to a local area to presort the mail, saturation walk sequence and carrier route presort are the two largest worksharing discounts offered, meaning they offer the most savings in postage costs. However, prebarcoding with the delivery point barcode can garner substantial discounts as well. The only mail that will be accepted for barcoding discounts is mail that is 85 percent delivery point barcoded. The USPS wants to encourage delivery point barcoding because automated sorting of the mail is expected to reduce costs further by cutting the sorting time for the individual carrier in half.

2-24
A box clerk sorting letters at the Long Beach, California General Mail Facility.

Bulk mail   There are two steps in preparing bulk mail for discount rates. One is sorting the mail pieces, and the other is traying or bagging. *Sorting* is the order of the individual pieces of mail and *traying* or *bagging* is organizing the sorted mail into groups for shipment. You can purchase software that can print labels or envelopes in the proper order for sorting and tell you how to bag the mail. Some software will even print your mailing in *production order*, meaning the order in which it has to be bagged or trayed, and will print the necessary labels for the trays or bags as well. This software is outlined in chapter 4.

By the way, the post office will be glad to supply you with all the materials you need which you can take back to your office and use to prepare your bulk mailings. These materials include stickers, heavy rubber bands, and canvas bags or trays.

At the time of this writing, 200 pieces are the minimum for bulk mail and 500 pieces are necessary to obtain first-class mail presort discounts. Sorting for both is similar, however. Once you have the required number of pieces, the locations where the pieces are to be delivered determine the discount. For example, the more pieces you have going to the same zip code, the better the discount. If you have a 500-piece first-class mailing going to 500 different zip codes, you will not get a discount from the first-class mailing rate. If you have a minimum of 10 pieces for each of the zip codes you are mailing to, then you can get a discount, assuming you sort the mail correctly.

You'll understand the sorting procedure better if you understand you're sorting the mail in the way the post office itself would sort it if you were mailing without discounts. A zip code order sort is required first, but then as many as three other passes are required to sort the pieces the way the post office would. The first pass is to group all pieces with the same first five-digit zip code together, but 10 or more are required for each five-digit zip code group. Once all the possible five-digit groups are made, bundles of 10 or 50 (depending upon your class) or more pieces with the same first three-digit zip codes are organized. Once all the three-digit groups are made, then all the pieces that go to the same states are grouped together. Any mail left over after this last pass is called residual mail and is grouped together.

The groups of mail are then labeled as to where they're going, as illustrated in FIG. 2-25 and FIG. 2-26. Bagged mail has a *bag tag*, while mail that is trayed is labeled on the front and with *stand-up tags*. Mail with the same five-digit zip code is labeled with the zip code and the city and state from the mailing pieces themselves. Three-digit groups go to SCFs, or to a city processing center uniquely identified with a zip code, where they are distributed to the individual five-digit postal stations. The city and state for each three zip code are identified on the label. Mail going to the same state is similarly labeled.

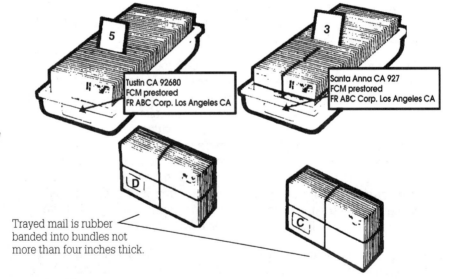

2-25
*An example of how
bagged mail is labeled.*

Metal bag closures also
hold labels for destination
of enclosed mail.

U.S. MAIL

5-digit label

TUSTIN CA 92680
3C LTRS
LOS ANGELES CA

3-digit label

Destination ——————
Contents ——————
Office of mailing ——————

SANTA ANNA CA 926
3C LTRS
LOS ANGELES CA

2-26
*An example of how trayed
mail is labeled.*

5

Tustin CA 92680
FCM prestored
FR ABC Corp. Los Angeles CA

3

Santa Anna CA 927
FCM prestored
FR ABC Corp. Los Angeles CA

Trayed mail is rubber
banded into bundles not
more than four inches thick.

Specific examples

Here are a few specific examples of how the postal discounts can produce
savings that could even pay for your services as a mailer. If you're mailing
over 500 pieces at a time first-class at $.29 cents to zip codes with the same
first three digits, you're losing money. A 500-piece mailing at $.29 costs $145.
The same mailing at the barcoded presort rate of $.233 cents costs $116.50.
There's $28.50 or nearly $60 per thousand that doesn't have to be spent.

Another example is an organization in the San Fernando Valley that sends out a newsletter to 6000 people four times a year, mostly to local residents. The newsletter is folded in half, measures 7 by 8.5 inches, and is addressed on the back across the bottom as illustrated in mailing piece A in FIG. 2-27. As it is now, the newsletter is considered too tall to be mailed as a letter, and it is not barcoded. That means the lowest possible rate it could be mailed for at current postage rates is $.233 per piece, or $1398.

Mailing piece A

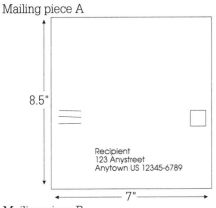

Mailing piece B
same piece as piece A, but folded in half, tabbed, barcoded

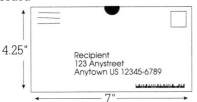

2-27
Thousands of dollars a year can be garnered from smart mail management. Piece A and piece B are the same, but B has been folded and held closed with a pressure-sensitive tab so the post office considers it letter-sized.

Estimated savings to mail 6000 B pieces	$522.00
Subtract $25 per 1000 to fold & tab	$150.00
Total estimated savings =	$372.00

Savings on four mailings = $1,488.00

However, if each piece was folded in half and tabbed, meaning held closed by a self-adhesive sticker, as illustrated by mailing piece B, it could be mailed for $.198 cents or $1188, a savings of $210. If it were barcoded and sorted by five digits it could be mailed for $.146 or $876, a savings from the original rate of $522. While it would cost $25 per thousand to have the piece folded and tabbed, that still offers a savings of $372.

Keep in mind, this organization is already spending money for printing the labels, money it could be spending with a mailing list service. So if you multiply the $372 times the four mailings, there's a savings of $1488. Even if the organization paid a mailing list service more than it's currently spending on mail preparation, it would still save a significant amount of money on postage. And you can bet an organization big enough to mail 6000 pieces four times a year has other mailings it does as well.

Also, the more automation compatible a piece is, the more money you save. That means if a piece is stapled, barcoding it doesn't do any good for discounts. A staple in a mailing piece makes it unable to go through some of the automation machines at the post office, and so knocks it out of the realm of automation compatible discounts. That means applying the barcode, while it might make it travel faster, doesn't get you any further monetary benefits.

Permits

Getting a discount is going to cost you. You can't just go to the post office, even with mail sorted correctly, and get the discounted rates. There are permits that must be acquired, which can be thought of as opening an account with the USPS. The post office doesn't care if you share the permit or let someone else use it, but in the end as the permit holder, you are responsible for the mail sent on your permit and for collecting from people you allow to use it. Figure 2-28 shows a permit application form.

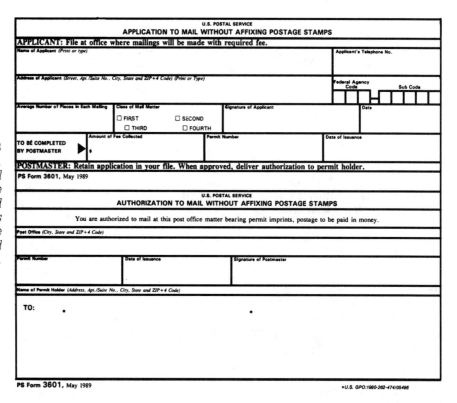

2-28
Shown is Form 3601, Application To Mail Without Affixing Postage Stamps. You are required to obtain and fill out this form from the post office where you wish to hold your mailing permit(s).

For bulk or third-class mail there are three possible permits. A processing fee of $75 is required to obtain a bulk mail permit, renewable annually for $75. Three bulk mail permits are available, one for use of precanceled stamps, one for a postage meter, and one for the permit imprint also known as the *Indicia*.

The precanceled stamp permit is the least expensive, but it requires you affix precanceled stamps, which can be purchased for $.10 each. However, $.10 each isn't all you pay. When you bring in your mailing, you pay the difference between the $.10 each for the precanceled stamps and whatever the mailing charge is. So if you have a 200-piece mailing at the basic rate of $.198, you've already paid $20 so you pay the additional $.098 per piece or $19.60.

When you make the payment, your permit account is credited with the $39.60, then deducted $39.60 for the mailing. You can choose to keep money in your permit account if you wish, but you might also just pay for each mailing as you deliver it.

A postage meter permit requires you have a postage meter, which you can estimate will cost you $20 or more per month and is usually billed quarterly. You may then buy postage for the meter at your local post office and meter the mail at your convenience. The post office does not sell or rent postage meters, but four companies in the U.S. are allowed to do so: Friden Neopost (formerly Friden Alcatel), Postalia, Pitney Bowes, and International Mailing Systems. Pitney Bowes is undoubtedly the largest of the four, but you'll find people with good and bad to say about all of them. While the USPS requires you fill out forms to have a postage meter, the company you rent the meter from usually handles all the paperwork for you. Examples of meter postage are shown in FIG. 2-29. Contact information for each of the postage meter companies is in appendix A.

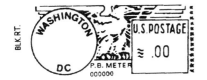  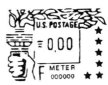

2-29
Examples of postage meter shown.

As a business mailer, you'll want a postage meter that can be set at hundredths of a cent, such as .189 cents. Nearly all of the discounted rates are broken down to hundredths of a cent as you can see back in FIG. 2-18. Most of the mailing services I talked with owned their own postage machine that seals and meters the envelopes and just leased a small, removable part of the machine which could be taken to the post office for the addition of postage.

The last bulk mail permit is for the *permit imprint* or *Indicia* which has the permit number on it and can be printed on the envelopes or made into a rubber stamp and stamped on like the imprints shown in FIG. 2-30. This is the most convenient for large mailers as it requires the least amount of physical handling. However, it says "advertising mail" all over.

2-30
Examples of permit imprint, also known as Indicia, are shown.

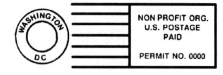

You can avoid paying multiple processing fees if you get all your permits at once. If you decide to change the type of permit you have, wait until you've actually gone down to your post office and changed it to make decisions. The bulk rate employees at my local post office told me a lady decided she would change her permit from a postage meter bulk mail permit to an Indicia permit. But before she did the paperwork with the post office, she had a printer print a 1000-piece mailing using her postage meter permit number. (You know what's coming don't you?) When she went to the post office to change the permit, the post office changed her permit number and she had to have stickers made with the new permit and put them on all that mail.

Also, permits cannot be transferred to another post office if you move or change your mind. You have to start all over again and pay the fee at the new post office. Not just any post office can offer you a bulk mail permit, so you'll need to check in your area which post offices do.

A presort first-class mail (FCM) permit also is required to take advantage of lower presort rates for FCM and it is $75 as well. The same three types of permits apply for FCM as for bulk mail: one each for precanceled stamps, postage meter, and Indicia.

USPS services

The post office has a vested interest in your success so it is offering programs, some free, for mailing lists. Free materials and subscription publications, even videotapes, are available for your use. The USPS has also set up help for business mailers in the form of Postal Business Centers.

Zip+4 coding help

The USPS is very enthusiastic about zip+4 coding for reasons we've already discussed. In order to encourage mailers and businesses to use zip+4 coding, the USPS has set up a service to do it once for free for anyone's list. After the first time, a per-name charge is levied. Lists submitted electronically or on paper to the USPS National Address Information Center located in Memphis, Tennessee will be processed and returned with updated zip+4 codes. In addition, each address will be standardized, meaning it will be changed to all uppercase and everything that can be replaced with an abbreviation will be.

Change of address (COA) information is also available from the USPS. Every year thousands of people and businesses move and they leave COA information with their post office. Each day the post offices send the changes electronically from Computerized Forwarding System sites all over the country to the USPS National Address Information Center (NAIC) in Memphis. The NAIC consolidates the information and places it on 9-track tapes which it then distributes to private licensees every two weeks, who then offer services to update mailing lists for a fee. An estimated one million changes, deletions, and additions are sent out by the USPS for each two-week period. The USPS NCOA licensees also receive the changes to the zip+4 code file from the NAIC once a month as well.

In addition, information on the saturation walk sequence addresses is available from the NAIC. The USPS will not give you the saturation walk sequence addresses, so to get them you have to follow a mail carrier, and write down his or her delivery route in order. You may also purchase this information from someone who followed the mail carrier once and is now selling the information. If you have 90 percent of the residential addresses or 75 percent of all possible deliveries for a carrier route, you can have the rest of the information compared to the USPS National Address Information Center's (NAIC's) computerized carrier delivery sequence (CDS) file.

Of course, you must get the proper forms to request these services and to find out how the USPS wants the information provided. You can request these forms and more information by calling the National Address Information Center at (800) 331-5746.

You can zip+4 encode addresses yourself with a personal computer and the proper software. The USPS Coding Accuracy Support System (CASS) Certification is a certification given to software developers after they pass testing given by the USPS. Several types and levels of CASS-certification exist, but for our purposes only two are notable, CASS DPC Certification and the POSTNET Barcode Certification. We cover barcoding certification next, so for now let's define CASS DPC certification.

CASS DPC Certification for zip+4 coding means the software has been tested to accurately determine delivery point codes, zip+4 codes, 5-digit zip codes, and carrier route codes for mail pieces. CASS DPC Certification means the software developer has taken and passed stringent testing conducted every six months by the USPS.

Attractive mailing discounts are offered for barcoded mail, but in order to barcode for discounts, the mailing list has to be zip+4 coded. In addition, you will not be allowed the barcoding discounts at the post office unless you have proof you used CASS-certified software to prepare the mailing. This proof is usually provided by a USPS Form 3553, a form you can get the software to print, or you can get Form 3553 at the post office and fill it out. The Form 3553 for your list is only good for a limited period of time, usually six months, after which updated CASS-certified software must be used on the list again.

Reference materials

The bible of the USPS is the *Domestic Mail Manual (DMM)*, available for $36 per year and updated quarterly. As a mailer, you need to subscribe to it and it is also available from the Superintendent of Documents. You can get it in a paper format from the post office or in an electronic format you can search with your computer from Window Book or from PC DMM, both of whom are listed in appendix B. You can expect to pay $200 to $250 a year for an electronic version of the *DMM*, and you can expect updates to be sent out four times a year.

Helpful publications include the "Postal Bulletin," which is published biweekly and contains current orders, instructions, and information relating to the USPS. Subscriptions are available through the Superintendent of Documents. "Memo to Mailers" is a free publication put out by the USPS and is one you should be receiving. You can request to be put on the mailing list by writing to US Postal Service, P.O. Box 999, Springfield, VA 22150-0999.

The other publication you should have is the *National Five-Digit ZIP code and Post Office Directory*. Published annually, it offers the most current information, including what post offices have been discontinued, delivery statistics, and other important information as well as five-digit zip codes for the entire United States.

If you can't come to the U.S. Government bookstore, the bookstore can come to you. A free catalog of government publications, including the ones mentioned here, is available by writing Free Catalog, P.O. Box 37000, Washington, DC 20013-7000.

Other helpful publications you can get by request are *A Guide To Business Mail Preparation*, *Mailer's Guide*, *Third-Class Mail Preparation*, and *The Small Business Direct Mail Guide*.

Postal Business Centers

To compete, the post office is supporting mailers and mailing list businesses. Of the total volume of the 165.9 billion pieces of mail processed in 1991, 105 billion pieces were processed under worksharing permits.

To facilitate businesses in worksharing, the USPS has set up sixty-three Postal Business Centers (PBCs) so far, with one in almost every major city, and that number is growing. The PBC has as its mission to help businesses cut postage costs. The staff of the PBC is dedicated to helping businesses streamline a mailing operation. If you are a large volume mailer, you might even be assigned a representative who will visit you on-site.

You'll want to get to know your PBC representatives because they are the ones who can help you with your sticky questions. They also can supply you with materials such as brochures and templates you might find helpful. Current PBC locations and phone numbers are in appendix D. A call to the PBC nearest you will get you started in getting information you need as a mailing business.

The biggest complaint I hear from the developers of software products for mailing is they run up against postal employees who don't know the nuances of the regulations and give their customers a hard time. Some developers said they regularly get on the phone on behalf of their customers to talk with postal employees to straighten out problems. However, the one person these developers say they can count on is the customer service support manager in the PBC, who will move "heaven and earth" to solve a customer's problem. You might make sure you get to know this PBC manager.

The Postal Customer Council (PCC) is a local group that meets once a month, usually for lunch, to discuss postal issues and is made up of the local postal leadership and the business mailers in an area. Often PCC meetings will feature speakers who offer information on postal issues. If there is a PCC in your area, the manager from the closest PBC will probably attend some, if not all, of the monthly meetings, and you can meet him or her there. If you don't have a PCC in your area, it only takes two people to start one: a person outside the post office and a postal employee. It might be in your interest to be the outside person to start the PCC.

Insider tips

The secrets of the mailing industry, the tips born out of long experience are what you'll find here. Many of these hints will save you aggravation and some could save you money.

Get your mail right

The French, unlike Americans, do not think it's cute or funny when someone mispronounces their language. Postal employees and mail are much like the French and their language. Postal workers deal with hundreds of people and thousands of pieces of mail every day, and while most of them I met were warm and friendly, some have little sympathy and even less patience with people who don't get their bulk mail prepared and sorted correctly. Their point of view is, as a mailer, you're getting paid to get it right and if you don't, they have to redo it.

The best way to worm your way into the heart of the Bulk Mail Entry Unit (BMEU) personnel is to get your mailing right. While you might be able to get past hurried employees at the Bulk Mail Center (BMC), if your mail is prepared incorrectly, you will be found out. That's because the machines examine each piece and improperly prepared mailing pieces stand out. You could get a call from the BMU personnel who will want you to fix your mailing and maybe even charge you first-class rates for delivery.

However, every mailing list service I talked with had a story about how they offer special treatment to the employees on the bulk mail dock. Sometimes they bring them a special treat, sometimes they write a letter of praise to the postmaster of the location when someone has been especially helpful, but everyone said they always, always make sure their mailing is right. If the mailing is wrong, the postal employees will make you redo it, right there, before it can go out and no amount of buttering up will earn their respect. One mailer I talked with said she had seven wooden flats, piled high with bags of sorted mail and wrapped with cellophane (such as the mail being loaded in FIG. 2-31), and the post office made her come back and unwrap each one to cross out two incorrect characters on the label of each bag.

2-31
Palletized bulk mail is dispatched into a 40-foot trailer from a Bulk Mail Center (BMC).

United States Postal Service

For praise or complaints about postal practices and services there is a form, USPS Customer Service Form 4314-C. While you can send the form to any Postmaster, mailing list services tell me they send their 4314-C forms to Washington, D.C., which means all you have to do is copy the return address on the form. The reasoning behind sending the form to Washington is it has to go through a longer list of bureaucrats that way, so hopefully more important people see it. You can obtain a 4314-C from your mail carrier or from any post office. Asking for one can be interpreted as a threat, so if you want one to report someone is doing a good job, you'll want to say that when you ask for the 4314-C.

Humidity can affect mail. If you have mail that is just under one ounce per piece sitting out on a humid day on a dock somewhere, it might weigh more than one ounce each by the time you get it to the post office. You're better off on humid days to keep the mail inside until you're ready to go.

Humidity

Bulk mail pieces have to be identical, meaning you should be able to open each piece of a bulk mailing and find exactly the same thing in each one. It is permissible to sign each piece of bulk mail and still have it qualify for bulk mail rates. However, if you decide to write the same exact personal note on each piece of bulk mail, be prepared to get a call from the post office. They weigh and open ten pieces of each bulk mail mailing and if it looks like a personal note is in there, it might hold up your mailing until you can straighten it out.

Bulk mail tips

Be sure your printer is configured correctly to your software when you generate barcodes. It might be a good idea to print a sample and take it down to the post office, just to be sure it works with the barcode reader.

Barcoding tips

If your mail is not machinable, it doesn't matter if it's barcoded. You might want to barcode so the mail travels faster, but if you have staples, or the piece isn't properly folded and tabbed, then there's little point in going to extra effort to barcode. It might look more professional, but it won't save you any money.

If you're using a postage meter, you will soon discover the post office is especially aware of the dates on mail pieces. That's because an independent auditor measures their performance by how long it takes a mail piece to travel to its destination. If it has an old date on it before they even get it, the old date can make it appear it took longer than it did to deliver the mail. However, it is very easy to forget to adjust the date on your postage meter, especially if you don't use it every day. And if the date is wrong on your mail, the post office will send you a couple of reminder notices, then they might return your mail to you to be correctly dated.

Postage meter tips

So what do you do if you meter the mail with an incorrect date? The answer is set the meter on $0.00 postage, correct the date, and meter each piece again on the bottom or the back. It is important the meter is legible, as the facing machines do not check dates.

You can also get postage back from items incorrectly metered, or spoiled in some way. This is especially important to tell to employees, who might throw away or destroy a spoiled envelope with metered postage on it because they didn't want you to see their mistake.

Get your money back from "spoiled" mail

You don't have to throw away money if you ruin mail you've metered. Here are the rules from the December 1992 issue of the *Domestic Mail Manual:*

What to Submit.

a Unused meter stamps are considered for refund, only if
   (1) The meter stamps are complete and legible;
   (2) They are on the portion of the envelope or wrapper bearing the name and address of the addressee, including the window on a window envelope;
   (3) They are accompanied by an application on Form 3533; and
   (4) They are submitted for refund within 1 year of the dates appearing in the stamps.

b. If a portion of the stamp is printed on one envelope or card and the remaining portion on another, the two must be fastened together to show that the two portions represent one stamp.

c. Meter stamps printed on labels or tapes that have not been stuck to wrappers or envelopes must be submitted loose.

d. Refunds are allowable for stamps on metered reply envelopes only when it is obvious that an incorrect amount of postage was printed thereon.

e. Submit separately, with statement of facts, envelopes or address portions of wrappers on mail returned to sender from the mailing office, marked "No such post office in state named, returned for better address" or "Received without contents," indicating no effort was made to deliver.

What Not to Submit.

a. Meter reply envelopes or cards paid at the proper rate of postage.

b. Meter stamps printed on labels or tape that have been removed from wrappers or envelopes.

c. Meter stamps without the name of the post office and state.

d. Meter stamps without the date printed on tape (see 144.47).

e. Meter stamps printed on mail that was dispatched from the mailing post office in regular course and returned to sender as undeliverable, including mail marked "No such post office in state named."

f. Meter stamps on mail addressed for local delivery and returned to sender after directory service was given or effort was made to deliver.

Business reply mail

If you want to prepay someone's response to you, you have two options. You can include a *self-addressed stamped envelope* (SASE) or postcard or you can get a business reply mail permit. Business reply mail costs more because you have the expense of the $75 permit as well as the expense of a $.40 processing fee and first-class postage of at least $.29 for each piece of mail that is sent to you. However, you know if you put stamps on each envelope, it is going to cost at least the one-ounce first-class mail (FCM) $.29 rate for each one and you lose money on every envelope never returned to you.

However, you might wish to appear as a larger business and so the Business Reply Mail permit might be worth it from that standpoint.

Deciding whether or not to prepay postage is simply a matter of arithmetic. If you think more than half of the recipients of the piece will send it back, it will probably be cheaper to prepay the postage in the form of stamps or meter than to use Business Reply Mail.

If you want to use Business Reply Mail, another option is the Business Reply Mail Accounting System (BRMAS) permit which costs $185 but you're only charged $.02 plus $.29 for each piece of mail returned to you. The rule of thumb at the post office is if you get more than 500 pieces of Business Reply Mail (BRM) a year, then your Business Reply Mail Accounting System (BRMAS) permit pays for itself. If you get less than 500 BRM pieces per year, the regular Business Reply Mail permit is cheaper.

A special permit is required for Business Reply Mail and it carries a $75 processing fee. Business Reply Mail is also covered in the bulk mail classes offered by the post office, and you'll find your best answers there. USPS Publication 25 also offers specific, detailed information about the preparation and design of Business Reply Mail pieces.

The Facing Identification Mark (FIM)

The discussion of the BRM permit leads us into the a discussion of the facing identification mark (FIM). The FIM provides a way for postal automated equipment to face and cancel letter mail that doesn't have the special phosphorus material used to face meter imprint mail or mail with postage stamps. The FIM is a barcode, but unlike the POSTNET barcode, it does not represent any portion of the delivery address. As of this writing, only three FIM barcodes, designated as A, B, or C patterns, are represented by long vertical lines printed at the upper right of the envelope. An additional function of the FIM is to indicate to postal automation equipment if the mail has a barcode or not so the determination of whether the mail should be sent to OCR or BCS equipment can be made by machine.

When you obtain a BRM permit, the post office will produce the appropriate A, B, or C FIM barcode for you, camera-ready, so it can be printed on return envelopes. If you will print the POSTNET code on your BRM mail, you'll get the FIM C pattern, and if not you'll be offered the FIM B pattern. The FIM A pattern indicates mail that is not prepaid, but has a barcode and may be obtained without a BRM permit. (If you decide to send prepaid envelopes, you can also get the post office to print a camera-ready POSTNET barcode for printing on your return envelopes to speed the return of your mail.) Some of the software available for mail automation will print your BRM, barcode, or the FIM on envelopes for you. The shop doing the envelope printing might also have the appropriate camera-ready FIM pattern available by request. An example of BRM with the FIM and POSTNET barcode is shown in FIG. 2-32.

BUSINESS REPLY MAIL

FIRST-CLASS MAIL PERMIT NO. 999 ANYTOWN, US

POSTAGE WILL BE PAID BY ADDRESSEE

Hot Stuff Mail Catalog
PO Box 123401
Anytown, US 12345-6789

NO POSTAGE
NECESSARY
IF MAILED
IN THE
UNITED STATES

2-32
Here is a sample of Business Reply Mail. The vertical bars on the top right are the Facing Identification Mark (FIM).

International mailing

International mailing is a whole different subject. The standards and the addressing rules change depending on the country you are mailing to and speed is measured in weeks instead of days.

However, the complexity of international mailing makes it more attractive to companies to pay someone to do it than to do it themselves. Here's an opportunity, a niche market within the mail sector, and perhaps one you'd like to pursue.

If you're thinking about international mail services, the book you need is the *International Mail Manual (IMM)* updated twice a year by the USPS and is $16 per year. It is printed by the Government Printing Office and subscriptions are available from the Superintendent of Documents or from a U.S. Government bookstore. Credit card orders by phone are accepted, and the contact information and an order form is printed in appendix B for your convenience.

So, now you have a history of how the postal system got started and an idea of what the USPS's goals are. All of these requirements are subject to change, which is another factor that can bring you, as a mailer, business. In general, you can expect the future to hold a move toward more and more automation required by the USPS on the part of the mailer, and higher rates for mail that isn't ready for automation.

Now that you have a foundation both in how the post office works and the terminology used, you're ready to move into how you can get started. The next chapter offers specifics on what you need to begin your own mailing list service.

References

Angus, Ian. 1973. *Stamps, Posts and Postmarks*. New York, NY: St. Martin's Press.

Compton's New Media. 1992. *Compton's Interactive Encyclopedia for Windows*, v1.01VW: CD-ROM. Carlsbad, California: Compton's NewMedia.

Encyclopedia Britiannica. 1984. *Macropaedia*, v14: p886-887. Chicago, Illinois: Encyclopedia Britiannica.

3 Getting started

Shirley Grose started as a homemaker who needed extra income. She had small children and had previously earned extra income from making and selling Barbie doll clothes. Shirley bought out a friend's automated personalized letter service when her friend's husband was transferred out of state, and when her customers transitioned from needing personalized letters to mailing services, Shirley transitioned, too. She now has a thriving mailing list service business in West Hills, California, with one entire room in her home and her garage dedicated to her mailing business. Her husband has taken an early retirement from his position as an engineer at Hughes Aircraft to help her, and she provides work to several of her neighbors. Shirley and her husband Gerald are especially grateful for the opportunity for profitable work together, because now Hughes Aircraft is laying off workers by the hundreds.

A.G. Pitsilos was working for his father and desktop publishing a newsletter on the side. He had to get a bulk mailing permit to do the mailings for the newsletter customers he was serving. Now he's on his own, has given up desktop publishing newsletters, and is concentrating on just the mail list service business because he says it's more profitable.

Kathie Edwards walked into the dentist office where she was office manager to discover she'd been replaced. She hunted around for a job and ended up working part-time for a mailing service. After four weeks she quit, went home and told her husband, "We can do this better ourselves." The Edwards have been offering mailing list services ever since.

Shirley and Gerald Grose
Automatic Total Service, West Hills, California

Shirley Grose started as an entrepreneur making Barbie doll clothes that a neighborhood girl sold in order to earn outfits for her own Barbie dolls. While the Barbie doll clothes helped Shirley and her husband, Gerald, take vacations, provide birthday gifts to each other, and gifts for their children, it didn't last. Barbie went out of style, but Shirley, with her talent for sewing went into alterations.

It was when Shirley was doing alterations that a friend started a business with a Flexwriter to do form letters for businesses. Shirley watched her friend start and build the form letter business, but suddenly the other woman's husband was to be transferred out of California. Meanwhile, Shirley was tiring of the alterations business. The idea came up that Shirley could buy the form letter business.

Shirley said she worked for her friend free for a full month before the business was hers and when her friend did move Shirley paid for the business and the equipment from her profits. The transition was so smooth, not one customer left, and some of those first customers are still customers today.

Form letters didn't last however. With the advent of the computer, companies started doing their own form letters. However, Shirley noticed her clients needed help with their mailings. So she adapted, switching to mailing services, getting herself a postage meter, and the necessary permits.

Shirley's husband, Gerald, is the one who brought computing into their mailing business. Gerald is acquainted with dBASE, a database program, and began helping in the business by taking customer lists and using dBASE to sort the names and print the labels for mailings.

Most of the time, Shirley's clients come to her through referrals, but she speaks very highly of her small ad in the local Pacific Bell Yellow Pages. She says she has tried different phone books, but for mailing services, the Pacific Bell ad pulls in customers every month.

Shirley believes in customer service. "We treat our clients like their money is our money. We believe in the golden rule." Shirley's back bedroom and her garage have been taken over and she hires her neighbors to do letter shop and fulfillment services. For one particular insurance company, Shirley is their outgoing mailroom. The company has their printed materials delivered to her home office, where she puts together new packets of materials and sends them to agents in the field. Shirley says she even trains new employees in company procedures. Another client who depends on her heavily is a bank who mails disks containing custom software. The disks have to go out and arrive in a certain time frame in order for the bank's branches to meet Federal Government reporting regulations.

Talking to clients and offering status reports is important, according to Shirley. She also requires payment up front from new customers until they've become established with her and always requires the postage in advance from all her customers. Shirley holds several mailing permits, which she alladdition we'll cover how to build products you can market and how to protect your investment from those who might want to steal it.ows her customers to use, and prides herself in her relationship with the Bulk Mail Center at the local post office.

In 1989, Gerald, employed with Hughes Aircraft, was made a one-time offer for early retirement. Both Shirley and Gerald weighed the decision carefully, and decided he should take the retirement and join the business full-time. The couple has expressed their appreciation for the mailing business because so many people have been laid off without the benefits of an attractive pension offer and without their own business to make up the difference.

Now the two of them work together and Gerald's database expertise is helping them expand into offering further barcoding and carrier route presort discounts to their first-class mail clients. Some weeks they put in 50 hours and others they put in 10, but their financial reports are healthy ones. Despite the economic downturn since 1989, Shirley and Gerald are experiencing some record-breaking months in their business, especially in the first few months of 1993.

Shirley and Gerald both said they know they could expand further, but they prefer to have time to play with their grandchildren in the afternoon and do volunteer work for a local non-profit group. "Knowing when to quit is the hardest part," Shirley said.

The opportunity is real and it is growing. While talking with mailing list service owners, I found these characteristics: they knew how to operate a computer, especially the ones who were the most successful; they were sticklers for making sure their work was accurate and delivered on time; and they were dependable. Many had a background in computer programming or database management, and while that isn't a prerequisite, it would certainly help.

All the businesses I talked with had taken the training offered free by the various agencies that offer it, but I discovered in sharing with each one that they learned as well from my knowledge of what others were doing. You'll have that advantage as well in reading this material.

What does a mailing list service do anyway? Who are their customers? How much can you expect to make doing this? The answers to those questions and others are here. In this chapter, we'll talk about the specifics of what mailing list services do, cover the basic concepts to get you on your way, what you can charge, and how to find customers in everyday places. In addition we'll cover how to build products you can market and how to protect your investment from those who might want to steal it.

Operating a mailing list service involves one or more of the following activities: list maintenance, list brokering, marketing, mailings, and consulting. While every mailing list service owner has done all of these at one time or another, the successful mailing list services pick one or two to focus on. Here is what each one involves.

List maintenance is doing the actual computer work with the mailing list. Usually a business will have a list of customers or contacts it needs to mail to either already in some computer format that you will have to convert and then maintain, or in a hard copy format, such as on invoices or sales receipts.

Design   You, as the maintainer of the list, will choose a program to use, set up what information from the records is important to have in a computerized format and the order that information is to be entered (known as designing the database), then enter the information or have it entered. Once the list is in the computer it is then a matter of maintaining the list, which involves making sure the addresses on the list are deliverable, entering new customers or contacts, watching out for duplicates, and sorting the list for use by the business.

Reports   Sorting the list, also known as *slicing and dicing* is not hard once you know how and can be profitable for you. Businesses might need reports from the same list of the names in alphabetical order, the names ordered by region (usually done by sorting by zip code), the latest names added to the list, and so on. This work can all be done by the computer once the list is entered, and you can charge for the various reports. In addition, sorting can also involve what the post office calls *pre-sorting* of the list. Usually labels are printed in the order the post office sorts the mail so when placed on the mailing pieces and properly bundled, the mailing can be sent at a money-saving discounted rate.

Data entry   Data entry is more involved than it sounds. One of the banes of the mailing list existence is getting a list where a secretary or receptionist has been assigned to design a list and then enter the data. This can result in problems such as inconsistent entry of data so a title such as Vice President ends up being entered as VP, v.p., vice pres., Vice Pres, or V. Pres. all in the same list. This makes it nearly impossible to go back later and pick out all the vice presidents on the list, because the computer looks for exact matches of text to do its sorting. It can also make it difficult to find exact matches by computer for purging duplicates. If you are in charge of getting the data entered, then you can see to it that the entry is consistent, which benefits you when it is time to produce reports, and the customer who gets a consistent appearance to the list.

List cleaning   *List cleaning* is the process of comparing the names to the post office records to be sure they are all deliverable. Several programs provide the ability to do this comparison. Lists can need cleaning for several reasons, such as cities change street names, carrier route numbers, rezone for zip codes, and the data could be entered incorrectly. The biggest reason for list cleaning is the crucial 20 percent of the people in any given area who move each year. A list that is not regularly cleaned can have a staggering amount of undeliverable addresses and mailing to such a list can mean money thrown away.

Merge/purge   *Merge/purge* is the terminology used for eliminating duplicate names from one list or combined lists in order to keep from wasting printed materials and postage. Duplicates on a single list are common and besides being a waste of materials, they can make the recipient feel as though the mailer is sloppy, inconsiderate, or both.

Profile

Geoffrey Hollander
Mail Pouch, Port Hueneme, California

Geoff said he had an intuition he should begin learning to use a computer, so he got a job with a software company. The software company decided to begin selling their product by direct mail and Geoff ended up involved in the process.

In doing investigation into the marketing end of mailing, Geoff said he discovered fascinating figures on response rates and studies on how a mailing piece should be done. When the software company started to do mailings, Geoff was ready to get involved. At the first meeting, when the boss stood up and told everyone the company expected a 10 to 30 percent return, Geoff recalls asking if those figures were optimistic considering the national averages were 2 to 4 percent. It turns out, those were very optimistic response rates.

"We did everything you were supposed to—personalized letters printed in 2 colors—we followed all the rules." The software company mailed between 50,000 and 250,000 pieces each month for 18 months. The lowest return they got was 0.5 percent, the highest return was 4.5 percent. The average was 2.25 percent—right in the range of the national averages! In addition, the software company experimented with prices from $49 to $495 and discovered they got the greatest return for their investment at the $179 figure—again, right in the range of the typical textbook statistics Geoff had been reading on direct mail!

Geoff said he was fascinated by the process, and one day it occurred to him people might pay him to handle mailings. He checked in the phone book and discovered no one else was doing it. Then he asked around, made some contacts with business friends who encouraged him, and started Mail Pouch in 1986 from his home.

Even with his previous computer experience, Geoff recalls it took six months to get everything working so a job went flawlessly. He said part of the time was spent learning more about the mailing business and part was spent learning the software. Now, Geoff claims mailing list services are easier to start because the software is easier to use and working at home is more accepted. In fact, minimizing his expenses by working at home was the strongest factor in his survival, Geoff asserts.

Blunders are part of the business. Geoff recounted how an old sailor once told him, "A professional is not someone who doesn't make mistakes. A professional is someone who knows how to correct his mistakes."

Geoff laughingly recounts the trials of the business. "I've reprinted entire rolls of 50,000 labels because of an 'oops' like I forgot something on the label. I count on mistakes, computer downtime, and oversights. Sometimes it's my fault, sometimes an oversight, sometimes you just get tired. I've had clients take a stack of labels five inches thick, pull open it arbitrarily, and say 'this guy is on here twice' and they're right. It's like psychic phenomenon."

"Regular customers are necessary so you're not always spending your efforts getting new customers." Geoff says he's struggled to get customers, but also admits he's moved the business three times. Mail Pouch started in New Mexico, relocated to Oxnard, California, and moved to settle in Port Hueneme.

Mail Pouch customers come from the company's Yellow Pages advertisement and from referrals. Geoff networks with other people doing the same type of work such as mailing houses, letter shops, and from businesses who might run into others to whom referrals can be made, such as printers. One of his most successful means of getting customers was a list of business and residents obtained from a business who was closing. Geoff describes how he "massaged" the list by updating it using the telephone company's records, added new names to it, and eliminated duplicates. "Each time I mailed that list, it was like printing money."

Most of Mail Pouch's business is divided between doing work such as postal coding and address correction on an existing list and list maintenance on a regular basis for businesses. Geoff does some list brokering and also spends time writing for mailing publications about the business. Mail Pouch doesn't do any letter shop work because Geoff wants to keep the space his business requires to a minimum.

Geoff charges an initial, minimum charge to deal with any new mailing list. This is so he can look over the list, test print some sample pieces, and try to get the "lay of the land." He has a per-piece price list for work the computer can do, such as locating duplicates and printing a report, and an hourly charge for work he has to be involved in, such as the actual elimination of duplicates.

Because Geoff doesn't do letter shop work, he's learned the hard way to ask for a sample piece before he sorts a list for a client. This problem came up because several times he sorted a client's list for one type of discount, such as an automation discount, and then when the client took the mailing to a letter shop, they were charged a re-sorting charge. The letter shop charged extra because the mailing piece was the wrong size and wouldn't qualify for an automation discount. That meant the entire mailing had to be re-sorted for a different discount.

The attraction for Geoff in mailing lists is the patterns. Being a former artist, patterns fascinate him and each list has a pattern of its own. For example, if the first 2500 names in a list have 10-percent duplicates, then it is safe to say the rest of the list will have the same percentage of duplicates. Database marketing is also intriguing. "There are secrets, information hidden in the patterns in lists that can be found if you know where to look."

In doing a mailing for a non-profit group, Geoff used Peoplesmith's Genderizer product on the list to see if he could find something out about the type of people who are on the list. Discovery of the type of donor would help the group rent or buy lists with donors who had similar characteristics. The assumption was made that donors without the "Mr. & Mrs." or without two names, such as "Bob & Mary," were single. Geoff noticed the single donors outnumbered the married donors two to one. Of the single group, the gender split was right down the middle—half the donors men, half women. On another donor list for a different group, the proportions were nearly identical. Geoff used these patterns to put the non-profit groups on to where they might find additional donors.

Geoff indicates list cleaning is an important sales tool for business. "When a business creates a mailing list, it is tempting to only think about getting to those people for the business they can bring. But the beauty about the mailing list is you can stay in touch with people. If you can make a customer feel like he is being contacted because you value him and not for what he can do for you, you'll be successful," Geoff maintains. "By being sloppy with the list, you can send the message that you don't value the customer and can in fact alienate the person. For example, duplicate pieces of the mail to the same person is a list cleaning problem that can send the wrong message."

Future plans for Mail Pouch include trying some direct marketing of mailing list how-to materials written in-house. In addition, Geoff's goal is to do further work in the database marketing field, uncovering patterns.

Mailing lists themselves have value and you can act as a broker, meaning you can be the party who brings two other parties, a list owner and a list buyer, together for a business transaction. Brokering mailing lists can involve representing a client to obtain a needed list of names for a mailing, representing someone who owns a list, or both.

Mailing lists are rented or sold, but ownership of the list remains with the source of the list. Lists can be rented for a single use, more than one use, or they can be sold, which allows the buyer unlimited use. However, the sale of a list does not allow the purchaser the right to rent or sell the same list.

However, list renters can build lists of their own that can be rented or sold. This is done by encouraging response to a rented list and then tracking the responses in a new list. Any responses to a mailing from a rented or purchased list become the property of the person doing the mailing.

Brokers often represent several list owners. You'll find list brokers in the Standard Rate and Data Service (SRDS) guides of direct mail list rates and data available at any public library. In looking through SRDS listings, you'll notice the names of the same brokers appearing again and again. You'll want to contact brokers who have lists of interest to you and ask for their catalog and any other information they have available.

Brokering

Here is a sample of what a typical SRDS listing might look like:

Sample SRDS listing

Pollution Control: Conscientious Disposal

1. Personnel
   List Manager:
   Hot Lists, 4785 Marketing Rd., Delphi, CA 91352
   Phone (310) HOT-LIST, Fax (310) GO-LISTS

2. Description
   Attenders at informational programs on hazardous material handling.

3. List Source
   Registrations

4. Quantity and Rental Rates
   April 1993

Total number	Price per/M	
Total list (1991)	35,000	75.00
1992	27,125	85.00

   Selections: state, SCF, zip code, attention line, 5.00/M extra; business, V.P., operations manager, president, manufacturing, chemical, 50.00/M extra; key coding, 2.00/M extra.

   Minimum order 300.00

5. Commission, Credit Policy
   20 percent to recognized brokers; 15 percent to ad agencies. Lists cannot be returned or exchanged. Cancellations prior to production subject to payment for work already completed. Net 30 days.

6. Method of Addressing
   4-up Cheshire labels
   4-up pressure sensitive labels, 8.00/M
   1-up pressure sensitive labels, 6.00/M

7. Delivery Schedule
   10 working days

8. Restrictions
   Sample mailing piece required for approval. Rental agreement; one-time use or one-year contract.
   Unauthorized usage billed at regular one-time rate.

9. Test Arrangement
   Subject to approval of publishers

10. Letter Shop Services
    Available on request

11. Maintenance
    Updated monthly

When you're representing a client looking for a certain type of list, you can expect to garner a percentage discount off the retail price from the broker you deal with, and then you in turn can charge the retail price to your client. The size of the discount will vary depending on the type of list and the amount of business you give that particular broker each year, but can be from 5 to 20 percent or more. Any additional handling of the list that you do for your customer, such as merge/purge of the customer's list with the list from the broker, you can charge for at your regular rates.

You can also become a list broker yourself, meaning you can represent list owners. Listings in the SRDS are free to brokers, which is what makes the publication such a good source for lists, but the real work in list brokering is in maintaining current information on the lists. This work goes further than just knowing the profile of the members of the list. Good list brokers know who has rented a particular list, how many times, and they follow up with list renters to see what was mailed and the kind of response rate the list produced.

The two basic types of lists are *compiled* lists and *response* lists. While *compiled* lists have value and can be organized from a number of publicly published sources, such as the new business listings in the newspaper, the most lucrative lists for rental are the *response* lists. Those lists are made up of people who are known to have responded to an offer made to them, usually by mail. The most valuable response lists are those of people who have purchased expensive items by mail, such as computer equipment or high-priced newsletters on particular subjects.

Your best bet as a list broker is to represent owners of response lists, such as a mail-order merchandise distributor or a magazine because you can charge more for these lists and make a higher commission. However, it is profitable to compile lists, especially if you can cross-reference the lists in some way, such as new business owners who own more than one piece of real estate, or female new property owners who live in neighborhoods where the houses are more than 15 years old. Anything that you can do to add additional information to the members of a list also adds value to the list. In addition, be prepared yourself to answer the questions I encourage people to ask brokers about the lists they represent.

Asking the following questions can help you determine if a list will be of value to you in addition to protecting you from misunderstandings. More detailed information is available in the reprint of the Direct Marketing Association's Guidelines in appendix H. These questions and the ones in appendix H are also questions you should be prepared to answer as a list broker.

What to ask when renting or buying a list

- Who owns the list? Do you have the names and addresses of other parties involved with the list such as the list broker, the list manager, and the list compiler or service bureau. Are all of the involved parties bound by the agreement about to be made?
- How was the list obtained? Is it a compiled list or a response list? How many records are available? If it is a response list, did the respondents purchase anything? What was the average amount of their purchases? Is there any other information about the members of the list such as age, occupation, employment, etc. Is that information available?
- Who else has used the list and for what? What were their results? When was the last time the list was rented?
- Can a portion of the list be tested prior to rental or purchase? Can a portion of the list be rented? Is there a minimum? Can a true random sample (a Nth number sample) be taken? Can the remainder of the list be rented or purchased without the random sample portion at a later time?
- What formats (including computerized formats) is the list available in? Are telephone numbers included? Can the members of the list be called after the mailing without payment of an additional fee?
- Is the list available already sorted? How can the list be sorted?
- What is allowable for use of the list? Can it be used more than once? Is a sample mailing piece required? To speed things up, can the sample be a copy of proofs going to the printer?
- Can the broker guarantee no one else will be mailing to the list during a specified time period? How long can be guaranteed? If not, can the broker guarantee no one will be mailing about a similar product to the one the list is being rented for during a specified time period?

- How is the list maintained? How often is it cleaned?
- How is payment for the list to be made? What percentage of the list is guaranteed deliverable? Is there any credit or refund for *nixies* (undeliverable mail) or duplicates?
- If the list is merge/purged with another, can credit or refund be offered for duplicates found on the rental list?
- What is the rental fee? Are there any minimums? Is there any provision for verification? Is there a discount for reuse?
- How long does it take to get the list? How will it be delivered? Are any materials to be returned? (The list broker might expect the return of 9-track tapes.) If so, when is return expected?

In general, if you are representing a client, you should be able to get a broker discount on the retail price of the list. It is also common for brokers to accept a copy of proofs going to the printer for the sample mailing piece, and some will even accept a design of the mailing piece before it is in production as a sample.

Most mailing list brokers want you to be successful with their list and will offer you not only the list, but sometimes marketing advice as well. They have seen a lot of mailings and keep up on what is working. So it is in your interest to begin talking with brokers as soon as you know you might want to rent or purchase a list for a client.

It is commonly accepted that any responses to the mailing belong to the list renter, i.e., your client. However, you should check to be sure. Also, it may be in your client's interest to offer some kind of giveaway to get members to the list to respond, even if they don't contribute in some way. That way you know they are a *responder*, and your client owns the name. It can cost as much as $.50 or more per name to get a response by the time you send a mailing piece and prepay its return, but if you think you might mail to that list often, it could be worth it.

In addition, buying a list usually costs twice as much as a one-time rental. If you know you're going to use the list at least twice, you might just want to buy it. However, once you buy it, the list is no longer cleaned by the owner and lists get stale quickly. If the mailings are going to be far apart, say more than six months, it might be better to negotiate for a multiple rental discount.

Smart thinking in renting a list can pay off as well. If you know you can only rent 5000 names from a 20,000 member list, try to rent the names that will not only offer you a postal discount, but might tell you something about where the most profitable places are for your next mailing. For example, if you're mailing locally, renting ten names from each carrier route is enough to get you a carrier route discount. If you track the responses to the mailing, you could discover certain carrier routes were more effective than others for your client's particular offer. So next time, you rent exclusively those carrier routes. You may want to go as far as to find out the characteristics of responsive carrier routes, such as average income, housing type, and so on and then, using demographic information, find other carrier routes that match the responding ones to hit as well.

Another function of the mailing list service business is marketing. *Marketing* has to do with expertise in bringing up the response to the mailing and so is more concerned with the appearance, the type of list mailed to, and the approach used in the mailing than with saving money on postage costs. This particular field will only be of interest and benefit to customers who are mailing for a response.

Marketing

Marketing overlaps with list maintenance and list brokering, and some mailers offer marketing advice as part of their services. Wayne Stoler, owner of Letter Perfect Information Services, Inc., insists that the more mailing services know about marketing, the more successful they'll be.

In dealing with clients who are mailing to sell a product or service, your expertise on trends, the types of offers that have been successful in your area, what response rates can be expected, where various types of lists can be found, and how to boost response can get you repeat business in addition to boosting your client's bottom line. But you have to know your stuff. Cecil C. Hoge, Sr., in his book *Mail Order Moonlighting* mentions the "slaughter of the mail order innocents" and says "a fool and his money are soon parted . . . super fast in mail order."

Most of the marketing knowledge you'll need can be found in the plethora of direct marketing books, available at your public library, and the current marketing trends are explained in trade publications. Some of the more popular ones are *Target Marketing*, *DM News*, *Direct Marketing*, and *Catalog Age*.

The types of marketing hints you'll offer customers might vary from the tip that a two-color mailing piece pulls better response than a single-color piece to helping a customer determine how soon they can expect responses and the half-life of the mailing.

For example, mailings within the continental U.S. usually reach their peak response in three weeks, according to Carol Grant, the Direct Marketing Manager for WordStar International, who mails millions of direct mail pieces a year. If customers are going to respond, the responses will begin about three days after the national mailing, continue to climb in number until three weeks after the shipping date, and then begin to drop.

A graph of the typical response is the bell curve seen so often in statistical analysis. The top of the bell is known as the half-life, meaning half of the total responses are in. By tracking the response to a mailing, you can deduce that when the response begins to decline, you've reached that midpoint. If you multiply the half-life by two, you can determine with some accuracy how many responses can be expected for the entire mailing.

It is also known that follow-up phone calls can increase response dramatically.

One writer of advertising copy said he wrote a 12-page letter on an investment product, and the next time the letter was sent it was made a bigger type size so it was 16 pages in length. The response to the larger type 16-page letter was greater by four to one than the 12-page letter.

Several publications specialize in marketing by mail and will offer tips and expertise you can pass on to clients. You can also pick up information at local PCC meetings.

Mailing

Also called *letter shop*, this is the actual preparation of mailings. Mailing includes all or part of putting printed or photocopied materials in order (collating), folding the materials, placing the materials in envelopes, printing or labeling the materials, sealing envelopes, putting on postage, sorting the envelopes according to the USPS requirements, making out the required paperwork, and delivering the mailing to the proper post office.

Letter shop work can also be done as the finishing touch to one or more of the other mailing services. Fortunately, machines are available that make letter shop work easier, but the machines also require space, such as a garage or warehouse. Regular clients of letter shop services often have the letter shop store frequently used materials, such as envelopes with the company logo or preprinted advertising.

Consulting

At one time or another, every mailing list service ends up being a consultant. Your understanding of the USPS automation system can be put to work so your customer's mail can be sent at the lowest possible cost. You'll be able to look at a mailing and say, if you'd fold that in half you could save $2000 a year on your mailings.

In many cases you'll give free advice as part of your service, but you can also charge for mailing consulting. Many mailing list services do have an hourly charge for sitting down and explaining the business to a neophyte or for helping a new customer who has expressed their interest in doing much of the mailing work themselves. In addition, you can teach classes, write articles, and do seminars on mailing which will not only help people who wouldn't otherwise use your services, but will promote you as an expert in the field.

While it doesn't take any special skills to start a mailing list service business, it does require you follow a few basic steps. To operate a mailing list service, you'll need to do research to learn the business, attend the classes your local post office gives on bulk mailing, get one or more mailing permits from the post office, buy a computer if you don't already have one, buy software, do a few mailings, decide what services to offer, and determine what to charge.

The first step, even before you get a computer, is to learn about the USPS and its requirements for mailing, since your business will be based on meeting those requirements. You're in the right place to start by reading this book, but there is no substitute for your own research. While I've tried to be as complete and as specific as possible in offering you facts, the information offered here is subject to change. I've included it anyway because it will give you a frame of reference to work from, but you'll need to check it with the appropriate sources (usually the post office) before you rely on it.

One of the ways to begin your research is to find out when the tours of your local post office are offered. The USPS is quite proud of its automation work and offers regular tours, especially through the larger and more automated facilities. In the tour, you'll learn the processes, meet some of the people you might be working with, and find out the locations where business mailers bring mail.

Another research source is publications who focus on specific aspects of mailing and direct marketing. Some are free, such as "Memo To Mailers," and others are available by subscription. I would strongly suggest you subscribe to as many as possible. Your success depends a good deal on know-how, so don't be stingy getting learning materials for yourself. The contact information for these publications is in appendix B.

You should take advantage of any free classes and free educational material offered by the post office. As you learn about the postal requirements, you can expect to take the free post office classes twice—once to get an idea of what is going on, and again after you've done some investigation so you can get specific questions answered. Even if the classes appear to be outside the realm of what you think you might be doing, you should go because the person instructing the class will probably be able to answer your questions, and they'll be a good contact for you in case of problems.

You'll also need a computer. If you don't have any computer experience at all, you'll need to get some basic educational materials on computers and begin to learn. Lots of educational material is available and adult education programs at night and on the weekends to teach computer skills are available almost everywhere.

Steps to building a mailing list service

Learn the business

Take USPS classes

Select a computer and buy software

Software is an integral part of the business, and you'll need some to start. While I recommend both a computer and software, I suggest you buy your software slowly, learning one package at a time. If you take an introductory computer class, immediately afterward is a good time to buy your software and computer, while your memory is fresh and you can make use of your new-found skills.

In the next chapter, I recommend what type of computer hardware to purchase. I also go through and explain what kind of software you'll need for the mailing list service and list many of the software packages available.

The more familiar you are with a type of computer software called a *database*, the more income potential you'll have. I spend an entire chapter on it in order to give you a solid background on the subject, but you'll need to do further investigation on your own by getting books on databases, taking courses, or both.

Obtain permits

In order to get discounted rates for mailing, you have to get permits from the post office. You might be able to put off getting the required permits if you start out doing work for someone who already has a permit, but you can expect to get at least one and as many as three permits from the post office. It will cost you between $200 and $300 for all the available permits, which have to be renewed once a year. The advantage to having all the permits is you can perform whatever work comes along. It is less expensive to get all the permits at once than one at a time, because you have to pay a processing fee no matter how many permits you get. If you decide to specialize in one or two areas, you can let the permits you don't want expire and only pay the annual fees for the ones you do use. The mailing permits available were covered in the previous chapter.

Do a mailing

If you're new to mailing, you need to get some experience. That is best done by offering your services at no charge or a reduced charge to a non-profit organization who needs help. You can expect to be warmly received, and they should pay your expenses, including postage.

This is also a way to work the kinks out of your skills and streamline your operation. One of the ways you can appeal to businesses is to be fast, but you can't be fast if you don't know what you're doing.

Determine the services to offer

Once you've done some mailings, you'll get an idea of what you can do and what you'd like to do. You'll need to decide what kind of services you can and desire to offer and resist the temptation to deviate. The most successful new businesses focus heavily on one or two areas. For example, if you decide you really want to just compile and broker lists, you might find it is a mistake to go ahead and take work doing labeling and collating, or vice versa. The extra time involved in developing the new skill might place you in a distracting position where you have to turn down other work or so you can't do the quality of job you prefer to do. You will also be in a position to reap larger profit margins if you can do similar types of work for several companies because you can get volume discounts on supplies and you won't waste time changing your setup to accommodate a new task.

Most of the mailing list services worked one of three ways. I'll outline those ways here, but it is important to realize these are simply guidelines. Also, all of the people in charge had performed all the tasks involved in putting out a mailing at one point or another, so they were familiar with the whole process. Each business had taken a particular angle depending on their interests and skills in order to distinguish themselves.

The first type of mailing list service offers specialized custom services. In these cases, they actually kept an inventory of printed materials for the businesses they serve so they could mail out needed materials on demand. These services offered special sorting for bulk mail discounts, printed and affixed the labels, and offered barcoding. They also offered to enter addresses into a database and maintain the information.

Other services were focused on the mailing list data itself. With a fast computer and fast printing equipment these services would check addresses, add postal codes, do merge/purges of large lists, barcode, and print labels. Services they avoided included affixing the labels after printing, collating, folding, envelope stuffing, and other letter shop services. Often these businesses were staffed by a single person who didn't want to hire other people.

A third type of mailing list service actually offered lists for sale or rent. This type of service hired people to do data entry work and offered specialized lists or would act as a broker of other lists to businesses wanting to use direct mail. Often this type of mailing service focused more heavily on marketing, offering inside tips to get better response from mailings. The idea here is to focus more on attracting customers for the client in question and less on saving money.

Determine what to charge

Most mailing list services are done on a per piece basis, meaning the faster you can get the job done, the more money you make. While everyone doesn't bid the jobs they get on a per piece basis to the customer, they usually base the estimate on a per piece rate.

Besides calling around in your area to see what other mailing list services are charging, you can lease the "Small Press Catalog" from Franklin Estimating Systems of Salt Lake City, Utah. The Franklin catalog is geared toward helping printers estimate printing costs for customers, but there's an entire section on addressing and mailing. Each step of the mailing process is outlined with a cost including oddball items like rubber stamping, matching and inserting various items (like checks) into envelopes, addressing by hand, putting on labels, and even delivering sorted and bundled mailings to the post office.

Franklin updates each section of the catalog once a year and leases the entire catalog for just over $100 a year. Estimating software can be obtained from Franklin as well, but at the considerable increase of about $700 per year. Franklin Estimating Systems may be contacted at (800) 346-7363 outside of Utah and at (801) 355-5954 in Utah, and by facsimile at (801) 322-5822. You can also request information by mail at Franklin Estimating Systems, P.O. Box 16690, Salt Lake City, UT 84116-9970.

As for services, rates are subject to change, but the rate for performing address correction, postal-code lookup, and merge/purge is about $.02 a name. Labels cost the customer between $.05 and $.06 each depending on whether or not the labels are self-adhesive, also known as pressure sensitive.

Entering mailing list information can be charged at as much as $.06 to $.07 cents per line, meaning between $.15 to $.20 per name. Some services charge a flat rate, such as $1 per name per year to maintain, update, and print the names a certain number of times.

Collating, folding, and stuffing envelopes can be charged per operation per page, such as $.01 per page. Usually, there's no extra charge for metering and sealing envelopes, other than the cost of postage. It is acceptable to split the postage savings with the client as well. Some services charge these services all together and most services require postage be paid up front, before any work is done, especially for new customers.

Duplicate checking is lucrative for both the owners of the list and the mailing list service. On the average, most mailing lists contain 10 percent duplicate names. In a large mailing of 1.5 million, the mailing service can reduce the duplicates by as much as 20 percent, so the mailing is about 1.3 million. The postage savings from just removing the duplicate names alone is a minimum of $70,000.

A.G. Pitsilos said he's calculated that by using a fast PC, the right software, and a large hard disk, he can make $2000 an hour serving clients with large mailing lists by checking addresses. He charges about $.02 a name and with his computer he can process 100,000 names an hour.

Rental rates for mailing lists vary widely. The SRDS can give you a starting place but extra information is worth more. The SRDS list prices vary anywhere from $10 a thousand to $125 a thousand (/M). The more specialized the list, or the higher the average amount spent by the members of the list, the higher the cost of the list. Keep in mind, however, while these lists seem very inexpensive, they usually require a minimum of three to five thousand names be purchased, and they require a sample of the mailing be sent them prior to use of the names. Your rates for 300 names might be higher per name, but lower overall in cost than the minimum these mailing list brokers charge.

If you have a list, can renting the list for extra income dampen the responses you'll get to your mail offers? Carol Grant, direct mail manager at WordStar International supervises the millions of pieces of direct mail the company sends out each year. WordStar offers their list for rent through list broker Worldata and Carol says the company's list of over a million names doesn't appear to be affected at all by renting. "People who are buying, are buying," Carol maintains.

Ed Burnett in *The Complete Direct Mail List Handbook* seconds the opinion that use of a list does not harm its responsiveness. In tests where a list has been split in half and only half mailed to repeatedly, the responsiveness of the unmailed half was the same as the rented half. The only difference between the two halves is one was producing extra income while the other wasn't.

The only exception to this is rental of the list to a direct competitor. Most list owners handle this by requesting a sample mailing piece before rental and by stipulating the lists not be used to sell a competing product.

So for example, a residential list which specifically targeted residents between 35 and 55 might be rented at $10 per thousand more than one which targets certain specific areas. You can charge extra for any information you can offer such as age, income, type of residence, length of residence, type of business, and so on. For a business list you might charge extra for contact names, a facsimile (fax) number, the number of employees, or inclusion of the government's Standard Industrial Classification (SIC) code.

Who needs mailing services anyway? There is hardly a business around who couldn't benefit from mailing services as a form of advertising, and many could save big money on services they're performing now with a little help.

Finding customers in everyday places

A source for mailing customers is the local Chamber of Commerce. Several mailing services mentioned the Chamber of Commerce helped them find leads and it has been a good source for referrals. Local printers are another good source.

As far as pinpointing the types of businesses who need mailing list services, mailers mentioned a variety of customers including: insurance companies, software companies, dry cleaners, non-profit groups, magazine publishers, janitorial and house cleaning services, beeper and paging services, answering services, doctors, dentists, chiropractors, opticians, gardening and landscaping services, accountants, chimney sweeps, plumbers, video stores, local grocery stores, dog grooming services, veterinarians, hotels, motels, caterers, public relations agencies, real estate agents, newsletter publishers, and stock brokers. The biggest mailers are businesses who use the mail as a way to attract customers. In terms of volume, most of the mail sent currently is bulk business mail, also known as advertising mail. Advertising mail is third-class because it can be discounted as much as 40 percent over the standard one-ounce $.29 cent rate.

Another source of customers are people who are remodeling, building, or trying to change the use of an existing property, such as converting a large home to an apartment building. Many of these changes require local zoning ordinance revisions, which require a mailing be done to local residents, businesses, and business owners affected by the change. Your source for who is planning changes might be the city records, but local architects will also be a potential source for referrals, if you let them know you are available.

Practice your craft

As I mentioned in the beginning of this chapter, one of the ways to practice your craft and get your name out is to volunteer or offer reduced rates for your services to one or several local non-profit groups. Often, people in those groups, like Children's Home Society, are influential members of the community who can bring you significant referral business once they get to know you. This can be a source of references for you as well, because common advice to those seeking mailing list services is to ask for references and check them out.

Also, according to sources at the postal service, the USPS may cut its costs by dropping the special non-profit mailing rate these organizations have enjoyed for so long. If you are a known quantity in the non-profit organization circles, you may be in a position to pick up the mailings these organizations are doing.

Use Yellow Pages advertising

Without exception, existing mailing list services told me the telephone company's Yellow Pages advertising brings them many times the work that an ad costs them. People looking for mailing list services usually start there.

A Yellow Pages ad is usually billed by the month, starting the month the phone books are delivered with your ad in them. That means if your local Yellow Pages is only updated once a year, it could take you six months or longer to be listed, so you need to get started right away. An ad large enough to say "I'm serious" can cost as little as $28 dollars per month, but bring in hundreds or even thousands of dollars of business each month. The Business-to-Business Yellow Pages is another good place to consider putting an ad, though if you have to choose one, the regular Yellow Pages should be your first choice.

Do your own mailing

One of the obvious ways to get clients is by using your services for yourself. Do a mailing.

A postcard has been an effective mailing for several of the mailing services I interviewed. Many said, to start out, they rented business names for $29 a thousand by renting mailing addresses of businesses in their area and sent a postcard that clearly outlined their services, location, hours, and telephone number. Postcards are effective because the entire message can be read quickly without opening an envelope.

Sending a postcard also means you'll have to plan your message to fit into the limited space. A clear message that says exactly what you can do for your customer is the most effective. Some examples other mailing services are using are, "We can make your mailing headaches go away," "If we can't save you money on your mailings, you don't pay," "Your advertising can pay for itself, the easy way."

Also, while spending a lot of money on printing an expensive postcard might boost your ego, direct mail experts say your money should be spent on your list.

Watch your mail

Watching your own mail is another way to pick up clients. Look for handwritten or misspelled addresses, and especially those mailers addressed to "Occupant," as those pieces flag businesses who mail, but could benefit from some expert help. For example, instead of occupant, it is just as easy using a computer to put "The Pizza Lover at" or "The Well-dressed Gentleman at" or some other phrase that targets the audience the piece is mailed to.

When you're out in your community, you should keep your eye open for opportunities. Watch for "Sign up for our mailing list" or the "Drop your business card in our fish bowl" notices. When you see one, you could ask to speak to the person in charge and find out what they do with those cards. Many times you'll discover the business doesn't know what to do with them, or perhaps after they attempt to do the mailing work, they might decide to give you a call.

Send an attention getter

You need to get attention and one way to do it is to send something memorable to potential clients. One of the most memorable pieces I can think of to send is the MP 4000 Postal Scale from Metalproducts Engineering of Los Angeles, California illustrated in FIG. 3-1. While this scale is not 100 percent accurate, the only time to be concerned is when the scale is exactly on a line, and then the letter might be heavier and need extra postage. The MP 4000 comes in a vinyl sleeve that can be printed with your logo by Metalproducts Engineering, or you might want to have pressure-sensitive labels printed yourself that say something like, "This scale is not 100 percent accurate, but we are."

The scale, developed originally by the Stansbury Company in the early 1970s was reportedly sold originally by post offices, but pressure from office supply stores forced the post office sales to stop. The MP 4000 is available in single quantities for $3.75 each plus $1.00 shipping and handling. The address and toll-free number is in appendix A.

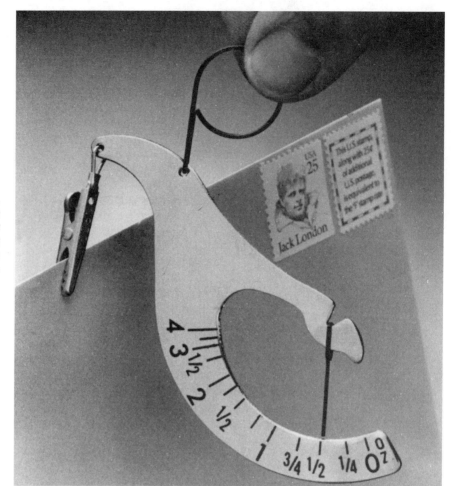

3-1
The MP 4000 Postal Scale from Metalproducts Engineering of Los Angeles, California, as an example of an attention-getting promotional piece.

Collect bulletin board ads

While you might think of putting your business card or a flyer up on a bulletin board in the office supply store or at the local post office, you probably won't think of mailing to those people advertising on the bulletin board. But that's exactly what Wayne Stoler, of Letter Perfect Information Services in Baltimore, Maryland, says he is doing to get new customers. He says he's gotten as many as 200 new contacts from the people advertising on the bulletin board and is getting about a 10 percent response rate from those names.

Use your personal knowledge

Facts that you know about certain types of businesses can help you get customers. For example, where I live in Southern California we have just ended six years of drought. Now that it has started raining, the homes 20 to 25 years old in my neighborhood with asphalt roofs are experiencing a severe need for reroofing. A mailing list service person in my area would be smart to target all the local roofing firms with a postcard saying something like, "The combination of drought and rain has created the need for home owners with asphalt roofs to reroof. I can help you target all the asphalt roof home owners in your area with an offer that will get you the business."

I also had the plumber out to unclog my sewer pipes. He told me there is more trouble with drainage problems during a drought. It seems all that conserving water means there isn't as much water to wash out the junk we send down our sewer pipes. Again, here's another opportunity for the mailing list service who could send a postcard to these local specialty services saying, "Let potential customers know a drought means they need your services more often."

A relative in the restaurant business told me things are very slow in January because people are eating at home. This could be an opportunity for restaurants to offer breads or specialty items people can buy and take home to spice up an otherwise ordinary meal. So in early January you send out a mailing that says, "You know things will slow down next month, but you can still grab some of those eat-at-home folks with a special offer."

Stan Golomb took his expertise gained by selling advertising in dry cleaning trade magazines and put it to work targeting only dry cleaners at first with his mailing list service. This means every person you meet is a potential source of information to help you promote your business. This will have the added benefit of making you more popular, as everyone loves a good listener.

Network

Someone approached me recently about paying $175 to join a group whose sole function was networking. I can't think of a bigger waste of money. I don't need to pay money to someone to make contacts, and neither do you. Some mailing list services I talked with said they did invest in getting to know people in the community by joining the local Chamber of Commerce, but that is a different matter. Other mailing services attend the monthly meetings held by the post office business centers, called the Postal Customer Council (PCC) even though there are other mailers at these meetings.

Often, a mailer with a large business load will look for a smaller business who can help during peak periods, and you could get that work if you get to know those businesses. You might meet those large mailers at PCC meetings. Sometimes a database expert is what they're looking for. One person mailing list services told me they've come to specialize in the data processing for larger mailing houses who do the manual work.

The opportunities in networking are real. However, everyone has seen the new guy in the Chamber of Commerce or PCC go around, practically drooling with greed written all over his face, passing out his business card. Don't be one of those people. You can expect it will take time to develop contacts and you'll need to give of yourself by listening and offering good advice.

Jay Levinson, author of Guerrilla Marketing, agrees. In his small business oriented book *Guerrilla Marketing Excellence: The Fifty Golden Rules for Small-Business Success*, Levinson says networking with the idea in mind you are going to sell yourself is the wrong way to proceed. His advice is to pick a small number of people to talk to and really talk to them. Ask them questions and find out what their needs are. He also says good networking is giving out excellent tidbits or ideas that help the other person.

Note the word "giving." No one likes the feeling of being used and people in business, especially in business-oriented groups such as the Chamber of Commerce, are experts at spotting and distancing themselves from the "users." If you are interested enough in others and their needs to offer really helpful ideas, you're on your way to winning respect and building your business.

Owen Edwards, of the mailing list service Kathie & Owen in Reseda, California, told me a networking story that illustrates this point. He frequently went to a local mail list broker to purchase business lists for his immediate area. After a few visits he got to know the receptionist. One day when he was waiting, she had time to talk and they struck up a conversation. She asked him what he did, and when he told her, she said, "I get people in here buying lists who ask for help all the time," and she asked for his card.

Ever since then, the Edwards have been getting referrals from that receptionist. Owen's experience just shows it pays to be kind and warm to everyone you meet, as you never know who might be in a position to help you.

Sweat the small stuff

The most lucrative work from the large mailers comes by getting to know someone who can recommend you when an opportunity comes up. Without exception, the successful mailing list service businesses obtained the lucrative work they have now through contacts they made with small jobs. In other words, they did good work on the small stuff and made contacts to get the bigger jobs. One service, a single-person operation, who does list cleaning and adds postal codes to addresses for companies as large as AT&T said, "They're not really buying the service, they're buying me."

Stick to established businesses

One last tidbit is that approaching new businesses has not been effective, according to mailing list services I talked with. It is the established business that wants to grow and is too busy to do mailings who sees the value in mailing services.

Kathie and Owen Edwards found the least expensive $29 per thousand business lists from a local list broker worked well for them. While those lists tend to have a high proportion of bad or nonexistent addresses, the hits you do make will be to businesses who have been around a while and now are established, since those will be the ones who haven't changed.

So, while you may be collecting new business listings for other clients out of the new business listings in your local newspaper, such as local office supply stores or office furniture outlets, you might find it unproductive to mail to them yourself.

As in every business, the mailing list business has its own set of special rules and terminology. You'll need to understand these terms and concepts in order to successfully navigate. The most important new concepts have to do with the mailing list, so that's where we'll start.

Things you need to know

Mailing lists themselves are considered property, just like automobiles or homes. Time and money goes into securing the names on the lists and maintaining the lists, so most lists are not sold, but are instead rented. The information on the lists is also considered private and should be treated in the same way valuable coins or precious stones would be, meaning access to the list should be limited and care should be taken to be sure the list is not stolen. More information on list security is listed in appendix H in the information provided by the Direct Marketing Association.

Mailing lists are property

Lists are usually rented for a specified period of time on a media which can be used by another computer. List rental means you as the list owner have the rights to the list, but the renter of the list has permission to use the list one time for a fee. Any responses as a result of the use of the list belong to the renter, and the list can be rented more than once to more than one person.

Usually lists are rented at a cost per thousand names (*per/M*). One of the best examples of list rental is the bible of the mailing list service, the *Standard Rate and Data Service directories*, commonly known as the *SRDS*. Carried by most public libraries and subscribed to by most larger mailing list services, the SRDS publications contain nearly all the larger mail list brokers and a startling variety of lists for rent. As many as 200 categories of lists are available in the SRDS, from Quality Control Engineers to Department Store Underwear Buyers. The SRDS is the definitive source for lists, because the SRDS prints information on lists without charge to the list owner or broker.

In the SRDS each list is described, such as buyers of high tech computer products or parents of preschoolers, and includes the name and contact information for the list broker. Occasionally the listing offers the average amount the people on the list spend on the products they've bought from the owner of the list, especially if the list is a result of a direct mail sales approach like a catalog.

Additionally, the price is per thousand (per/M) names, the computer-readable formats the list is available in, and any minimum number of names that must be purchased is listed. Extra information available at additional charge, such as phone numbers or titles, is listed as well as the specifics on how much more that information costs. Information on how long it takes to get the list once ordered, where the data came from, and how it is maintained in the SRDS listings can also appear. You'll also notice a *sample mailing piece* (SMP) is often an item required by brokers listing in the SRDS before the list can be rented.

Most public libraries subscribe to SRDS publications and dispose of old copies at the end of a six-month period. This means you might be able to pick up old copies for a nominal charge or without charge.

In looking at the SRDS, you'll see the *Standard Industrial Classification* (SIC) codes. The SIC is a coding system developed by the Federal Government for identification of businesses used to distinguish companies by the type of business. For example, a bakery would have an SIC code of #5463 while an attorney would be #8111. A current list of SIC codes in use by the Department of Commerce as of June of 1992 is listed in appendix G.

Testing a mailing list

List testing, or *sampling*, is a common practice and a prudent one, especially if it is a large list. Testing involves sending a portion of the list a mailing to see what the response rate is, before mailing to the entire list. A continuation is a guarantee for renting the rest of the list if the results of the sample are satisfactory.

In sampling, instead of taking the first 1000 names, the most common practice is to ask for an *Nth sample*, meaning every twentieth name or every hundredth name depending on the size of the list and the size of the sample desired. For example, to get 1000 names from a 30,000-name list, the sample would be every 30th name. The idea is to get a random sample of the list, rather than the names in the order they were entered, because the order the names are entered might not be random. If a mailing was done and the responses from a certain area came in first, those first 1000 names might all be from the same area. Sampling might also be done if the buyer likes the list, but the list is too large for the buyer to rent all of it.

While the Nth number sample is the preferred way to get random sublists from another list, it is sometimes difficult to accomplish. An alternative to the Nth number sample is to take the last one or the last two digits of the five-digit postal code, also known as the zip code, and pull the names based on that. Ed Burnett, author of *The Complete Direct Mail List Handbook* recommends this approach because it is just as random, but easier to do.

The most important issue to consider when looking at any mailing list is the cleanliness of the list. Cleanliness refers to whether or not the addresses on the list are deliverable. Because people and businesses are constantly changing, lists are constantly changing as well. While your mail carrier may be as good as mine and something gets to you even though it was incorrectly addressed, you can't count on that. Missing apartment numbers, missing directional indicators (is it North 42nd Street or South 42nd Street), misspelled street and city names, transposed numbers, incorrect or missing zip codes, and a hundred other possible ways an address could be incorrect all make for undeliverable mail or *nixies*. *List cleaning*, then, is checking through the addresses on the list making sure the addresses are correct. Because some classes of mail are not returned if they are undeliverable, list cleaning is very important.

Up there with a dirty list is a list full of duplicates. Lists are often combined, or *merged*, to form one list. Usually, lists are merged because they have something in common, which also means the chances of duplicate names appearing on the merged list is high. *Purging* is eliminating the duplicates. The operation of combining lists and eliminating duplicates is called *merge/purge*.

If you delve into list brokering, about the only way to know if a mailing list is being misused is to place a few dummy names on a rented list, also known as *seeding* or *salting* the list. The idea is to attempt to catch anyone who is using the list more times than they've paid for or catch the mailing of something different than the sample piece submitted. The dummy names should be to people you can check with beforehand, and they should be unique enough that they're a flag to the recipient.

Protecting lists from list thieves

While any seed can be found by an experienced mailer, an attempt should be made to avoid obvious mistakes. Such mistakes might include adding a seed that is the only address being mailed to in a certain state. Simple changes to an existing name on the list are attractive as seeds, such as adding a middle initial to make a known contact name a seed. But if the mailer decides to drop first names and mail to the "Pizza Lover at," then your middle initial scheme is done for. Another commonly recommended piece of advice is to place your own name in the list, assuming you can place it in among other names going to the same area. Mailing to yourself has the added advantage of allowing you to monitor how long it took the mailing to arrive, which gives you an idea of when you and your client can anticipate results.

How many seeds do you need? Two per thousand is the number commonly recommended, but Ed Burnett admits in practice one seed in five thousand is more common. You'll need at least two seeds to prove that an unauthorized use of your list has occurred, so keep that in mind.

Most mailers don't bother to look for seeds, so even the most obvious ones are mailed to. Attempts to remove seeds from a rented list are considered to be dishonest in the industry, despite any arguments mailing to seeds is a waste of the mailer's postage.

Another type of misuse is for an unscrupulous mailer to ask for several small numbers of your list, mailing each time the specified mail piece, then order a large number of names or the entire list and mail a different piece. Because you were expecting them to use the same mailing piece, you don't expect they'll use a different one. Also, some question can arise as to whether or not you have reason to complain since you didn't ask for a sample mailing piece the last time.

But, like any other business, the mailing world tends to be a small one and word gets around pretty fast about unscrupulous firms. Bigger problems are to be found within the organization of the broker or mailer. These include willful destruction of data by disgruntled employees and theft of data. Ed Burnett recites an incident where he was approached by a young man with a tape containing names and dollars of interest reported to the Internal Revenue Service. This was obviously unauthorized information taken without the knowledge of the Internal Revenue Service, and Burnett recalls he couldn't get the young man out of his office fast enough.

People in your employ will soon discover the value of a good mailing list and should not be permitted unlimited or unauthorized access to your data. You also want to prevent unauthorized access to lists you have custody of whether you are brokering the lists or not. Most of the better mailing software programs discussed in chapter 4 allow you to assign a password to your list. Without the password, access to the list is restricted. Some programs go as far as to code the data (called *encryption*) so the list looks like a bunch of garbage and a copy made of the list won't work without the password.

Passwords are easily thwarted if they are carelessly chosen and maintained. According to experts at the Lawrence Livermore Laboratory, the five most common places people put their passwords are stuck on a sticky note near the computer, in their top desk drawer, under their computer keyboard, or in an address file beside the telephone under "P" for password. But passwords should be treated just like any other valuable and placed under lock and key.

The most popular excuse offered for why better care isn't taken with a password is the trouble in remembering it. People try to choose passwords they can easily remember, such as their own first name or the names of family members, especially if they're not allowed to post it somewhere. The problem with passwords like those is anyone who knows you can easily discover the information and try it as your password. According to password experts, a good choice of a password is one that has both letters and numbers and is not a common name, yet is easy to remember. One such choice might be a description of something in your environment, like the two brown upholstered chairs in your office. Such a password, "2brownchairs," is easy for you to remember and almost impossible for anyone else to guess. Passwords should also be changed at least every six months. More information on steps to secure your computer data are listed in the materials from the Direct Marketing Association reprinted in appendix H.

The best security measure and the one most commonly neglected is backups. A *backup* is simply an exact copy of the data. Backups should be made regularly and stored in a secure area on site, and backups of critical materials should also be stored off-site, in case of fire or some other disaster. Periodically, a "snapshot" of your computer system with everything, including the operating system, software, and data, should be made. Then, if you have a customer come back in two or three years who asks you to perform the same operation again, you can reproduce the complete environment the work was done in, even if you've made changes to the system since the work was performed. The easiest, fastest, and cheapest way to do this is to use tape backup drives, discussed further in the next chapter.

It is the software and hardware tools in addition to knowing how to use them that will make the process of performing these tasks not only easier, but interesting and even fun. Nothing beats that feeling you get when you have gotten the computer to produce the work! These tools are outlined in the next chapter.

References

Brumbaugh, J. Frank. 1979. *Mail Order Made Easy*. North Hollywood, California: Melvin Powers Wilshire Book Company.

Burnett, Ed. 1988. *The Complete Direct Mail List Handbook: Everything You Need to Know About Lists and How to Use Them for Greater Profit*. Englewood Cliffs, New Jersey: Prentice Hall.

Cecil C. Hoge, Sr. 1988. *Mail Order Moonlighting*. Berkeley, California: Ten Speed Press.

4 Tools of the trade

The mailing list business requires a computer, a printer, and some type of software for list management. This chapter presents more than just those basic components because mailers add additional equipment and software to help them do more after they've built their business. But to start, that's all you need. So please don't conclude that you must buy the additional software and hardware mentioned here. You should know about what's available, and buy what you need as your business grows.

The computer

We know a computer is a necessity in the mailing list service business, but which computer should you get? While it is possible to use your child's old Commodore that's stored in the back closet or an old KayPro your Dad has stored in his garage, you're going to find it difficult to get software or components that will work with those older machines. The mechanics of the business, however, will be very much the same regardless of which computer you use, so you'll find help in the following material even if you decide not to purchase the computer I recommend. If you need to purchase a computer, here are some tips to save you time, money, and aggravation in choosing it and planning for related hardware tools you might need later.

If you don't have any experience with computers, you should take some classes to learn before you buy. The basics of operating a computer are outside the scope of this book, but many fine classes and books are available on the subject. It is usually best to take a class before you buy a computer, if you're in the market for one, because you'll have a better feel for what you like and what the trends are in this fast-changing market. Also, if a certain type of display monitor looks fuzzy to you, you need a bigger screen, or you find a certain keyboard feel is more comfortable for you, you'll know what you want when you shop. The least expensive classes are offered by adult education programs in high schools and junior colleges and are usually scheduled in the evenings and on the weekends.

The majority of computers used in small business are either IBM-compatible personal computers or *PCs* (also known as *DOS-based computers*) or Macintosh computers. IBM and compatible PCs, known hereafter as the *PC*, offer more bang for your buck because a wider variety of inexpensive software is available for the PC, it is widely supported, and many times it costs less than other types of computers. PCs are also the computers used most in the mailing list service business, precisely for those reasons.

Macintosh computers exclusively from Apple Computer of Cupertino, California, are also a possibility. While there is software available to do mailing list functions, it is more expensive and there are very few packages available. Some of the mailing list service businesses said they dealt with Macintosh computers, but only in the context of the ability to move information from a client's Macintosh to the PC used by the service. The Mailer's Software catalog from Melissa Data, listed in appendix A, does have a couple of mail software packages for the Macintosh. However, if you're buying a new computer, I recommend you stick with PCs.

Understanding the basic components of the computer is important when making a purchase. You need to know what the following terms mean; CPU, RAM, hard disk, floppy disk drives, expansion slots, and monitor. The next section explains.

Things you should know

The CPU The basis of the PC is the *central processing unit* (CPU) or *microprocessor*. The computer's speed is based on how much information the CPU can process at a time (measured in bits) and how fast it can process that information (measured in megahertz). What does all this speed stuff mean to you the user? Well, a slower computer means you will spend more time waiting for it to get back to you once you tell it to do something. While you're sitting there waiting, you can't usually be doing anything else. Besides being annoying, the wait can cost you money.

RAM The components of the computer, such as the storage space, called the hard disk drive, and the *random access memory* (RAM) will also make a difference in how long you wait. *RAM*, sometimes referred to as *memory*, can be thought of as work space for your computer in much the same way a workbench is work space for a carpenter or a kitchen counter is work space for a cook. Nearly everything the computer does is done in RAM. When RAM is limited, the computer has to swap things in and out to perform tasks in the same way a crowded workbench or limited counter space would slow down a carpenter or a cook. Too little RAM can mean some programs just won't work at all, while more RAM means the computer can get more done faster.

The hard disk   As RAM is the work space, the *hard disk* can be thought of as the cabinets where the various tools are kept. Software programs are copied to the hard disk from floppy disks distributed in software packages. When called upon, the software program is copied or *loaded* from the hard disk drive into RAM, where it is used by the computer to perform tasks. Hard disks are slower than RAM, yet occasionally hard disk space is allocated by the computer for use as RAM in order to get a job done. The larger the hard disk, the more programs and information you can store on it.

Floppy disk drives   The *floppy disk drives* are for moving information to and from the hard disk and to other computers. The drives usually come in 5.25-inch 1.2 megabytes (Mb) and 3.5-inch 1.44Mb.

The monitor   The monitor is for you, to allow you to see what is going on. Most mailing software programs don't require you have a state-of-the-art monitor, because most of them are not based on visual output although they do make use of color if you have it. However, other software programs for the PC are requiring more sophisticated monitors. The standard monitor is the *video graphics array* (VGA) monitor. The number of pixels the screen can display determines the sharpness of the image and VGA ranges from 640 by 480 pixels per inch to 1024 by 768 pixels per inch. The more pixels, the better the resolution. Other factors affect the appearance of the display, such as the dot pitch and the refresh rate.

The *dot pitch* is the width of the dots that make up a pixel. The smaller the dot pitch, the sharper the image. The accepted dot pitch is $\frac{31}{100}$ of a millimeter (.31mm), but smaller is better.

The *refresh rate* is how often the monitor redraws the screen. Like television screens, the monitor is drawing the screen line-by-line faster than the eye can see. If the refresh rate is high, the image has a better quality to the eye.

Expansion slots   Make sure the PC offers expandability. This is not the time to buy a laptop or a portable computer. You'll need room inside the case to add other devices to your system. This type of business will require you at some point to add peripherals such as a modem, a *compact disc read-only memory* (CD-ROM) drive, or a 9-track tape drive, and each of those components is connected to the computer through expansion slots. (I talk about each of these peripherals later in this chapter.) Expansion slots allow you to add the components which interface the peripherals to the computer and are commonly termed *cards*, *boards*, or *circuit boards*. Just because the outside case of the computer appears to be big enough doesn't mean you can add the devices you need. You need to know if there are expansion slots available and how many there are.

In a survey of new PC, buyers Dallas, Texas-based Channel Marketing said of the top five items new PC owners wish they had gotten, more expandability was number one. Too few internal expansion slots and external drive bays was the biggest complaint with 62 percent of the respondents and was only discovered when an additional device was purchased for the computer system.

Next on the list was a better quality monitor. While the monitor won't make or break you in the mailing list service business, you are going to spend a lot of time looking at it. You'll want at least a video graphics array (VGA) monitor with 640 by 480 pixel resolution, although Super VGA at 1024 by 768 is better.

You'll find two environments available for PCs. One is the operating system, called the disk operating system (DOS) and the other is a graphical user interface (GUI) called Microsoft Windows. There are a growing number of software applications for the Microsoft Windows graphical operating system environment, but Windows requires more memory than DOS. The third most common complaint among new PC buyers was they hadn't gotten enough memory. Many purchased systems with Windows preconfigured on the system, but with only two megabytes (Mb) of RAM. With so little RAM, they had difficulty, or simply could not run the applications desired, or found they needed four or more megabytes of RAM to run two applications at a time.

Even more disappointing was the fact that some users had to purchase all new RAM, as the additional RAM could not be used in conjunction with the RAM they already had. That's because many PCs are equipped with SIMMs (*single in-line memory modules*), which come in varying capacities that do not mix. For example, you cannot put six 1Mb SIMMs with a 2Mb SIMM to get 8Mb of RAM. To get 8Mb of RAM, you must have eight 1Mb SIMMs, four 2Mb SIMMs, or two 4Mb SIMMs. If the motherboard of the PC is only equipped with two slots for SIMMs, then to upgrade from 2Mb to 8Mb, the user would have to discard the 2Mb SIMMs completely.

The next biggest complaint was a hard disk drive that was too small. Hard disk storage is very important in the mailing business as customer mailing lists tend to use up disk space. Microsoft Windows is also disk space hungry, so the larger the hard disk, the better. Windows takes up 5Mb to 8Mb of hard disk space. Many of the Windows applications, such as WordPerfect for Windows or Microsoft Word for Windows, will take between 6Mb and 10Mb of hard disk space each. On a 40Mb drive, four applications and Windows takes up nearly the entire hard disk drive storage space. If you can afford it, a 200Mb or larger hard disk drive is preferable, and many mailing list service businesses purchase 500Mb or larger hard disk drives.

The final complaint was the computer was only equipped with either a 3.5-inch or 5.25-inch floppy disk drive. New PC owners said they discovered they needed both in order to use software they already had as well as new software, or to exchange shareware programs with other users. You will need both size floppy disk drives as well so you can read any disk a customer might hand you.

The overwhelming majority of users surveyed said they could have avoided these problems had they more seriously considered the applications they were going to use. Many users said they were trying to avoid additional expense at the time of purchase. Channel Marketing reported many users who said they had attempted to upgrade the computer they bought and discovered they were unable to do so. Of the users who responded, almost all said they would have saved a significant amount of money had they simply bought a PC with the options they needed instead of upgrading later. So don't make the same mistake those people did.

Ergonomics

Repetitive stress injuries are real, but you can avoid them by taking some precautions. The most important thing to remember in purchasing office furniture is one size does not fit all. Everyone is different and adjustability is the key to avoiding repetitive injury.

One of the most important investments you can make is an inexpensive wrist rest placed in front of your computer keyboard to keep your hands and wrists supported while you are typing. Some people have simply rolled up a towel until it was the necessary height and placed it under their wrists. A good, adjustable chair with back support is also important. You want to avoid leaning forward or bending your wrists to type.

What you should buy

The safest way to buy a computer is to look at the software you want to use, then buy the computer the software requires. For the purposes of the mailing list service business, the minimum computer you should consider is a 386-based PC with 8Mb of random access memory (RAM) and a 200Mb hard disk drive. If you can afford a 486-based PC at 25 megahertz (MHz) or faster with 8Mb or more of (RAM) and a hard disk 500Mb in size, you should buy it. You should get at least a VGA monitor, both 3.5-inch and 5.25-inch floppy disk drives, and a minimum of four expansion slots.

One additional tip on the purchase of a computer is that you might want to consider a tower such as the one housing the 486-based Dell computer in FIG. 4-1 or mini-tower configuration like the 486 AST Advantage! in FIG. 4-2. The tower takes less space on your desktop and is easier to work with when it's time to add new devices. Many times the instructions on new devices, such as CD-ROM drives are simple enough; you can make the addition yourself by following the instructions. A tower configuration makes adding new components simpler because it is easier to open up and it is easier to get to connections on the back of the case.

4-1
The Dell 486/T is shown in a full-height tower configuration equipped with both a 5.25" and 3.5" floppy disk drive and a tape backup drive.

Dell Computer Corporation

4-2
The AST Advantage Plus 486DX 33 in a mini-tower configuration has a 3.5" and 5.25" floppy disk drive and a Colorado 120Mb tape backup drive with a tape inserted.

Peripheral devices are components you add to the computer to offer you the ability to get information in a different format or to expand what your computer is capable of doing. The most common peripheral devices in the mailing list service business are a modem, a CD-ROM drive, a 9-track tape drive, and a tape backup drive.

Peripheral devices

The modem A *modem* uses the phone lines to transfer computer readable information to and from your PC. Its speed is measured in *baud* rates, with the most standard modems operating at 2400 baud or 9600 baud. You might need a modem because some list maintenance programs allow you to use the modem to update small mailing lists with zip+4 codes by phone.

The CD-ROM drive Much of the mountains of information used in mailing list services is offered on *compact disc read-only memory* (CD-ROM) and on 9-track tape, especially if the information is from the government. CD-ROM drives read information stored on disks much like the audio CDs, and the drives are read-only. Read-only means your computer can read what is on the CD-ROM, but you cannot erase or alter the information. Information from the CD-ROM can also be copied to the hard disk, if there is room, and this is attractive because the hard disk offers faster access than the CD-ROM. Figure 4-3 shows an external CD-ROM drive and a CD-ROM drive for internal mount in the computer's case.

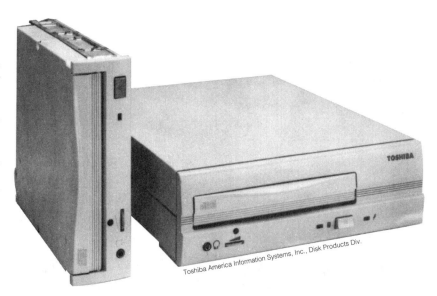

4-3
Toshiba's XM Series double-speed CD-ROM disc drives are some of the fastest in the industry with a 330-kilobyte-per-second transfer rate and a 200-millisecond random access time. A drive for internal mount is shown on the left and an external drive is on the right.

Toshiba America Information Systems, Inc., Disk Products Div.

The storage capacity, in excess of 600Mb, makes the CD-ROM attractive for distributing large amounts of data, like an entire set of encyclopedias with photographs and video clips or all the zip+4 mailing addresses in the United States. Most mailing list software which allows you to qualify for the big postal discounts is distributed with a CD-ROM disc.

For this reason, you might want to consider purchasing a *multimedia PC* (MPC). The MPC is designed for use with video and graphics, but comes equipped with a CD-ROM disc drive, usually a larger-than-usual hard disk, a better quality monitor, a sound card, and more RAM. While you won't need the sound capability for the mailing list service business, you might find an MPC is less expensive than having a PC with the components you want custom built for you.

The 9-track tape drive

About half the mailing list service businesses in my survey owned 9-track tape drives. Much in appearance like the big reel-to-reel tape recorders of the past, the 9-track tape drive is used heavily by the government and businesses with large computer systems because it is an inexpensive way to distribute lots of data. If you obtain a 9-track tape, you will have to copy the information to your hard disk using the 9-track tape drive in order to be able to make use of it.

The 9-track tape drive is available for PCs, but it can cost anywhere from $2500 to $10,000. Used 9-track tape drives are around for less than $1000. Once you have a 9-track tape drive, you've opened doors to pick up business from large corporate users who store their data on 9-track tape, to purchase large mailing lists for less, and get information from the Federal Government at a low cost.

One drawback to 9-track tape drives is they come in two basic capacities, 1600 *bits per inch* (bpi) and 6250 bpi. While a 6250 bpi drive can read tapes created by a 1600 bpi drive, it doesn't work the other way around. The 6250 bpi tape drive can also create tapes formatted at 1600 bpi, but you may or may not be able to talk the company you're working with to format the tapes at 1600 bpi so your 1600 bpi tape drive can read them. So, if you're buying a tape drive, you'll want to know its capacity. Also, most 9-track tape drives require a separate interface card, which will take up an expansion slot on your PC. However, some plug in to existing ports on the back of the PC.

You can also pay to have the 9-track tape data converted to a format your PC can read without buying a tape drive. However, this eats into your profits quickly.

Tape backup drives

The only way to truly protect information on a computer is to make a copy of it and store the copy away from the computer. The copy, known as a *backup*, can then be restored to the computer if some disaster befalls your data. Disasters come in many forms, from power surges in the electrical system that short-circuit your computer to hard disk failure. The most popular types of backups are tape backup drives, which store relatively large amounts of data, such as 120Mb or more, on tapes that look very much like cassette tapes. Both the AST Advantage! mini-tower in FIG. 4-2 and the Dell computer depicted in FIG. 4-1 are equipped with tape backup drives. You can expect to pay $200 to $300 for a tape backup drive and $20 to $30 each for the tapes themselves.

Printers

Along with a computer, you'll need a printer. The type of printer should be a dot matrix printer, ink jet, or a laser printer, though as your business grows, you may end up with more than one type of printer.

Dot matrix printers, such as those illustrated in FIG. 4-4, are also known as *impact* printers because they work by hitting ink-soaked ribbon which then strikes the paper and makes an impression, much like a typewriter does, but with dots instead of letters. An "inside" view of a new type of dot matrix printer with two print heads for faster printing is shown in FIG. 4-5. Dot matrix printers come in 9-pin and 24-pin print heads. The more pins, the better the print quality the printer can produce. Dot matrix printers also come in wide and narrow carriage widths, such as the printers in FIG. 4-4.

Epson

4-4
Shown are two of Epson's line of dot matrix printers. The Epson FX-870 at top has a standard width carriage while the Epson FX-1170 has a wide width carriage.

Laser and *ink jet printers* are similar in appearance. However, a laser printer works much the way a photocopy machine does by using heat to fuse toner to the paper. An ink jet printer is different as it "draws" on the paper with ink.

There are also small convenience printers, such as the Avery Personal Label Printer depicted in FIG. 4-6 or the Seiko Smart Label Printer Pro shown in FIG. 4-7. While these printers certainly won't hurt your business image, they're mainly for producing one or two labels at a time. They're also expensive as

4-5
The Advanced Matrix Technology Accel-290 series printers offer two 9-pin print heads for high-speed printing.

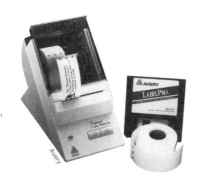

4-6
The Avery Personal Label Printer is designed for producing a small number of labels quickly. It requires special labels and is too expensive to use for large numbers of labels.

they cost between $200 to $300 each, and special labels must be purchased for use as well.

The safest type of printer to get, if you can only get one, is a dot matrix printer with a wide carriage. You might need to fill out forms with multiple carbons, and only a printer that makes an impact will work. Also, labels come in wide widths, such as four across, and the faster you can print labels, the more money you make. Because a wide carriage printer can also print on

The safest printer investment for mail

4-7
The Seiko Smart Label Printer Pro can quickly print a small number of labels, but is too expensive to use for large numbers of labels.

Seiko Instruments USA, Inc.

paper that is not as wide, as in FIG. 4-8, the wide carriage dot matrix printer offers you more options.

Dot matrix printers are usually either 9- or 24-pin, the pins being the objects that strike the ribbon and produce the characters on the page. Twenty-four pin dot matrix printers produce a finer image overall than 9-pin printers do, but they also cost more and are slower.

With the right software, a 24-pin printer can produce an image almost as clear and crisp as a laser printer. Because it doesn't use heat, you don't have to buy more expensive special labels required for laser printers that can take heat without burning.

Many dot matrix printers also come with fonts built in, although they usually have to be selected by pressing buttons on the front of the printer. Usually the software used to print the document is unaware of the font the printer is using and therefore cannot compensate for line spacing and character size.

Epson

4-8
A wide carriage printer can print both standard size paper and sheets of labels with several labels across, such as this Epson LQ-1170.

The easiest printer to use is a laser printer. The most elegant looking output comes from these printers as well. The most popular laser printers are made by Hewlett-Packard (HP) and are supported by almost all software programs, although other companies make laser printers as well. The Hewlett-Packard 4 LaserJet printer depicted in FIG. 4-9 has built-in support for Microsoft Windows to make printing faster.

4-9
The Hewlett-Packard LaserJet 4 prints at a resolution of 600 dots-per-inch at a speed of eight pages per minute.

Printers, especially dot matrix printers, can be difficult to work with because they can be more difficult to configure. Configuring a printer involves coordinating the software with the printer so both understand each other. Your printer might speak several different dialects or maybe even different languages, and your software might do the same. When a printer speaks the language developed specifically for another brand of printer, it is said to *emulate* that printer. If your software doesn't have your brand and model of printer specifically available to choose from, you must select an alternative from the printers your printer can emulate. The two most popular brands of dot matrix printers to emulate are the IBM ProPrinter and the Epson series of printers. In the ink jet and laser printer world, the popular brand to emulate is Hewlett-Packard. Hewlett-Packard has developed several versions of a page description language it calls *PCL*. The newest version of the PCL language is PCL5, but the software may still be programmed to talk to laser printers that support PCL4. The good news is any laser printer that will speak PCL5 will also work with software that uses PCL4.

Printer emulation problems can cause you trouble. One business in particular had printer problems with an older 9-pin printer that would emulate both an Epson 9-pin printer and an IBM ProPrinter. The problem was, the software thought it was talking to an IBM ProPrinter when the printer was configured to be emulating an Epson. So when it came time to print labels with barcodes, the barcodes were too short and the mailing did not receive the discounts it should have. This particular printer was difficult for a novice to configure because it required programming (creating a Basic program) to change the emulation. While all the instructions were available for the creation of the program, only someone with some programming background would know how to get the Basic interpreter that comes with the operating system on a PC started and how to correctly copy the commands.

Fortunately, the newer dot matrix printers are easier to configure. Most have a sequence of keys on the front or a switch inside to change the emulation. It is of particular importance to know what the printer's emulation is and to be sure the programs you have are all set to talk to that type of printer.

High-end fast printers

Speed is important when you get those big clients in the mailing list service business. While you might not need a fast label or envelope printer now, you might want to keep one in mind.

Most laser printers print at 8 *pages per minute* (ppm). At 30 labels per page, that's 14,400 labels per hour. Envelope printing on a laser printer is slower at the rate of about 8 per minute or 240 per hour. Also, laser printers cost more to run because the toner costs $100 per cartridge and gives you between 30,000 and 50,000 pages—about the same cost as photocopying.

Many options are available, but high-end fast printers start at $1000 and go up to $4000 or more. These high-speed printers become specialized and are designed to print a specific product, such as only letter-sized paper, only envelopes, or only labels. An ink jet printer specifically for envelope printing is shown in FIG. 4-10. High-speed ink printers are popular because ink costs less than the toner used in laser printers, but can often produce better looking results than dot matrix printers.

Some of the high-end dot matrix printers produce Cheshire labels, which are paper labels made to be affixed by machine. These printers can print labels at

4-10
Some printers are designed for particular types of printing. This Address Express inkjet printer from CoStar is specifically designed for envelope printing.

CoStar Corp.

upward of 10,000 to 30,000 per hour and have ribbons that will last for 200,000 labels.

By the time you move into the high-speed printer arena, you will have already decided which direction you want to head and will have specific needs. Magazines for mailing are the best places to find the right products when you're ready and several distributors can also help. *Mailer's Review* has reviews and advertising of key products, the Melissa *Data Catalog* offers hardware products to mailers, and so do other industry publications. Trade shows, such as MailCom, are also a good source for what's available. Information on industry publications and trade shows is listed in appendix B.

Ray Melissa   Profile
Melissa Software, San Juan Capistrano, California

Hundreds of wrong numbers turn out to be right after all.

The Mailer's Software Catalog offers a collection of software geared toward mailers, including zip code finding programs, local market demographics, and map programs. However, the same company offering the catalog also offers a catalog of items personalized with the name "Melissa," an idea which came literally out of hundreds of wrong number calls.

Ray Melissa, who owns Melissa Software and produces the Melissa Catalog, said: "Once we put in the 800 line, we started getting 30 to 40 calls a day from young girls, junior high to high school age. We couldn't understand it, and we were going to change the 800 number until we accidentally stumbled on why they were calling."

The 800 number is (800) MELISSA, a number Melissa hoped his customers would associate with his mailing software catalog. Instead, Ray discovered the young girls calling all had one thing in common—their first name was Melissa. They were simply picking up the phone and dialing their first names toll-free.

Ray said he knew there was an opportunity here. "Here are all these customers calling, there had to be something we could offer them." After some thought, Ray decided to do another catalog, this time with personalized items for girls named 'Melissa.' "When they call now, we get their address and send them a copy." In the first month, the Melissa catalog already garnered a two percent response with the personalized clothes selling the best, but Ray says he can do better.

Knowing what he does about mailing and lists, Ray went to a list broker who said he could specially sort a list of US high school students to just pull the names of 126,000 girls named—you got it—Melissa. Ray said he is preparing 50,000 catalogs to send to a subset of that list.

By-the-way, Ray got another 800 number for his software catalog that doesn't spell out into a word; (800) 443-8834. But it makes you wonder how an (800) JENNIFER number would do.

Other tools

You have to have a computer and a printer, but the rest of these tools offer a savings on your back and hopefully on your wallet. Remember, the more you can produce, the more money you can make.

If you think you might be doing letter shop work, the basic tools are a labeling machine and a folding machine. Labeling machines are ingenious devices that make the pressure sensitive labels peel away from the paper so you can easily grab them and stick them on. When you pull off the last label in a row, the machine advances just enough to make the next row of labels available. This machine speeds up pressure sensitive labeling enormously. Dispensa-Matic Label Dispensers, a division of Commercial Mailing Accessories, sells the label dispenser machines. They are listed in appendix A, have an 800 number, and offer a free 21-day trial. These machines are practically indestructible and are often available for sale used.

A labeling machine for chopping computer printed paper into 1-x-4-inch rectangles and gluing those labels on to the mailing pieces was invented by Cheshire, who has the distinction of having the printed format for the labels his machine uses named after him. The Cheshire label machines can label up to 10,000 pieces an hour and are pricey for the home-based business. New Cheshire label machines can run approximately $40,000 to $50,000, while used models can be obtained for $10,000 to $30,000, depending on their age and condition. However, the term Cheshire label is a common one in the mail business because in very large quantities Cheshire labels are significantly less expensive than pressure-sensitive labels.

Folding machines come in a number of types and are designed to fold paper a myriad of ways. Folding is also one of those operations that can offer big postal savings. Several manufacturers offer folding machines, which are also nearly indestructible and can often be bought used. Some of these manufacturers are GBR Systems Corporation, Martin Yale Industries, Pitney Bowes, Friden Neopost, and Postalia, whose addresses and contact information are listed in appendix A.

As a final note, it is always best to proceed cautiously in purchasing business equipment and to begin investigating the purchase of a piece of equipment before you actually need it. If you know something about what you're after, you'll be more apt to make a decision that is of true benefit to you.

Software

Software is an essential part of computing and necessary to take advantage of the capability of the computer. Software comes in two basic forms, system software and application software. Both are necessary for the operation of the computer.

Computers are worthless without software, but the good news is lots of software is available for PCs that can help you with your mailing list service. Every computer requires both system software and application software. We'll start with the system software, then talk about the tasks application software can perform for you, and then list how the software packages available help you do those tasks.

Software that operates the computer system is called *system software*. This type of software "talks" to the hardware directly and all other types of software must interface with the system software in order to work. You should get the system software with the computer when you purchase it. You should also get documentation.

System software

DOS (Disk Operating System) is the most widely used operating system on PCs and the latest version is DOS 6.0 shown in FIG. 4-11. If you buy a new PC, you should get DOS 6.0, or higher, with it.

C:\>ver

MS-DOS Version 5.00

4-11
A screen shot of the disk operating system MS-DOS version 5.0.

C:\>

The latest trend in PCs is the move toward the *graphical user interface* (GUI). Microsoft Windows is the most popular of the GUI interfaces on the PC and requires you have a pointing device called a *mouse*. With the mouse you move an arrow on the screen to point to pictures or objects to give the computer instructions. Windows requires DOS in order to operate and works best with DOS 5.0 or higher. For most mailing list processing activities, Windows is slower than DOS. However, gains in productivity due to the fact that Windows is easier for new users to work with than DOS could make up for the slower processing speed. Application software is started in either DOS or Windows by giving a command. In DOS, the user types a word and presses the Enter key on the keyboard to start application software running. Windows allows users to start application software by offering pictures users can point to and click quickly twice on a button on the mouse to start, as shown in FIG. 4-12.

Mailing list services don't really need Windows, and few services used it. Windows is demanding of the computer and requires more memory than just DOS alone in order to operate, which means it costs more to use. None of the major mail list applications required Windows. However, some interesting

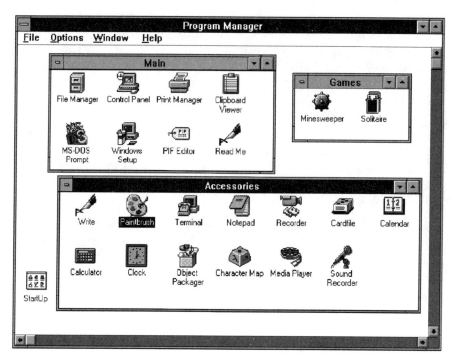

4-12
A screen shot of the Microsoft Windows graphical user interface. Users move the pointing device by using a device called a mouse to click on objects that represent programs or commands.

and beneficial mail-related software products for Windows are available, and those products will be covered as they pertain to the mailing list business.

Application software

Software designed to perform a special task is called *application software*. It can be thought of as software that applies the computer to your problem. Application software requires the system software, DOS, and it might require Windows as well in order to operate. Sometimes application software is spoken of as being loaded on top of DOS or Windows. However, the user is often unaware of this hierarchy and only sees small parts of the system software, spending the most time with the application software. Figure 4-13 illustrates.

Mailing tasks you can automate

You could do all of this mailing work by hand, but the idea is to do the work of several people all by yourself by getting the computer to do the work. But what tasks can we expect the computer to perform, and how does having software help? First, we'll have to outline the tasks involved, and then we can talk about the application software that can perform those tasks for you.

Data entry The first task in any mailing list is entering the information, also known as *entering the data*. Somewhere, someone had to enter the data into the computer, and the computer can often help you with the data entry. Some of the software packages are smart enough to automatically capitalize words for you, allow you to type abbreviations that the software turns into

The computer's point of view

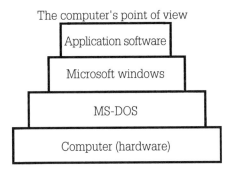

4-13
The computer requires operating system software be loaded before any application software can be used. From the user's point of view, however, the application software is the most important.

The computer user's point of view

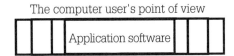

the full word, or warn you if the entry might have something wrong. But no matter how you slice it, the grunt work of data entry still has to be done.

If you're lucky, someone will have already entered the data for you and you'll have it on a disk. But it is seldom indeed that you'll get a disk with the data ordered the way you want it. What if the names are entered last name first or the company name is before the name of the person on the list or there's extra data you don't need? Well, as long as it was done consistently, meaning every name is last name first or company name first, it doesn't really matter. You can tell most mailing list software the order of the data and the software can reorganize it.

If you think you might be doing a lot of data entry work, consider a package like DynaKey from North Scituate, Massachusetts-based Peoplesmith Software. DynaKey allows you to type everything in uppercase and then translates it to upper-and lowercase. It also allows you to type simple one- or two-character abbreviations which it translates for you into the full words, as illustrated in FIG. 4-14. The product stores data in dBASE format, but offers translation into other common formats as well. Using DynaKey means you'll have an extra step, as you'll be faced with moving the data into whatever list management package you happen to be using. DynaKey costs around $400 and is available from Peoplesmith Software, 18 Damon Rd., P.O. Box 384, N. Scituate, MA 02060, telephone (617) 545-7300.

If you're renting lists and find them full of abbreviations, such as those in FIG. 4-15, DataLift, also from Peoplesmith Software, can help you convert those cryptic abbreviations into more readable and personable text. This is important to give the mailing a more personal look.

4-14

Shown is an example from Peoplesmith's DynaKey product of how the product can speed data entry by expanding abbreviations to their fully spelled counterparts.

```
DynaKey   -   Power-Assisted Data Entry System

-> Mode L - Expands, punctuates, converts to Upper/Lower Case
   Mode U - Expands & punctuates; leaves data in UPPER Case
   Mode F - Forces to UPPER CASE but does no other processing


MR C L MCHUE JR PHD              Mr. C. L. McHue, Jr. Ph.D.
EVP                              Executive Vice President
NET                              New England Telephone Co., Inc.
UST BLDG                         United States Trust Building
S BOS MA 02016                   South Boston, MA 02016

     Welcome to DynaKey - Please touch any key to begin
```

4-15

Rented lists often come laden with abbreviations. Many of the high-end list management products offer the capability to decode abbreviations. Peoplesmith's DataLift product, shown here, is designed especially for this purpose.

```
D a t a  L i f t    --    File Converter/Refiner

-> Mode L - Expands, punctuates, converts to Upper/Lower Case
   Mode U - Expands & punctuates; leaves data in UPPER Case
   Mode F - Forces to UPPER CASE but does no other processing


M/M ABE LINCOLN PRES             Mr. & Mrs. Abe Lincoln, President
THE WHITE HOUSE                  The White House
1500 PENNSYLVANIA AV             1500 Pennsylvania Avenue
WASH DC 20500                    Washington, DC 20500

     Welcome to DataLift - Please Hit any key to begin
```

Importing and exporting data   Getting someone else's list of names from the disk into your software and back out again is called *importing and exporting*. You're going to find yourself doing a lot of import/export work, even with data you entered yourself, so you'll need to find software packages that will do it. Most of the better software for mailing or data management offers import and export capability, but the thing to watch for is an import but no export. If the software only imports, you might be faced with doing double duty to maintain two lists if you have a client who doesn't use the same format as your software package does.

Merge/purge   You'll want to find duplicates and eliminate them. If more than one list is involved, the lists are joined (*merged*) and then the software for comparing the names and addresses on the list is put into motion. Most software packages require you look through the suspected duplicates before elimination, but some can be set to allow the computer to make the decision to eliminate the duplicates automatically. In addition to finding exact matches of names, the more sophisticated packages offer phonetic checking such as looking for names that sound alike such as "Dover" and "Dovor." The problem with allowing the computer to make the decision is it might eliminate the wrong name as it can only guess as to the identity. However, if you have a million names, it might be too difficult to sit down and look at 100,000 duplicate names and addresses to determine which should be eliminated. You'll find duplicate checking in most packages, although there are entire software packages geared just to duplicate checking, such as Dupe Eliminator from Group 1 Software.

Mail merge   Personalized documents, such as letters or coupons are done electronically by a process called a *mail merge*. The computer is able to generate a document that says the same thing, but one personalized copy is printed for each person on your list. Sometimes these computer-generated documents are called *form letters*. Actually, creating labels and addressing envelopes is also a form of mail merging.

You can get your mailing list and a word processor together to do mail merging. A word processing software package will make your correspondence and your mail merge documents look as appealing and up-to-date as possible. This is the arena where Microsoft Windows-based word processing software applications shine, because what you see on screen is what will print, also known as *what-you-see-is-what-you-get* (WYSIWYG).

Mail merge documents are easier to create with a Windows-based word processor, because the help is more extensive and much of the work is done for you. If you don't want to make the investment in Windows, you can certainly use one of the many DOS-based word processing packages to do mail merge, such as WordPerfect, Microsoft Word, or WordStar. More information on the mechanics of mail merging is offered in chapter 5. This combination will probably produce better looking output than using other packages for mailing that offer integrated word processing, because you can use different fonts to make the document look appealing. Word processing software is designed for producing appealing documents and popular packages include Microsoft Word, WordPerfect, Ami Pro, and WordStar to name just a few. All of these packages have Windows versions.

A word processor is also useful as a troubleshooting tool. Often you can use your word processor to take a quick peek at a list without changing it to see what's there.

Reformatting   If the data is entered in all capital letters and you need it to be in upper- and lowercase, you can get software to change the data for you without reentering all of it. The software can usually change the data either way, so it is all capital letters or not, depending on what you want. Often the software can correct other formatting problems, such as data entered full of abbreviations, such as D/M for Dr. and Mrs., as the data you might rent from a broker might be.

Printing   Once you have the data, and it's in the format you want it in, you'll need to print it out. Software is required to print the data, whether you're doing labels or form letters.

Also, software can allow you to print the barcodes and Business Reply Mail pieces as well. If you have a Business Reply Mail permit, you can print the Business Reply Mail postcards or envelopes as you need them using software developed for that purpose. Some of the software packages that do this printing are geared exclusively toward laser printers, but others will work with ink jet or even dot matrix printers. Laser printers are going to produce the best looking output, however.

Envelope Manager, from PSI Software, will allow you to enter your Business Reply Mail permit information and will print out Business Reply Mail materials as you need them. Postmark from RAM Solutions of Temple, Arizona and Jet Reply from Jet Products offer similar functionality.

Sorting   The data for labels or envelopes can be printed in zip code order, zip code sort order, or production order. What's the difference? Zip code order sorts the names in ascending order by zip code. The second type of sort, zip code sort order, organizes the zip codes in the sort order the post office requires, such as 10 or more with the same first five digits together, but doesn't take bundling, sacking, or traying into account. Production order means the zip codes are sorted the way the post office wants mail sorted, bundled, and sacked or trayed. Production order is dependent on the size and weight of the mail pieces as the mail cannot be bundled too thin or too thick, and once the mail is bundled it has to be placed in specially labeled sacks. A software package that offers production order sorting will ask you for a brief description of the pieces, including the size and weight of the pieces and will then sort the list taking those factors into account so no further sorting is needed. Production order software is updated as the post office changes its requirements, so you can expect it to cost more. While almost any mail-oriented software programs will zip code order the printed pieces, not all will place the pieces in zip code sort order, and few programs offer production order sorting.

USPS reports   Once the mail is bundled and sacked, reports are required on the mail for the post office. The reports include the number of pieces of mail and the zip codes. If you want barcoding discounts, you'll have to fill out a report to show specially certified software was used to prepare the mailing and the percentage of zip+4 coded addresses. These are tasks the software should do for you.

List cleaning   A clean list means the addresses have been checked and are deliverable addresses. The only check for deliverable addresses is to attempt to zip+4 encode those addresses. In order to perform list cleaning, CASS-certified software must be used.

The only way to conveniently distribute the USPS database of nationwide address information required to list cleaning is on the laser format of CD-ROM (discussed earlier under the hardware section). This not only requires the user have a CD-ROM drive, it also requires updates as often as quarterly to keep the national address information accurate.

This also means the CASS-certified zip+4 coding software is going to cost you more. You'll need a CD-ROM drive, and you can expect to pay about $1000 per year for the software. The ability to do all the zip+4 encoding right on your desk is definitely convenient, and it is certainly something you'll want to consider as a mailing professional. This is the activity A.G. Pitsilos said he could make $2000 an hour doing, at $.02 per name with the computer whipping through 100,000 names per hour. Pitsilos has a large one-gigabyte (Gb) hard disk to which he copies the entire contents of the CD-ROM disc and the lists from clients and then sets the software to work on the list.

The leading list cleaning packages in the PC world are ZCR 2000 from the Business Computer Center in Libertyville, Illinois, and AccuMail from Group 1 Software of Greenbelt, Maryland. There are others, but they all offer on CD-ROM the zip+4 and Carrier Route data for the entire United States and each is CASS-certified. The Business Computer Center licenses its CD-ROM from First Data Resources (FDR) who also supplies CD-ROMs to the USPS. AccuMail offers its own CD-ROM.

The post office provides a list of current CASS-certified software vendors twice a year. You may request a copy of the CASS-certified vendor list from the National Address Information Center at (800) 238-3150 or you can write to the National Address Information Center, US Postal Service, 6060 Primacy Pky. Suite 101, Memphis, TN 38188-0001.

If $1000 per year seems a little steep right now, there are alternative ways to get the zip+4 information for any given list. One is to send your list in on disk to the USPS who will code it for you. The list has to be in special format and mailed on a disk to the Memphis, Tennessee, USPS National Address Information Center (NAIC) facility, who will add the zip+4 coding the first time for free and after that will charge you about $50 per 1000 names. This process takes about three weeks. Your nearest Postal Business Center may also be able to do it for you, and more quickly. You can also mail your data directly to the company that does the processing for the USPS National

Address Information Center (NAIC) where you can have not only zip+4 coding done, but you can also get the USPS National Change Of Address (NCOA) information that is pertinent to your data. This means if anyone has moved on your list and notified the post office of the move, you will receive the new address information. You can mail your list on disk to the NAIC, who will forward it to a licensee, FDC, Inc. of Minnetonka, Minnesota, who will then forward it to its licensee Lorton Data of Minneapolis, Minnesota. Or you can simply send it directly to Lorton Data who will send it back in about seven days. The forms you must fill out for this service may be obtained from the NAIC by calling (800) 238-3150, and in Tennessee the number is (800) 233-0453. Lorton Data is at 43 Main St. SE, Suite 408, Minneapolis, MN 55414-1029.

One other option is to add the zip+4 code by modem. As of this writing only PSI Software in Palo Alto, California, develops software programs for between $40 and $150 that support modem lookup, a service the company calls Dial-A-Zip. The company offers two software programs, Envelope Manager for DOS and DAZzle, a Windows software package. Envelope Manager offers list cleaning, list management, and barcoding. A call to PSI can get you the number of the nearest Postal Business Center (PBC) which has the dial-up service. The dial-up zip+4 services are offered at no charge (except for the call) however, the USPS has put a 100-name limit per call restriction on the service because they didn't want the free dial-up services to compete with the CD-ROM distributors. The company's Windows product, DAZzle, shown in FIG. 4-16, is designed for doing one piece at a time. One address at a time is too slow for the type of mailings we're talking about here, even though it only takes an average of 15 seconds to dial-up and get zip+4 information, but DAZzle is not geared toward production work. As a side note, PSI Software originally marketed the software to the USPS for postal centers and postal employees to use and even has a version that prints envelopes for franking.

If you send your data off to the USPS, a Postal Business Center, or one of the USPS licensees to be zip+4 encoded, you will be provided with a Form 3553 which you can photocopy for mailings.

Key coding   Any zip+4 CASS-certified list cleaning product, will generate codes to tell you how each address did when compared to the zip+4 data. The codes vary somewhat from product to product, but once you've seen and understand one set of codes, you'll be able to quickly catch on to any other package's coding scheme. For the sake of illustration, we'll use the key codes generated by ZCR 2000 depicted in FIG. 4-17. ZCR 2000 generates three codes: the flag code, the address record data code, and the slush code.

A *flag code* is a letter, A, B, C, and so on, much like the letter grades students earn. Another code, sometimes known as the *address record data code*, tells you if the address is a company, an apartment building, a post office box, a rural route, and so on. ZCR 2000 adds error codes, also known as *slush codes*,

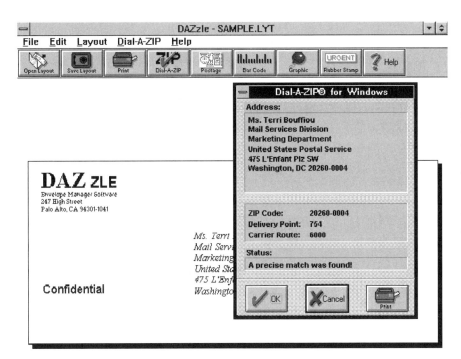

4-16
DAZzle for Windows makes use of a modem to dial up and access zip+4 information centers at post offices. However, it is only designed to look up one address at a time and is geared mainly to printing envelopes.

to indicate more detailed information as to why the address was rejected or wasn't an exact match for zip+4 coding. Each of these codes are normally added at the end of each name in the list, after zip+4 processing.

Why might you get an error code? There are lots of reasons but all of them have to do with missing or misplaced information. If the address is incomplete, such as the numbers in the street address are missing, you'll get a "multiple responses" error code meaning the address could be one of two or more possibilities. Other missing information that might produce a "multiple responses" error code could be a missing company name. While a missing name of an individual won't produce an error code, a missing company name might because some companies in large buildings are assigned individual zip+4 codes. If you have an individual name but not a company name, you might get the "multiple responses" error code, or a "default match" code, meaning the software gave you the generic zip+4 for the building, but you might be able to get a closer match if you have more information. However, the default match is acceptable to the USPS.

If the address is in a location where the mail carrier doesn't deliver, like a rural route where people pick up their mail at a centralized location or a parcel of land with no building on it, you'll get a five-digit code zip code and an exact match slush code message, but a "w" flag code, meaning the address is undeliverable. You can see why the post office allows 15 percent of the addresses in a barcoded mailing to get by without zip+4 coding.

Footnote Flag

Flag code	Meaning
A	ZIP code corrected
B	City/state spelling corrected
C	Invalid city/state/ZIP
D	No ZIP+4 assigned
F	Address not found
H	Missing apartment/suite number
I	Insufficient/incorrect data (multiple response)
L	Street too long
M	Street abbreviated
P	Previous ZIP+4 not found
R	City abbreviated
S	Incorrect secondary number
T	Street address line corrected
U	Unofficial PO name
V	Unverifiable city/state
W	Invalid delivery address

Address record data type

Record type	Meaning
F	Firm
FR	Firm range
H	Building/apartment
P	Post office box
PR	Post office box range
RR	Rural route
HC	Highway contract
S	Street
GD	General delivery
PM	Postmaster

Slush codes

Slush code	Meaning
10	Invalid dual address
11	Invalid city/state/ZIP code
12	Invalid state
13	Invalid city
21	Not found
22	Multiple addresses
31	Exact match
32	Default match
33	Non-deliverable address

4-17
The key codes let you know how successful the zip+4 coding was for each address in the mailing list. These codes are the ones used by ZCR 2000, but most zip+4 coding software will use similar codes.

Besides helping you troubleshoot what's wrong with an address, you want these codes to protect yourself. With the error codes in hand, you can go back to your customer and say, "Look, here's what's wrong with these addresses." Then your customer can decide whether or not to fix the addresses or simply pull them from the list. Also, if your customer's list falls below the 85 percent of zip+4 coded addresses, so it doesn't qualify for barcoding discounts, you're going to have to explain why. Even if you're not doing barcoding or carrier route mailings, this will prevent a huge pile of nixies from coming back to your customer.

Barcoding   Once you have the zip+4 coding, you can make use of barcoding software. CASS-certified barcoding software is available, but the USPS is more concerned about CASS-certification for zip+4 coding than it is about the POSTNET Barcode Certification because the printed barcode either works with the postal equipment, or it doesn't. Even barcodes printed with CASS-certified software won't work if the printer is producing poor output.

The POSTNET certification focuses exclusively on the ability of the software to get the printers it supports to print the POSTNET delivery point barcode accurately and correctly so USPS barcode readers can process it. This involves getting the bars the right height, not too close together, not too far apart, not too thin or too thick, and in the right place. Remember, printing of the POSTNET delivery point barcode requires that the zip+4 and the address information is already available and that the printer is working according to the manufacturer's specifications.

Some software is offered specifically for barcoding, such as Bar-Lite from PostSaver systems of Rochester Hills, Michigan, or BarRight, specifically designed for 9-pin dot matrix printers from Scriptomatic of West Conshohocken, Pennsylvania.

List maintenance software   The list cleaning software, while useful, doesn't handle the list management or data entry functions. To offer a complete package to customers, developers of the list cleaning software have come up with companion products to interface with the list cleaning products and offer the list maintenance functionality. Other products from other companies also offer the list maintenance functionality and some even work with the list cleaning software.

The Business Computer Center offers Mail Manager 2000, which interfaces with its own ZCR 2000 or Group 1's AccuMail for zip+4 functions. Group 1 offers ArcList or PostSaver (FIG. 4-18), both of which work with AccuMail.

Most of the list management software offers data input services such as inserting the city and state if a zip code is entered or vice versa, and performing address standardization on the fly if it is used with one of the list cleaning CD-ROM products or Dial-a-Zip. CASS-certified list maintenance packages Envelope Manager from PSI Software (mentioned earlier) and MailMiser Plus from Kestrel Enterprises are examples of list maintenance software that will work with the list cleaning CD-ROM products mentioned earlier.

Because the number of five-digit zip codes is much smaller, most list maintenance software includes all of the five-digit zip codes and will insert the five-digit zip if a list cleaning product is not available. The lists created by these software packages can always be cleaned later by list cleaning software. Also, most of the list cleaning packages offer the option of exporting the data in a format for either the National Address Information

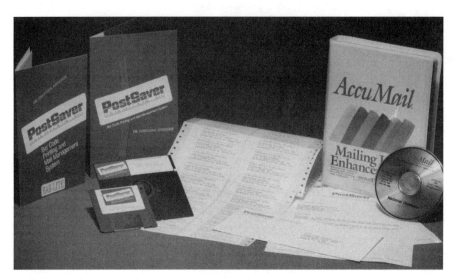

4-18
All of the zip+4 coding packages have their own companion list management software packages. Here Group 1 Software's product PostSaver mail list management software is shown with the company's AccuMail CD-ROM.

Center (NAIC) or the National Change Of Address (NCOA), so you don't have to understand either format.

These packages also offer some kind of duplicate checking during data entry. In addition, the software will perform reformatting of the data, including automatic capitalization, so you can do your data entry in all lowercase and the software knows when to capitalize. Most mail list maintenance software can also convert a list in all uppercase to upper- and lowercase characters, or vice versa. Sampling, including Nth number sampling, is sometimes built in and the list can either include the Nth sample, or offer all the names except the Nth sample. Label design is also offered, and some of the packages even have the most common label types built in so you can just pick them off a list. Password protection of each list is usually included for data security, and some mail merge capability is also offered for personalized correspondence.

Some of the packages don't offer production order sorts of the list, just zip code sorting. Of the ones that offer the production order sorting, some will even ask you how thick your mail piece is and how much it weighs and will then print special reminders in between labels to tell you when to bundle and when to sack what's bundled. You can also expect the software to print the sack or tray tags. Some list maintenance packages will support a 9-track tape drive, such as Mail Manager 2000, and most offer customer support for the first year. You'll even find a few toll-free numbers for customer support.

If your budget is tight to start with, you may only be interested in the less expensive software packages, which sort for the most basic discounted mailing rates at the post office and cost between $50 and $100. If you know your lists are not going to be larger than about 30,000 names, and you don't want to track much information about the members of the list, you will find several good products to choose from. Some are specifically designed for mailing, such as MyAdvancedMailList from MySoftware or Avery Label Pro from Avery, the folks who also make mailing labels and office products.

List information software   No listing of software packages for mailers would be complete without software for list information, such as determining the sex of the names on the list. Software is available to help you determine the sex of the person from their first name, even with unusual first names. Software just for the task of splitting names, such as D/M Tom Jones into the two separate names Dr. Tom Jones and Mrs. Tom Jones, is also available. The purpose is to create more personal mailings when processing large numbers of names, especially from purchased or rented lists. Knowledge of the sex of the individual can also be valuable information to know for targeting new customers. Peoplesmith makes two products for this purpose, Personator and Genderbase. Genderbase offers just genderizing, while Personator offers both name splitting and genderizing functions.

Mail software purchasing tips

No matter what list management software package you purchase, you'll have to learn to use it and that just takes time and support from the software vendor. I recommend you call the companies you're interested in first to see how they treat you before you buy, especially with the more expensive packages. You'll find the Melissa Data catalog has an entire line of software and hardware products all geared toward mailers. Also, most of the software vendors advertise in the publications geared toward the mail industry, and these publications are listed in appendix B. The major publications in the industry, such as *Mailer's Review*, *DM News*, and others also offer reviews of the current software.

If you decide to use a mailing list management package and the package says it barcodes, you need to look for two things. One is CASS-certification and the other is a money-back guarantee within a certain period of time (usually 30 days) if you can't make it work. Be sure you hang on to the receipt so you can prove when you purchased the software. CASS-certification is important if you're barcoding. Believe it or not, some of the packages say they barcode, but they're not CASS-certified, and the barcode they print isn't readable by the USPS barcode readers.

That money-back guarantee protects you if you discover the software won't produce USPS readable barcodes with your equipment, even if the software is CASS-certified. You'll save yourself much embarrassment and aggravation if you produce a few experimental pieces with barcodes and take them down to your post office to be sure they work before you run an entire mailing. A number of things can prevent the barcodes from being readable, such as a printer ribbon that's over-inked and is smudging, an old or dried out ribbon, a dot matrix printer with a print head in which the pins are bent or not hitting the paper at all, incorrect printer emulation, and so on. A test will tell you for sure if your barcoding software and printer are working. If the problem is your printer, then no software will fix it, but if the problem has to do with the way your software talks to your printer, then you'll want to have the option of taking it back. If you get it working, then over time you'll need to watch for changes in the barcodes you print that might make them unreadable.

CD-ROM lists   If you have a CD-ROM drive, you can purchase on CD all the U.S. Yellow Pages listings, all the U.S. White Pages listings, nationwide demographic information, as well as other lists. Most of these CDs let you view all the names, but limit you a certain number of listings, such as 20,000 after which you must pay the publisher of the CD an additional charge to access any more listings. Somewhere between 9 and 35 million listings are offered on a single CD-ROM and prices vary from $100 to nearly $5000 depending on how up-to-date the lists are and how they were obtained. Newcomers to the CD market are offering CDs with unlimited access, but they will admit the lists on such CDs are older.

Software for you   As a business owner, you'll find you can use your computer for contacting your clients and tracking your own business. You'll need a way to generate invoices, a financial management program, a way to track who you've talked with and who you need to get back to, and you'll need to be able to generate correspondence. Most of the word processors will allow you to do some of these functions if you're clever in the way you use them. But eventually, you'll find yourself with less time to create everything you need from scratch, and you'll want the computer to do more of the work.

A quick list of popular software packages for small business follows. For small business accounting, Quicken is a very popular package and widely supported. Both DOS and Windows versions of Quicken are available. For tracking your own customers there are contact managers such as ACT! for Windows or DOS from Carrollton, Texas-based Contact Software International or PackRat for Windows from Polaris Software of San Diego, California. PackRat also offers time management and financial tracking as well. MySoftware offers an inexpensive package called MyInvoices to track your invoices, produce customer statements, and track who owes you.

In order for you to make full use of your software products in offering mailing list services, you need to know something about databases. That's what the next chapter is all about. In it, you'll find the definitions you need to make sense of the terminology you're bound to run into, valuable time-saving tips, and references to further information. You can save yourself some headaches and some work by reading it before you start working with lists or doing data entry.

5 Databases
Maintaining your mailing lists

You can get into this business without a lot of knowledge, but the more you know, the better. The big profits in the mailing list service business are made by people who understand and know how to make use of database software to automate the gathering and insertion of information into a mailing list. To do this, you need to understand what the concepts of a database are, how mailing lists fit into those concepts, how the computer sees your mailing list, and how you can get the computer to do the grunt work. The basics of mailing list mechanics, or *database manipulation*, are provided here.

To present you with this basic information, I am making a few assumptions about things you already know. I am assuming you know what a file is and how to use DOS commands such as DIR, COPY, and TYPE. If you don't know what those things are, this chapter will still help you, but you should take some basic computer courses as I've already mentioned, then reread this information. You also should seriously consider taking courses or getting materials on databases and how to work with them, as you can turn all that knowledge into income.

A *database* is a collection of data organized to serve a particular function. A mailing list is loosely called a database and in our case the function is to mail material to the addresses on the mailing list. But a database can be used to track almost anything that can be organized into a group, from inventory in a store to a baseball card collection.

What a database is

Databases come in many forms such as object-oriented databases, hierarchical databases, network databases, and relational databases. Most of the database application software tools for the PC use some form of the relational database, so that type of database is what I will focus on here. To explain the basics of a relational database, first I'll explain the terms used and what parts of the database those terms refer to, then I'll talk about database formats, common operations performed using a database, and database design issues.

Common terms

The database is made up of entities, fields, records, tables, keys or key fields, and it can be ordered various ways for viewing by indexing. Let's take these terms one at a time.

Entity   *Entities* are things in the real world, such as people, companies, baseball cards, cars, etc. The purpose of a database is to process information about entities. In the mailing list business, the only entities we are interested in are people and maybe companies.

Attributes   Each entity has *attributes*, which are the characteristics of the entity that are meaningful to us. The people represented in our mailing list have first names, last names, company names, street addresses, cities, states, and zip codes, among other things. Some of a baseball card's attributes would be the card's year, the player, the condition, and perhaps the value. Not every attribute is of interest to us. For example, a characteristic of people is hair color, but for the purpose of the mailing list, that is not an attribute that has meaning. However, the person's carrier route is a characteristic of the person we would find of interest.

Table   Entities exist in the real world, but we need a place the computer can use to store information about the entity. In a database, a *table* is that place the information about the entity is stored. Figure 5-1 shows a mailing list table in a database application. An important guideline to understand about databases is each table should only contain information about one kind of entity. In other words, a database will contain one table for each entity you want to track.

Fields   Within a table, *fields* store information about the entity's attributes. Notice within the table in Figure 5-1, I have divided the information about each address into separate parts, and each part is in a column. These columns are called fields, and each field is given an individual name to identify the data. Notice how each last name is in the field Lastname, each first name is in the Firstname field, and so on.

When creating a new table, you have to determine how long the fields are. Most of the time this is done by looking at the data and figuring out the largest number of characters, including spaces, you would put in a field. Fields that are too long are cumbersome and waste space, but fields that are too short make it difficult to enter the necessary information.

Records   One *record* exists in the table for each instance of the entity. Each row in FIG. 5-1 stores an individual occurrence of the entity, in our case each name and address in the mailing list, and these occurrences are called records.

Index   The beauty of a database is its ability to deliver to you the information you want, no matter how that information was originally entered. Most mailing lists store the records in the order in which the information came into the firm collecting the data. However, when you offer the database application the proper commands, called *querying*, you can view the records in the table in any order in which it is convenient. Notice how in FIG. 5-2 the database application software displays the records in the table in alphabetical order by last name and in FIG. 5-3 the database displays the records in zip code order. The data is still stored in the table the way it was originally entered, but the software presents the data in any way you would like to see it.

If the way I have viewed the records is a view of the mailing list I'd like to see often, I can *index* the database on the particular fields, meaning I can see that view without waiting for the computer to visually reorganize the records every time.

An index of a table is like the index in the back of this book. When you're looking for something specific, instead of searching the entire book, the location of the information is stored in the index so you can go right to it. The database application creates an index by obtaining the location of the records based on the sorting criteria, then storing the locations. As new records are entered, the index or indexes must be updated to include the new records. Indexes can be changed as records are entered, or the process can be done all at once. Many indexes can be set up, so the table information can be viewed in a variety of ways. However, each index requires disk space. The speed at which database software can index is a source of comparison between competing database products. Indexing also makes looking up individual records, such as a customer name, very fast.

Keys   *Keys* are fields that uniquely identify a record. While you might not need to concern yourself with keys in order to handle a mailing list, you will hear the term used. Usually a number is used as the key since it is easy to generate a unique number for each record. The primary key is the main, unique field used to contain the information that uniquely identifies that record from all other records in the database.

Formats

Different database applications store table data in file formats that vary from one product to another. The three formats that are of the greatest concern in the mailing list service business are the ASCII delimited, the ASCII fixed-length, and the dBASE or .DBF file formats. The most universal is ASCII delimited in either comma delimited or tab delimited types, but the other two are found frequently as well.

ASCII comma-delimited   The most vanilla format is the *ASCII delimited*, sometimes called just *ASCII*. A carriage return/linefeed (which is what you get when you press the Enter key on the keyboard) signals the end of a record in ASCII. But how do you know one field from another one? The *delimiter* solves this problem. It is placed between fields in the table to separate one field from another one. Almost any character can be used as a delimiter, but the most common character is either a comma or a tab. *ASCII comma-delimited fields* use a comma as the delimiter. No matter how long the fields are, only the actual data in each field for each record is copied into the ASCII comma-delimited format, as shown in FIG. 5-4.

Some fields might have a comma in them, such as the name William Smith, Jr., in FIG. 5-4. To keep the database application from thinking the comma inside the field is a delimiter, quotation marks are placed around the field. Some application software programs play it safe and place quotation marks around every field when generating an ASCII comma-delimited format. An empty field in a file that has quotation marks around every field will just have a pair of quotation marks surrounded by commas.

```
"Xavier","Jones","Mr","","","355•Main•Blvd•#•D","Boynton•Beach","FL","33435-6671"¶
"Baker","Martha","Ms","","","PO•Box•3000",Humacao","PR","00792-3000"¶
"Hauser","Douglas","Mr","","","13300•Tamiami•Trl•E•Lot•191","Naples","FL","33961-8731"¶
"Long","Gabriel","Mr","","","390•301•Blvd•West","Bradenton","FL","34205-1234"¶
"Song","Crystal","Ms","","","238•San•Carlos•St","Nokomis","FL","34275-1519"¶
"Thavin","Ronald","Mr","","","2930•Tan•Oak•Cove","Germantown","TN","38128-7338"¶
"Grant","Carry","Ms","Dr","Medical•Towers","Box•236a","Pelkie","MI","49958-1234"¶
"Smith,•Jr.","William","Mr","","","13867•Bromwich•St","Arleta","CA","91331-6120"¶
```

5-4
An ASCII comma-delimited file is displayed by a word processor that shows all characters, including spaces as dots and carriage return/line feeds with paragraph symbols.

ASCII tab-delimited The *ASCII tab-delimited format* is very similar to the ASCII comma-delimited format, except the character generated when the tab key is pressed on the keyboard is the character that acts as the delimiter. ASCII tab-delimited is found more often on the Macintosh platform, though it is used frequently because, unlike the comma, the tab character rarely appears in a field. A blank field is indicated by two tabs in a row, as shown in FIG. 5-5.

```
Xavier →Jones  →  Mr  → → →  355•Main•Blvd•#•D → Boynton•Beach →  FL  →  33435-6671 ¶
Baker → Martha → Ms → → → PO•Box•3000•  → Humacao PR   →  00792-3000¶
Hauser→Douglas→ Mr → → →  13300•Tamiami•Trl•E•Lot•191  → Naples → FL →  33961-8731¶
Long  → Gabriel → Mr  → → →  390•301•Blvd•West → Bradenton FL  →  34205-1234¶
Song →  Crystal →  Ms  → → →  238•San•Carlos•St → Nokomis → FL →  34275-1519¶
Thavin →Ronald → Mr → → → 2930•Tan•Oak•Cove → Germantown  →  TN  → 38128-7338¶
Grant Carry → Ms  → Dr → →  Medical Towers →  Box 236a→  Pelkie → MI →   49958-1234¶
Smith,•Jr.→ William→ Mr → → →  13867•Bromwich•St → Arleta →  CA  →   91331-6120¶
```

5-5 *The tab characters are displayed as arrows separating fields in this ASCII tab-delimited file.*

ASCII fixed-length *ASCII fixed-length format* means every field is exported with the maximum number of characters each field is designed to accommodate, and each record ends with a carriage return/linefeed. If the data in a field is not long enough to fill the field, spaces are inserted until the required number of characters is reached. Fields that are blank are all spaces.

DBF The *.DBF* standard, often also known as the *dBASE format*, got its introduction when now defunct Ashton-Tate used it in the database application software dBASE II. Since then .DBF format has become a standard in the PC database industry. Standards for the .DBF format are still being discussed and worked out by the *American National Standards Institute* or ANSI (pronounced "an-see"), an agency founded in 1918 that proposes, modifies, approves, and publishes data processing standards for voluntary use in the United States.

The .DBF file format includes information at the beginning of the table, called a *header*, as to the number and type of fields and other pertinent information about the database designed for a database program to read. There are no carriage return/linefeed characters and no delimiters, because the header offers all the information about how long the fields are. Most often the extension of a dBASE compatible file is .DBF.

Since dBASE first introduced the .DBF format, it is currently the measure against which .DBF files are compared. Those tables created in other programs that work without modification in dBASE are said to be *dBASE compatible*. dBASE is marketed by Borland International, headquartered in Scotts Valley, California.

Operations

Certain operations are performed over and over again in the process of manipulating the information in tables in a database. The most frequent operations, and the ones you'll hear the most about, are importing, exporting, adding, updating, deleting, querying, and joining. Let's examine each one.

Importing   One of your most frequent activities and your biggest challenge as a newcomer to the mailing list service will be getting the data given to you into a program you have so you can make use of it or *importing* it. Most database application software products require you to create a new database, defining each field, before you can import any data.

This means you'll need to know what the fields are, what type of fields they are (such as character, date, or numeric), and the maximum length of the fields in order to set up your database to receive data. This information should be given to you in printed form by the owner of the data along with the actual data on disk and will look something like the sample in FIG. 5-6. The field names are sometimes limited to 10 characters, and each field name must be different, which explains the cryptic field names you sometimes see. If you don't get a printed report of what the field names are, you might find it difficult to import the data. Occasionally, if the database is simple, you can guess by looking at the data with a word processor, but you can't count on being able to do so.

Exporting   *Exporting* is an operation you perform from inside a software application. You export for one reason and that reason is to make your data readable by another software application program. The application program may be one that belongs to you, or one that belongs to someone else.

To export, one of the first things you need to check is how much disk space you have. If you are exporting, the table may take up less disk space than the original, but the only way you'll know if you have enough disk space is to check and see if there's enough room for another copy of the current table. Even if you are sending the database out to floppy disks, you'll probably have to write it to the hard disk first anyway unless you are experienced with exporting.

You'll also want to get your software to print out a copy of the names, lengths, and type of the fields you're exporting and put it with the disks you

FIELD_NAME	FIELD_TYPE	FIELD_LEN
LASTNAME	C	018
FIRSTNAME	C	022
SALU	C	034
TITLE	C	034
COMPNAY	C	034
ADDRESS2	C	034
DELIVADDR	C	034
CITY	C	019
STATE	C	002
ZIP	C	010
DLVPT	C	002
SCF	C	003
ZIPTYPE	C	001
COUNTY	C	019
CNTYCODE	C	005
BUSPHONE	C	013
FAX	C	013
HMPHONE	C	013
OTHPHONE	C	013
CODE1	C	004
CODE2	C	004
CODE3	C	020
ADDDATE	D	008
CHGDATE	D	008
PRNDATE	D	008
CARRT	C	004
FOOTNOTE	C	010
TYPE	C	002
PRE	C	001
CKD	C	001
DUP	C	001

5-6
A typical printout of the structure of a table. The "C" stands for character, the "D" for date.

send out. Most database programs will print a report of the database fields names, types, and lengths, and you'll usually find the terminology used for the report is to *copy structure*. Sometimes you must copy the structure of your table to another table or to a file which you can then print out. You'll probably want a copy of the structure for your own files anyway, so it might be a good idea to learn how to get the program you're using to print the structure before you need to.

If you're exporting to get the NCOA data from the USPS, you'll need to fill out the form the post office requires you fill out describing each field and its length and export the data in ASCII comma or tab delimited, ASCII fixed-length, or .DBF file formats. Probably the easiest format to send out is the .DBF format, although you will get the data back in an ASCII format. You can make special arrangements to get the data back in a more custom format at an extra charge by calling Lorton Data at (612) 623-3130.

Adding   *Adding* records to a database is an ongoing process. You must give the database software a command to let it know you want to add information, usually by choosing an add command. A new, blank record will be made available into which you can type in the data you wish to add. Typing in the data, or *data entry*, is where the most future work can be avoided, if it is done correctly.

Duplicates get into the database here in ways that are not particularly obvious. Let's take a person in the database, Richard Smith. Like most people, Richard Smith goes by several different names. He is R. Smith, Rich Smith, Mr. Richard E. Smith, R.E. Smith, and probably other names we can only guess at. Most database software allows for some type of duplicate checking, but the computer will not necessarily recognize every duplicate. The problem is further complicated since two names can be the same without being duplicates. For example, R.E. Smith of 12726 Mariposa Lane is probably an entirely different person than Rich Smith of 1265 Martin Avenue. Even if the duplicate checking doesn't catch everything, it is better to attempt to do some duplicate checking at the point of entry than later, if possible.

It is also important to enter the data as consistently as possible. For example, you don't want Street abbreviated St., Str., Strt., and St. The database software has the ability to search within fields for certain character strings. The varied abbreviations of the word "street" make it difficult to search for in the database. If you want everyone on Main Street, for example, it becomes more difficult to search if the data is entered inconsistently. If you are going to abbreviate while adding records, you should use the abbreviations used by the USPS, which are listed in appendix F for your convenience. The date the record was added is also a useful piece of information.

Updating   A mailing list is about people and people change. Those changes need to be reflected in your mailing list tables. To update records you can usually have the application software look for the record you want if you enter a search criteria, such as find all the Smiths.

Also, from what you now know about mailing lists, you know that 20 percent of the records a year or more old are probably incorrect and need to be checked and updated. When a record is updated, the date of the update should be part of the record, so you know when that information was changed.

Deleting   For one reason or another, you will be deleting records from the mailing list. In the dBASE world, deleted records are marked deleted, but can be retrieved at any time. An operation called *pack* is what permanently removes records marked for deletion from the database and frees up the space the deleted records were using. It is wise to delete, but wait to pack for a few days until you are certain the records you've deleted really should be deleted. Once the records are packed, you can no longer retrieve them.

Querying   The whole point of using a database is to be able to get the information you want out of it. That process is called *querying*. You have to know something about the database and about how computers look for information in order to perform a successful query. The idea behind a query is to find records that meet a certain condition. For example, we might ask the database for the names and addresses of everyone whose state field contains the letters MA for Massachusetts. The database won't change the order of the records, but will allow us to view every record whose state is MA. Of course, the database wouldn't be smart enough to know that Mass or Massachusetts were also equal to MA unless we told it, or the designer of the database programmed it to recognize all the possible ways Massachusetts could be abbreviated.

We also might want to find information within a field. In our example with Massachusetts, we could have queried the table for all the records where the state field started with Ma* (the asterisk is the *wildcard*, meaning ignore the rest of the word), but then we'd also get Maine and Maryland. If we had a client who wanted a random sample of the database, we could ask for just zip codes where the fourth and fifth digits are 42 by querying for *42. Asking the database to look for characters or letters within a field is called *parsing*.

More complex queries are possible that mix two or more sets of conditions. For example, we could ask for a certain five-digit zip code and all the persons whose last names begin with M. Every record the computer finds that matches both of those conditions will be displayed. Once the desired records are displayed, they can be imported, exported, updated, deleted, or printed. Queries can be done that exclude records as well, such as all states except Massachusetts. The jargon for querying in the database world is *slicing and dicing*, meaning you can take the data and manipulate it a number of different ways.

Tutorials on how to perform queries are offered in several of the database products and in the manuals for the software for mailing list management. One important query language is the structured query language SQL (pronounced "see-qual"). Its most frequent use is to access database data stored on a mainframe computer. Its use is outside the scope of this book, but you will run into the term when working with databases.

Joining   *Joining* is a process that combines information from tables in your database to create a logical table. Two or more tables can be joined or *related* (hence the term *relational database*), if they have one key field that is the same in each one, such as an identification number. Why might you want to relate two tables? If you are tracking the orders that come in from a mail order catalog, rather than create a new record for each order and repeat the name, address, telephone, and so on in each record for every order, you could set up two tables. One is the mailing list information, and the other holds all the orders that have come in listing the product ordered, the invoice number, method of payment, and so on. If each customer is given something unique to identify them, such as an identification number stored in an ID field in the mail list, then by creating the same field by the same name in the order table, the field can be used to relate the information in the two databases, as illustrated in FIG. 5-7.

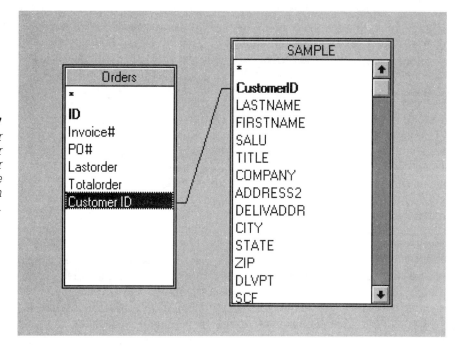

5-7
Two tables are related or joined on the customer identification number duplicated in the CustomerID field in each one.

Not only does this eliminate duplicate information, but it makes performing common tasks, such as updating a customer record with an address change, a simple matter. Instead of changing every place that customer name appears in the orders table, a single change may be made to the mailing list table. Order entry becomes easier as well, as all that is needed is the customer ID number, which the mailing list table can provide, and then that ID number and the order information is all that needs to be entered in the order table to identify who made the order. It also makes some sophisticated sorting possible, such as viewing the purchases each customer has made. This is a very common procedure and you may also see it referred to as *relationships* or *relate tables* instead of join.

Smart database design & planning

Much of what you'll do in working with mailing list software will be defined for you. You will seldom be faced with starting from scratch, having to decide what each field in your table will be and how many tables will make up your database. However, it is prudent to have some familiarity with how it is done.

Design   When setting up database fields for the first time, the software will want to know what type of data you plan to put in the field. Basic types of data for fields are *alpha* (for alphabetical) also known as *character* or *text*, *numeric* (for numbers only), both alpha and numeric, and *logical* fields. The logical or *true/false* field is a field for information that is either a yes or a no and is usually just a single character in length. While logical fields don't have a big application in mail list service business applications, you need to know about them. Other field types built into database products, such as *date*, *time*, *currency*, or free-form text fields known as *memo* fields, are an extension of those basic field types.

Determining the field type depends on the data that will be stored there. For example, you may want to set up a city or state field to be alpha only, meaning the software won't allow you to enter numbers in those fields. Since entering a number in one of those fields would be a mistake, this offers some error checking during the entry of information. A numeric-only field might be a phone number or a zip code, although zip codes outside the United States do sometimes contain alphabetical characters. Both alpha and numeric means the field will accept both letters and numbers.

Most database software programs will allow you to set up a *template*, or a form, for your field. This is helpful in fields where the information is in a repeatable format, such as phone number and social security number fields. You can set up a phone number field with the first three digits surrounded by parentheses ( ) and the dash put in automatically after the next three digits, so you don't have to type those characters.

Determining what fields, what type of fields, and how long each field in the database should be is not difficult, it just takes planning. Usually, you create as many fields as you have attributes or individual pieces of information for. You can get an idea of the type of table design common in mailing list services by looking at the fields in the commercial mailing list packages mentioned in the last chapter. The order of the fields is pretty much determined by the order you would enter data into them, so you could put address, city, state, and zip before name if that was more important to you.

The USPS indirectly offers some guidelines for mail list design as it will only work with fields of a certain length for its one-time address correction service. The USPS will only accept name, secondary address, and a delivery address field with a maximum of 48 characters. For the city field, the maximum the USPS will accept for its one-time address correction service is 28 characters. For the state field, the maximum is 2 characters and for zip code, 10 characters (including the dash) will be accepted. If you choose to add a carrier route field, and that seems like a very good idea, the maximum length the USPS will accept is 4 characters. Certainly, this is not the only length or even the best way to set up the fields, but it's a starting place. However, if you're using list management software, those decisions will be made for you.

Once the database has the fields defined, you can then begin entering the data you have or import data from another application. If a field in a database you're importing is longer than you've set your corresponding field to be, the field will often be *truncated*, meaning the data will simply be cut off after the number of characters your field can hold.

If you design your table poorly, you've created work for yourself. If you decide you need a field you don't already have, you might have to create a new table with all the same fields and the new field you need, and then import the data from the old table into the new one.

As you gain experience working with tables and databases, you'll find planning and design gets easier. However, the easiest way for new people to get started is to purchase and learn to use a database application already built for their business, like the mailing list management packages already mentioned.

Troubleshooting   While importing and exporting isn't hard, it does require a certain amount of expertise on your part. If you happen to be working with someone who knows what they're doing, you can hardly go wrong by asking for or delivering data in an ASCII delimited format. However, if the data is a mess, then you've got a problem on your hands.

What could be a mess? Well, how about someone who put the city, state, and zip code in a single field. To get your CASS-certified software to work with this data, those fields have to be separated. Also, if the data is intended for a single area, you'll need the information in separate fields to add carrier route presort information. Carrier route presort information is also important for demographic information. Sometimes new users will create a table with fields the same length and simply enter the data for each record the way they want it to print on the envelope. This means one record might have a company name in the first field, then a name in the second field, a post office box in the third field, then the city, state, and zip code in the fourth, fifth, and sixth fields. The next record could have a first and last name in the first field, a street address in the second field, the city in the third field, the state in the fourth field and the zip code in the fifth field. The example in FIG. 5-8 is one such table. Adding information like this will work for a single printing, but it is a horrible mess to attempt to sort or maintain.

If the data is consistently misentered, you can usually fix it in the table or by exporting it in ASCII and using a word processor to do a global search and replace. A global search and replace means you have the word processor go through the table and for every instance of a certain combination of characters have it substitute a different combination of characters. For a simple example, if the two-digit state code and the zip code are in the same field, then separating out the two is simply a matter of putting a comma in place of a space. Sometimes, however, there's no way to fix a database mess but to just get in there and physically reorganize the data by hand.

Some software packages for the mailing industry offer fixes for messy databases. The leader in the mailing list service business for troubleshooting problems is Peoplesmith Software. The company offers products such as Right Fielder, which is designed to have the computer standardize a table where data has been added in haphazard order, such as the one shown in FIG. 5-8.

F1	F2	F3	F4	F5
227 DUFFIELD ST CORP	C/O V CHATEL	227 DUFFIELD ST	BROOKLYN NY 11201	
ABE NAMEONLY	52 REMSEN ST	BROOKLYN NY 11201		
D MISTLINE	ABC CO		123 MAIN ST	COHASSET MA
FRANK O CONNER	AR DEPT	160 NUMBER CO LTD	446 STATE ST	GARP BLDG
HARRY NOSTREET	CEO	BIG CO	SMALL TOWN, SD 67002	
HARRY NOSTREET	CEO	BIG CO	SMALL TOWN, SD	67001
HARRY NOSTREET	CEO	BIG CO	SMALL TOWN	SD
HOME SAVINGS	151 HAMILTON AVE	BROOKLYN NY 11231	ATTN: BOOKEEPING	
HOME SAVINGS	151 HAMILTON AVE	BROOKLYN NY 11231		ATTN: BOOKE
JOE SMITH	JANET JONES, TRUSTEE	ROCKLAND TRUST	123 MAIN ST	SMALL TOWN
JOE SMITH	% E OSBORNE SMITH INC	50 E 42 ST	NEW YORK NY 10017	
JOE SMITH	PRES	% E OSBORNE SMITH INC	50 E 42 ST	SUITE 100
MR. UNDELIVERABLE	319 VAN BRUNT ST	BROOKLYN NY		
MR. UNDELIVERABLE	123 MAIN ST			
NOTHER ASSOC	% E OSBORNE SMITH INC	50 E 42 ST	NEW YORK NY 10017	

5-8
Inconsistent data entry, fields that are not thought out, and inexperience produce a table like this one. The problem is creating the correct fields and moving the data into them without having to reenter all of it by hand.

In order to understand how databases work, you have to understand the basics of the coding schemes used by computers to represent characters to us. Every computer uses numbers to represent the alphabet, called a *coding scheme*. There are two coding schemes that concern us in the mailing list service, and those are ASCII and EBCDIC.

Coding schemes

The *American Standard Code for Information Interchange* or *ASCII* (pronounced "ask-ee") is the "universal" language in the PC world. It was created in 1965 by Robert W. Bemer and defines each alphabetical and punctuation character with a unique number between 0 and 127. Each character on your keyboard is represented by one of 128 decimal numbers. The easiest way to test this is at the DOS prompt hold down the Alt key on your keyboard and type the number 65. When you let up on the Alt key an uppercase A will appear on the screen. To get a lowercase A, type the number 97 with the Alt key held down.

ASCII

Later, another 128 characters identified by the numbers 128 through 255 were added, called the *Extended ASCII Character Set*. Most of the extended character set is used to represent commands to printers to turn on and off special functions such as bold or italic lettering, as well as other functions.

Also, the Extended Character Set is used to draw the boxes you see on your screen in DOS applications. For example, the number 205 represents a double line, while 200 and 201 make up corners of a double line box.

What does all this have to do with databases, you ask? Well, first of all it is important to note that everything you type on your keyboard is represented by a number to your computer, even though it is not necessary to know exactly what number represents each character. Even a space, which you can get by holding down the Alt key and typing 32, is a character to the computer, not just a blank in the way we learned to think of it in typing class. That means when typed it has to be stored and takes up space. It is also important to note uppercase letters of the alphabet are different to the computer than lowercase characters.

Formatting

You'll hear the term *formatted*, or *formatting*, in relationship to data transfer. Formatting is the addition of characters, usually outside what is on your keyboard, to indicate special functions to a software program or printer. Because formatting characters in one program seldom mean the same thing in a different program, formatting creates problems when you're trying to exchange text. Many software programs will allow you to remove the formatting, leaving just the text, spaces, tabs, and the carriage return/linefeeds. Some people create their mailing list in a word processing program, and you will need to have them save the list unformatted before they give it to you to work with. Other terms for unformatted text include *ASCII*, *text-only*, and *DOS text*.

EBCDIC

The version of ASCII on mainframe and mini-computers is the *Extended Binary Coded Decimal Interchange Code* or *EBCDIC* (pronounced "ebb-sa-dik"). EBCDIC is important to mailers because some lists from mainframe computers are put on 9-track tape in EBCDIC. Like ASCII, EBCDIC is a coding scheme using numbers to represent alphabetic characters, but it uses different numbers to represent the same characters. This requires a translation process from EBCDIC to ASCII that has to take place before EBCDIC data is readable on a PC.

Often 9-track tape drive software will offer a translation utility or the mainframe can translate it before the information is recorded to tape. It is a common practice to do this type of translation, but you need to know who is going to do the translation if you happen to end up working with data on 9-track tape.

Common mistakes to avoid

Now that we've been through enough of the database concepts and terminology to have a background, we need to talk about the most common mistakes made and how to avoid them.

Professionals make copies of whatever they are working with, also known as *backups*. Unfortunately, one of the common mistakes to make is to start working with the only copy of a table before a copy has been made of it, and inadvertently make some change or corrupt the data. Even just pulling the data into your database or word processing program to look at it can be potentially dangerous without a backup. Lots of things can happen that will alter or destroy the data, some in your control and some beyond it. The potential embarrassment alone of having to call your customer and say, "I need another copy of your data because I lost it," ought to be enough to motivate you to always, always make a backup of the data, even if it is just copying it to your hard disk and looking at the copy from there.

Of course, you need to back up your own system as well. Your business depends on your software and you need to be sure you have a copy of it. Because you're working with other people's information, the potential for you to become infected with a rogue program called a *computer virus* is greater. In addition, there's the fact that equipment fails, hard disks crash, power shocks through the electrical lines fry computer systems, internal components fail, and you have to be able to get back up and running quickly if something does happen.

Sometimes the most unexpected and trivial things can cause the loss of important data. One person told me a plant over her desk had just been watered and a big truck came by the building jarring her plant and knocking it off onto her computer. The water in the plant shorted out her computer and ruined it. Someone else was the only person in the city whose house got hit by lightning during a thunderstorm, and all the computers were fried as well as every other electrical appliance. You just never know what will happen.

That's why I recommended a tape backup in chapter 4. You should have snapshots of your entire hard disk at different points in time so you can go back to that point if something happens. You should also always back up your system before you add any peripherals, such as a 9-track tape drive, a new hard disk drive, or a CD-ROM drive, or any device that necessitates opening up the computer's case to get inside.

You also need to get into the habit of saving your work periodically. Sometimes you can set your software to automatically save what you're working on at certain time intervals, but be sure to save! I have a favorite horror story when a new computer user friend of mine was doing work for a big corporate chain, typing in page after page of their employee manual and suddenly his system locked up. He tried to determine what was wrong, but every time he hit the keyboard, it just beeped at him. He had typed in 60 pages of information and hadn't issued the save command, which gets the information written from the computer's memory to the hard disk. He had simply typed in so much that the computer's memory was full, and then he didn't have enough memory left to issue the save command. He had to reboot the computer and start over. Don't let this happen to you!

Mistake 2—Using a spreadsheet for a database problem

This is a common mistake because so many people are familiar with spreadsheets. The reason an individual will do this is because most of the time it is simply easier to use the spreadsheet they're familiar with than the database they're not. The reasoning is usually that they're not interested in doing a lot of slicing and dicing, and they don't particularly care about sharing the data with anyone else.

The problems usually start where the spreadsheet ends. And no matter how big a spreadsheet program is capable of expanding, there's a limit to the number of rows and columns. Once you hit that limit, that's it. Also, a spreadsheet tends to be more error prone. If you're working with someone who has done this, chances are you can export the data into something made to handle it. If not, it simply has to be reentered.

Mistake 3—Not enough room to grow

Money, or lack of it, is usually the reason for starting with a software program that won't grow with your needs. The problem is, while you can make some products work for quite a while before you have to move on to another product, you must have some expertise and some time to make the jump when you need to.

If you're getting started and you need to generate some income before you can afford to buy another software package, it makes sense to buy something inexpensive like MyAdvancedMailList from MySoftware, knowing it is not CASS-certified and it won't expand when your clients do.

However, you have to learn the software and spend time using it. If all your data is in MyAdvancedMailList and you get that big client you've been working for, you're going to be faced with learning to use a package with the power you need, like Mail Manager 2000. This is going to cost you precious time, and might cost you the client if you can't move fast enough.

Sometimes you don't have a choice. You simply have to get started and there's not time or money to fiddle around with more complicated programs. But you need to recognize that if you grow, you will be faced with updating your software to meet the needs of your expanding client base.

Mistake 4—Too much data in one field

Hopefully, you'll have enough background after reading this chapter to avoid the most common design problems, such as putting all the city, state, and zip code information in one field, or putting the first and last name in the same field.

Unfortunately, most design problems are not that simple. It takes time and thought to design a database and while fields you hadn't thought of before can be added, you often have to create a new database with the new field and import the old database into the new one in order to get a field added.

For example, a beginning database user just looking at a mailing list might not think to put in a carrier route field. If you happen to be tracking sales information as well, you'll need to be sure and add a table to track the type of payment used, as well as what was bought and when, especially if you plan to offer the list for rent. You might also need a database of the lists you rent with descriptive information about each one and who's sampled the database, who continued after sampling, and what the results were.

It is best to spend some time and write down on paper what you want to track or how the database will be used before designing your database. This can save you much in the way of time and headaches later.

If you know you're going to be doing lots of data entry, you'll want a database product that makes it easier. Mail Manager 2000 is designed specifically for mailing list data entry and so are other products. Mail Manager will automatically capitalize proper names, even Irish names like McHenry. You also want something that will allow you to set up repetitive information, such as setting the state to California unless you change it. Then if you happen to be working with 100,000 names in California you don't have to type "CA" 100,000 times.

Mistake 5— Database poor for data entry

Most database programs will allow you to set up repetitive operations to minimize the time you spend entering data. After all, the idea is to get the computer to do the work, right?

You don't want to get locked into someone's proprietary database standard. A proprietary database means someone has made up this format, and no one else uses it. If you can import and export, that's better than nothing, but the best arrangement is to be able to import and export ASCII and .DBF. However, if you can import and export an ASCII delimited file, you can at least get your data out without retyping all of it.

Mistake 6—Getting a proprietary database

Most products allow you to import, but some won't let you export. Often, when you receive a database from another PC user, you'll find it in a compressed format to save space. The details on compression are next.

Data compression is a relatively new item, but an important one in any discussion of databases. *Compression* is the practice of using the computer to translate data into a format that consumes less space.

Compression

By nature, databases tend to be disk space hogs and moving one from one machine to another can be time-consuming and tedious. However, they lend themselves well to compression techniques, often compressing down to be stored in a fraction of their uncompressed size.

Older compression techniques were only used for storing the data, so it had to be decompressed to be used. However, recent advances in data compression allow the compression and decompression to occur "on-the-fly." Data is stored compressed on the disk, decompressed when read from the disk into the computer's memory, then compressed again when written to the disk. This process can be done without the user noticing a difference in the performance of the computer because the compression/decompression time is offset by time saved in reading and writing to the disk. The new version of the DOS PC operating system, MS-DOS 6.0, offers a compression utility called DoubleSpace that performs this function.

You'll find in exporting that disk space is hard to come by and that floppy disks become limiting very fast when you get several thousand records. You might find you need to split the table into sections and only export a portion at a time. However, another technique for transferring large files is compression.

It is a common practice to compress database files transferred from one party to another. The practice is especially common between individual PC users. Compressed files often have extensions such as .ZIP or .ARC, which let you know the files are compressed.

Some of the popular data utilities, such as PC Tools, FastBack, or Norton Utilities offer data compression, but in order to get the data uncompressed, the person you give it to has to have the same program you used to compress the data. Other popular file compression application software includes PKZip, Arc, or LHarc.

PKZip and Arc are *shareware*, meaning these programs are offered for distribution on a try before you buy basis. If you like the program, a message within the program encourages you to send a registration fee to the author and gives you an address. LHarc is *freeware*, meaning no registration fee is required. When files are compressed with shareware, it is customary to include a copy of the shareware used to compress the files so the recipient can uncompress them, unless some other arrangement has been made beforehand. Reputable shareware software distributors charge between $5 and $8 per disk for copies of shareware. If you are transferring data between PCs equipped with MS-DOS 6.0, you can use DoubleSpace to compress and decompress the files.

Mail merge

Insertion of the names, or personalization, is an important concept in direct marketing and one which is becoming more and more sophisticated. The more you can personalize the mail, the more likely it is to get read. That's the reason handwriting fonts are popular among mailers. Changing the content of publications to make them more attractive to residents in different regions of the country is already occurring. Computerized automation of printing operations means magazines are already producing regional versions with content varying according to where the magazine is sent. Talk is already starting of personalization so sophisticated that readers might find their own name in advertisements in magazines to which they subscribe.

Another term for personalization of mail is *mail merge*. The idea is to take a list and a document and merge the two, creating a personalized document. You see such mailing pieces in your mailbox all the time.

Almost any word processor offers the ability to take an ASCII comma or tab delimited file and do a mail merge. A *placeholder* is put in a document, usually the name of the field from the table that you want placed there. Once you have your table and your form with the placeholders, you tell the word processing software to mail merge. The software does the job of replacing the placeholder with the actual information from the table in each letter, producing a copy of the letter for each record in the database.

Examples of simple mail merge documents generated in Microsoft Word for Windows and Ami Pro for Windows are shown in FIG. 5-9 and FIG. 5-10 respectively. As you can see, the data is the same but the placeholders are the field names set apart by special characters that vary slightly from one word processing program to the next. Yet each generated the same letter shown in FIG. 5-11 from our SAMPLE.DBF file. Mail merge of documents is a standard feature available in the major word processors for Windows, including Microsoft Word, Ami Pro, and WordPerfect as well as the DOS versions of these and other word processing products. Mail merge operations can also allow you to perform logical types of operations, such as leaving out the title if there is none, or only printing letters to people from a certain city or carrier route. In the example, the word processors were set to avoid leaving a blank line even though the record for Martha Baker in the SAMPLE.DBF file did not contain any data in the ADDRESS2 field.

<<Firstname>> <<Lastname>>
<<Address2>>
<<Delivaddr>>
<<City>>,<<State>> <<Zip>>

Dear <<Salu>>. <<Lastname>>,

     Mailing costs seem to be another one of those inevitable expenses in life, especially these days. But what if you could discover ways you could cut your mailing costs, move your mail faster, and even increase your business while you're at it. Sound too good to be true?

5-9
A mail merge document from Microsoft Word for Windows is shown here. Note the field names from the SAMPLE.DBF are acting as placeholders and special characters called chevrons surround the placeholders. Word for Windows allows the field names to be picked by the user off a list rather than the user having to remember and retype the field names.

Another example of a mail merge document, this one from Ami Pro for Windows. Ami Pro will also allow use of .DBF format files as well as ASCII-delimited files. Users can pick field names from a list for insertion into the mail merge document.

<Firstname> <Lastname>
<Address2>
<Delivaddr>
<City>,<State> <Zip>

Dear <Salu>. <Lastname>,

      Mailing costs seem to be another one of those inevitable expenses in life, especially these days. But what if you could discover ways you could cut your mailing costs, move your mail faster, and even increase your business while you're at it. Sound too good to be true?

5-11

Both word processing programs produce the same result. Note the spaces, commas, and punctuation need to be added to the mail merge document in order to print, and the word processors ignored the blank ADDRESS2 field in this record.

Martha Baker
PO Box 3000
Humacao, PR 00792-3000

Dear Ms. Baker,

      Mailing costs seem to be another one of those inevitable expenses in life, especially these days. But what if you could discover ways you could cut your mailing costs, move your mail faster, and even increase your business while you're at it. Sound too good to be true?

One thing about a mail merge is the printer is going to print exactly what you tell it. You'll need to remember to add other characters you want to print between the placeholders, such as a comma and a space between the city and the state fields. It is also a simple matter to generate envelopes for the names on the mail list, if you don't care to barcode, with a word processing program.

Anything you can print, you can mail merge, including postcards, labels, envelopes, letters, nametags, and order forms. Several of the leading word processing, mail management, and database products also include the most common Avery label products by number so you don't have to design the label.

The main advantage of a mail merge is that it is fast. Even the world's fastest typist can't compete with a computer doing a mail merge. In fact, you might not even notice a difference in speed between the mail merge and the printing of regular documents. Even at the four-page-per-minute speed of low-end laser printers, mail merging is unrivaled for speed.

You're not limited to just a single page either. A mail merge can encompass as many pages as you're inclined to print. This means legal contracts and other lengthy documents can be mail merged with the appropriate names or information inserted where necessary.

The biggest problem in doing a mail merge is having either enough data or the appropriate data. You can only merge what you have in the database. For example, let's say you want to do a personalized letter to car buyers that says, "I saw a red Corvette the other day and thought of you," but you want to replace the color and model with the color and model of the car the person purchased. In order to do that, you have to have the color and model information in your database. If the information isn't already there, you have to put it in.

Adding fields for new data to a database requires you create a new database, then import in the old database to the new one. Once the old data is in the new database, you can then go through and add the information to the new fields.

This means doing effective, personalized mail merging requires you set up your database correctly. The more information you have and the more detail, the more you can personalize your offers. For example, you can set up a form letter with an or statement that tells the computer that if the car is a Corvette, to add a paragraph you've written about the features of the new Corvettes coming in. If the car field does not equal Corvette, then the computer can leave the paragraph out or insert another paragraph about the service department.

So, we've seen how databases are an essential part of personalizing mail. But more information can be stored than simply items for personalized letters. As previously discussed, an entire new discipline, *databased marketing*, is emerging. Herman Holtz in *Databased Marketing* describes the database as the "Swiss army knife" of marketing. Holtz predicts, "The versatility of databased marketing will ultimately astonish its most enthusiastic supporters. It may prove to be the absolutely indispensable marketing weapon."

For you, the database is a tool, and a profitable one if you know how to use it.

Roger Crafts, Jr.   Profile
Marketing Dimensions, Situate Harbor, Massachusetts

Roger Crafts has been in the mailing list business for 18 years. His company, Marketing Dimensions, has a different slant than other mailing list services because it focuses heavily on databased marketing.

Marketing Dimensions offers in-depth building of data files and plans a marketing program for its clients. About one-third of the company's business is working with textbook publishers and another third is from non-profit groups.

For textbook publishers, the initial contact is through response to advertising aimed at college professors. When follow-up with a professor is made by a sales representative, Marketing Dimensions has a program for the sales representative's laptop computer where critical information can be taken down during the visit. The key marketing data collected includes the size of the opportunity (meaning the number of students who might potentially buy the textbook), the book being used now, whether the decision to buy is made by an individual or a committee, the probability of changing the current text, and the level of satisfaction the professor has with the current text book materials.

The company then uses the key data collected to prepare personalized sales letters. Roger said a typical letter to a professor might include statements such as, "You mentioned you're using _____ book and you said your interest in the text was at _____ level," with the blanks filled in by the data the sales representative entered in the database. The information about the textbook in use by the professor is also compared to the book published by the company Marketing Dimensions to show how a switch to it could be advantageous.

For the non-profit groups, the databased marketing work is more focused on qualifying leads by comparing a number of source materials. Sometimes as many as 40 sources go into a merge/purge, Roger said. These files could be business lists, residential lists, telephone information, donor files, and so on.

In order to do the type of databased marketing work the company offers, many of the programs used have been written in-house in dBASE IV. Sometimes more detail is needed and the computer languages C or low-level Assembler have also been used, Roger added.

To get clients, the company uses its own database marketing techniques. "We try to sell programs, instead of commodity services." The company does limited Yellow Page advertising, Roger acknowledged, because it has gone after vertical markets.

The danger and advantage to the mailing list service business is in the *front log*. "Hardly any program lasts longer than six weeks, which means you can't have much more than six weeks worth of work lined up at a time. This means you have to get continuing business and stay very busy," Roger stated. "If you have fixed overhead expenses and no heavy backlog of work, you can lose your shirt."

However, the future looks bright for Marketing Dimensions. One of the new markets the company is pursuing is the healthcare industry. Roger's goal is to go after Health Maintenance Organizations (HMOs) by obtaining a list of the decision makers within the organization and then using the company's own marketing techniques to get customers.

Getting more help

If you're new to databases and all of this seems a little overwhelming, you're not alone. This chapter is meant to give you an overview of the terminology and the basics. Serious database training is not the focus of this book, but plenty of it is out there.

Probably the easiest way to begin to learn database particulars is to take a course. Again, the junior colleges and high schools offer adult education programs, and most will have some form of database training. Most of the major database programs on the market have books written about them by third parties, which can also be helpful.

You'll want to choose a product that is well-known and well-supported. Several of the mailing list service businesses used DOS-based products like Nutshell from Stoughton, Massachusetts-based Fairhaven Software, Q&A from Santa Clara, California-based Symantec, or Alpha Four from Alpha Software of Burlington, Massachusetts because they felt these products were easier to use. Others used dBASE IV from Scotts Valley, California-based Borland or FoxPro from Microsoft of Redmond, Washington. Still others were moving to Microsoft's Windows-based database programs such as Access or the new FoxPro for Windows. Nutshell, Q&A, and Access use their own file formats, although they can import and export the major file types. FoxPro, Alpha Four, and dBASE use the .DBF file format. dBASE as of this writing has the largest portion of the DOS-based database market, so classes and books on it are plentiful.

To really learn the particulars of a database, you'll have to commit to a product. Again, let me stress that your income potential can be directly influenced by the amount of expertise you can gain in the area of databases and their use—the more, the better.

Reference

Holtz, Herman. 1992. *Databased Marketing*. New York, N.Y.: John Wiley & Sons, Inc.

6 Marketing tips that sell customers

If you're going to make this business work, you've got to have ways to sell your services and yourself. You must answer the following questions for your potential customers:

- Why should I manage the mailings I do?
- Why should I start direct mailing?
- Why should I let you do my mailings for me?

If you don't know the answers to those questions yourself, you'll never be able to answer them for your customers.

Why manage mailings

The reason to be concerned about managing mailings is, frankly, if you aren't, you're wasting money. Fear of loss is a strong motivator, but in this case it's reality. You have not only the concrete costs in terms of paying more for the same service, but also soft costs involved when mail isn't managed. If you're not managing your mail, you're throwing money away.

Reduce postage costs   Management of mailings starts way back before the piece is even in hand. While a mail piece is still in the design stage, you can help clients save money because you're the one who knows what the post office wants. No matter how good a piece looks, if it's poorly designed from a postal point of view, it is going to cost more to mail and move more slowly through the mail system. If you can give the post office material easy for them to handle and meet your client's needs, you can garner discounts which can translate into significant savings. Sometimes only the smallest modification is needed to produce big savings.

When you look at a mailing, one of the things you're looking for is how the piece fits the postal size and automation requirements. The closer to letter size, the better. If the piece is too high, too long, or too thick it is going to be charged a $.10 surcharge, above the $.29 rate.

Reduce soft costs   *Soft costs* are those unexpected costs, difficult to measure, but just as real, and incurred when mail comes back. Proper management of mailings is designed to do the delivery work before that mailing piece is ever touched by the post office so it gets to its destination without delay.

The USPS estimates 20 percent of the mail on any given list has addresses that are no good. What does the post office do with mail that is undeliverable? If it is bulk mail, or third-class mail, they throw it away. If it is first-class mail, the post office is supposed to send it back, but that doesn't always happen.

Industry mailers I talked with said 20 percent bad addresses in any given list is optimistic. A realistic estimate on a good list is 30 percent of the addresses are no good. Some lists can be as high as 40 percent undeliverable. That means out of 1000 addresses a whopping 200 to 400 are a waste of money to send to because that mail will never be delivered. Even at discount rates, in a 1000-piece mailing 200 bad addresses can cost as much as $46.60 in postage alone, not to mention the soft costs businesses you don't see of handling nixies (undeliverable mail returned to sender), the wasted materials, wasted printing costs, wasted time, and so on.

Also, mail carriers cannot tell third-class mailers the mail is returned. If the addresses are bad, the response to the mailing has to be lower than it could be. I've had USPS workers tell me they throw away half the mail of some customers, just from bad addresses.

But, what about requesting address correction? Address correction is an option the post office offers for first-class mail in which the mail is forwarded but the sender is sent a notification of the new address. It is usually placed on the return address on the envelope, as illustrated in FIG. 6-1. Unfortunately, address correction is still painfully expensive. Anyone who has used address correction can tell you it can take months for the address corrections to trickle back to the sender from a single mailing. It is easy to mail several other pieces to the same bad addresses at an extra $.29 each in address correction costs because you didn't get the first correction in time.

How can you help businesses keep that money instead of throwing it away? If you use software to apply a zip+4 code to each address before the mailing is done, you know those addresses are good. If a zip+4 code cannot be applied to an address, that is an indicator something is wrong with the address. Most of the zip+4 software offers some intelligence so it will correct mistakes, like putting "Street" instead of "Lane" in an address. But if a critical

Balloon Masters
123 Fourth St
Los Angeles, CA 90026-1234

Address Correction Requested

$0.29
PLACE
FIRST-
CLASS
POSTAGE
HERE

First Class

Mr. Marvin T. Runyon
Postmaster General
Office of the Postmaster General, Rm 10022
US Postal Service
475 L'Enfant Plz SW
Washington, DC 20260-0004

6-1

*An example of an address
correction request in a
return address.*

piece of information is missing, your software won't be able to find the address to zip+4 code it, and that means the probability is very high the mail carrier delivering it will never find it as well.

In fact, the most economical way to handle zip+4 coding is to do it before the mailing materials are printed. The discovery that 20 percent of the addresses are bad means you need to print 20 percent fewer materials for mailing. That reduction can save a client significant printing costs, especially on a large mailing.

Why start direct mailing

Almost any business that isn't using direct mail to build its client base and hang on to existing customers should start. Here's why.

People who study learning will tell you something new has to be repeated six times before the average person will remember it. Advertisers know this, and that's why you see the same commercial over and over and over again. Businesses should know it, too. One of the most striking stories of success using mail is related by Zig Ziglar in his book *Zig Ziglar's Secrets of Closing the Sale.*

Ziglar mentions Joe Girard who was credited at the time for holding all automobile sales records even during two recessionary periods, but without fleet sales. Each sale was to an individual.

One of Joe's secrets included the use of direct mail. Every month he dropped a card in the mail to every one of his customers. He sent Christmas cards, birthday cards, anniversary cards, Easter cards, even "Happy Fourth of July" cards.

Joe sold an average of over 1300 cars per year for the last six years he was selling on a full-time basis. His tactic was to stay in front of his customers. Direct mail will keep a business in front of its customers like no other medium. It's more personal, more targeted, and less obtrusive than any other form of advertising. Let's look more closely at the benefits of direct mail.

You can expect objections to using direct mail in four main areas: direct mail is too expensive, it is annoying "junk" mail, it invades a person's privacy, and it is a waste of natural resources. But each of those objections can be turned around to view direct mail in the true light of its benefits. Let's look at the benefits of direct mail one at a time.

Direct mail is economical   Direct mail is less expensive than radio or television by far for the audience it targets. While a television commercial might be cheaper than mailing out to the three million people watching it, unless it is of very general interest it's missing the mark with millions. Direct mail is much more focused as opposed to the shotgun approach of radio, television, or newspaper advertising—if it is done correctly. Even the general interest advertisers, such as pizza chains, use direct mail in addition to television advertising. Their direct mail pieces are focused specifically on a targeted marketing area where the customers are available for a specific outlet of their nationwide chain. Direct mail also can be done in smaller increments, so for example, a mailer can hit as few as 200 potential customers at a time, which makes it more economical.

Direct mail is unobtrusive   While it might be a hassle to pick up the pile of advertisements from the mailbox, direct mail is unobtrusive to the customer. It doesn't come up at high volume late at night during his or her favorite show, doesn't repeat some annoying jingle five times an hour, can be read at the consumer's convenience, and even saved for future reference. The direct mail piece doesn't ask the customer to remember the phone number, location or the benefits to the service it promotes—everything is right there. It can also be passed on to someone else.

As far back as 1988 the average household received five pieces of direct mail a day. Yet the average person is bombarded with over 1000 advertising pieces per day from every imaginable source such as radio, television, bus stops, billboards, buses, automobiles, and direct mail. I recently counted 14 commercials in a row during a single prime-time television show. Surely direct mail is less obtrusive.

Direct mail is wanted   According to the USPS's Household Diary Survey, a majority of Americans read their direct mail advertising, also known as third-class mail. The survey also said they found it useful or interesting and are very satisfied with the shop-at-home experience. More than half of the adults in the United States, nearly 96 million, made a shop-at-home purchase in 1991. Obviously more than just a few people like direct mail.

The Direct Marketing Association has hinted that most of the attacks on direct or "junk" mail have come from the newspaper industry, which might be losing advertising dollars to the growing direct mail market. Yet 40 percent or more of a newspaper is advertising along much of the same vein as direct mail pieces. Some direct mailers have labeled vendor promotion in newspapers as "junk" advertising.

Issues concerning personal privacy and direct mailing lists do have some merit, but sending mail to someone's address who lives within a mile of a certain dry cleaner is a far cry from cross-referencing lists and credit records for such purposes as selecting who will receive an offer. Companies who offer such information are receiving sharp criticism.

While some sources are expecting the Federal Government to step in concerning privacy, the fact is the small mailer who is helping local businesses offer services to clients is not the target of the privacy campaign. If privacy legislation forces the splitting up of information from various sources, the home-based mailing service business might become even more important as lists might not be as easily or cheaply obtained, and businesses will still need to contact potential as well as existing customers.

As a measure to try to prevent government intervention in direct mail, the Direct Marketing Association (DMA) established in 1971 the Mail Preference Service (MPS) and in 1985 the Telephone Preference Service (TPS). Large mailers are expected to subscribe to the DMA MPS. In addition the MPS was recognized by the Presidentially appointed Privacy Protection Study Commission as a legitimate and effective alternative to legislation.

Consumers who want to be on the MPS and/or TPS DMA lists may register by writing to the Mail Preference Service or the Telephone Preference Service at the Direct Marketing Association, 11 West 42nd Street, P.O. Box 3861, New York, NY 10163-3861. Those requesting to be registered on the MPS must offer their complete name, including apartment number and zip code. Consumers registering for the telephone preference service should also include their phone number with the area code, as well as their complete name and address.

Customers of any establishment should be given the right to opt out of having their names sold or rented to other direct mailers or solicitors. A provision should be made so customers can choose to have their names withheld, such as a check box on an order form. It is the responsibility of the mailer to see to it those names remain confidential and a certain amount of security is expected in handling any list of names to protect the privacy of the persons involved. As a help in determining what is ethical and what kind of security measures should be taken, *The Direct Marketing Association's Ethical Business Practices, Mailing List Practices, and the Fair Information Practices Checklist* is reprinted for your convenience in appendix H.

Direct mail conserves resources   As for natural resources, the direct mail pieces can be produced on recycled paper, which doesn't damage or destroy any existing resources and is available in increasing supply and variety. But even if the mailing materials were not reproduced with recycled paper, the paper that was used can be recycled afterward. Also, mailing reduces driving, a much more critical threat than paper making. The reduction or elimination of sales calls coupled with the reduction in driving on the part of literally millions of individuals in search of needed products and services can result in a significant reduction in the amount of pollution generated by automobiles. The evidence of the reduction in individuals driving to purchase items is provided by the millions of Americans who are now shopping by direct mail.

We've talked about how good management can save money and speed up the mailing process. We've explored why direct mail is effective. Now the big question your customer will want to know the answer to is why should they use you to do their mailings? The three big reasons are: You know the postal regulations, you know the technology, and you know the tactics for successful mailings.

Why customers should let you do their mailings

Keeping up with the USPS or any branch of the government is a challenging, full-time job. Since you do it for more than one business, you can afford to spend all your time hassling with the recent changes in the way the post office handles mail.

You can also make sure all the mail lists you handle are clean. It is your business to learn the software it takes to do management of mailings right.

In addition, you can be of value because you can help produce successful mail campaigns that bring in new customers and get more mileage out of existing customers. These all add up for your customer into a lower cost using your services than they can obtain doing the job themselves.

It's your job to be sure the mailing is going to the right audience, that it has the best possible chance of being read, and that the mailing is followed up in effective ways to increase response. You'll also want to have some effective approaches for your client's advertising materials and be sure you follow basic principles in mailing. Here are the basics and the resources which will help you in your search for marketing ideas.

12 tactics for a successful direct mail campaign

Determine your break-even point An important service you can offer your customers is helping them decide if they can afford the mailing. Especially when selling by direct mail, if the item for sale falls below a certain point in value, it is not really worth the time and effort it takes to try to sell it. In a storefront business, this doesn't really apply, since the idea is to get the customer in. Knowing if the offer of the product or service has any chance of paying for itself is certainly worthwhile, however, and should be pursued.

There is a simple formula to figure out what the break-even point is on a mailing, shown in FIG. 6-2. You want to divide the mailing expenses by the net profit per order to determine the number of responses needed for the mailing to pay for itself. The *net profit per order* is determined by subtracting the expenses in getting the product to the consumer, including the amount

6-2

These break-even analysis formulas should help in determining how many responses are needed to break even on a mailing and if the mailing can be profitable.

Applies only to direct marketing.

Before you do a mailing, you should determine how many people must respond for you to break even.

$$\text{Break even} = \frac{\text{Mailing expenses}}{\text{Net profit per order}}$$

Net profit per order	Mailing cost per piece	Number of addresses	Mailing expenses	Break even	Break-even rate
$5.00	$.50	1,000	500	100	10%
$20.00	$.50	1,000	500	25	2.5%

the product itself costs the seller, from the amount the product sells for. The mailing expenses are what it costs to do the mailing, including postage, labor, printing, list rental and so on.

Let's take a simple example. Using even numbers, we'll say a client has a product whose net profit per order is $5, and it costs $.50 per piece to do a mailing to a list of 1000 addresses. It costs $500 to mail to the 1000 addresses, which divided by $5 leaves us with a break-even of 100 responses. That means 100 people out of our mailing of 1000, or 10 percent, have to respond to make our mailing profitable. Knowing what we do about mailing and average response rates, we know there's not much of a chance of getting a 10 percent response rate. So we know that as it stands, the customer doesn't have much of a chance of breaking even on this mailing. If our customer was able to market something with a net profit per order of $20, then the break-even on the same mailing would be 2.5 percent, which is within the realm of what we know is possible with direct mail.

While it is great to make money on a campaign, a break-even campaign is very good. No matter how you slice it, the word about the products and services any business offers has to get out there in order to just stay even. That's because customers are lost to moving, changed circumstances, or just plain inertia and need to be replaced. If a campaign to attract customers breaks even, it is still profitable to the business because those customers are worth more over time than just whatever it costs to attract them. This leads us to the concept of buying customers.

Buy a customer   Some mailings do not break even and purposefully so. These mailings are designed to *buy* a customer. While it might not be a break-even proposition to attract a customer, if the product or service is an ongoing one, the new customer might still be profitable in the long run. This is the concept used in those record and tape clubs where you get so many records or tapes for a ridiculously low amount—like a dollar—but you have to sign up for a year. Someone discovered attracting a customer was worth more than the cost of the offer.

In order to determine if it is worthwhile to buy a customer, the business has to know how much and how frequently its average customers buy. The amount spent to buy the customer is then based on those calculations.

Rate your customers   It's a fact that mailing to current customers, especially the more active ones, produces a better response than prospecting for new customers. This is true for obvious reasons, such as current customers are already familiar with the business and are more receptive.

This leads us to the problem of tracking who the most regular customers are. The standard formula mentioned in almost any direct marketing book is the RFM formula, for frequency, recency of order, and monetary value of orders. Each customer is assigned an RFM score, which is a cumulative value based on the point scale shown in FIG. 6-3.

Recency

3 months	25 points
6 months	20 points
12 months	15 points
18 months	10 points
24 months	5 points
25+ months	0 points

Frequency

6-3
The point scale used in determining each customer's RFM rating.

Every month	50 points
Every 2 months	45 points
Every 3 months	40 points
Every 6 months	30 points
Every 12 months	15 points
Every 18 months	5 points

Monetary

$100	25 points
$75	22 points
$50	18 points
$40	15 points
$30	10 points
$20	5 points

Customers are scored based on points for how long ago they bought, how often, and how much. For example, customer A may have been in six months ago, comes in about once a year, and buys about $200. Customer B was in last week, comes in every month, and buys about $20 each time. Customer A receives an RFM score of 20 for recency, 15 for frequency and 25 for monetary for a total of 60. Customer B receives 25 for recency, 50 for frequency, and 5 for monetary for an overall score of 75.

According to the RFM point scale, Customer B is actually more valuable to the business than Customer A, even though Customer A buys more at once. The idea is to mail more to the customers with higher RFM scores, because they're most likely to respond.

The sticky part of all this is tracking the RFM. And if you're really going to do it right, you need to track more than just RFM, you'll need to also know how the customer paid (with a credit card, check, what?), how the customer was attracted to the business in the first place (they're a resident, they responded from an offer from a list purchased from a certain magazine, and so on), if they came from another mailing list (which list), and what offers they've responded to. This is especially critical in mail order, such as catalog sales, as there's no way to know what offers are working without some sort of tracking system in place.

Here's an opportunity, if you happen to be or are willing to learn how to be an expert with a database. The direct marketing publications recognize the complexity of tracking this information and advise mailers to seek out someone to help them. While it is not necessary you know how in order to offer mailing services to customers, this could be an opportunity and you should at least be aware of the issues involved.

Target the right audience   The worst possible thing you can do in mailing is send it to the wrong group of people. Targeting the right audience becomes a clear issue when you take a simple example. Let's say a roofing company comes to you with a mailing and you notice the area they want to target has houses with tile roofs. Unless they specialize in tile roofing, they're not reaching customers who need what they have to offer. Now, you may think no one would be so naive as to do something like that, but you'd be surprised.

Think about how often you get mail of no interest to you at all. The shotgun approach is used all the time. Yet the response to a mail piece is directly proportional to how well it targets the audience to which it is sent, and response is the key to making money on the mailing.

Because the list is the most important factor, how can you be sure your customer gets a good list? It depends on what is being sold, but the best way to gauge the profile of the list you want is to look at who is buying the product now and try to find lists who fit the profile of those people.

Know your client's customers   If the business doesn't know who its customers are, finding that out is the obvious first step. This can be true in businesses that serve many customers and are cash-only operations such as restaurants. Any business that is taking checks or charge cards should know who its customers are. If the business isn't tracking its customers who write checks or use charge cards, you've got an opportunity for your services right there. Offer to do it for them.

However, in those situations where cash payments are used, the most recommended way to uncover the identity of customers is to come up with a giveaway of some kind, such as a drawing for a free lunch or some other product the business offers in order to get people to sign up. The type of giveaway depends on the type of business.

Many of the larger companies have determined the effective means of getting responses via giveaways, and an effective campaign by a large chain can often be scaled down or adapted to fit your customer. Perhaps each customer who fills out a card is allowed to reach into a bowl and pull out a coin marked with the amount of a discount they'll receive on their current purchase.

An added benefit to such a campaign is the customer has to do something. If you can get the customer to take an action, no matter how small, such as rubbing off a coating with a coin to reveal a discount or reaching in to draw out a marked coin, the action increases the customer's interest and therefore increases your chances of getting a response. This is an effective direct marketing technique, and if you watch your mail you will see it used often.

While the business might think they know who their customers are, a more careful look might surprise them. For example, Prodigy released the results of a study it had done which said almost half of computer owners have children, a surprising fact since many computer-related services were assuming the typical "computer nerd" made up the majority of computer owners.

Prodigy's research indicates there's a predictable correlation between computer owners and parents. Direct marketers look for correlations because lists of people who have children or people who have computers are not difficult to obtain.

Once you know who the current customers are, it's simply a matter of finding more like them. A certain amount of deductive reasoning is involved. The direct marketing mindset would take the Prodigy research and deduce computer owners would be a good target for items geared toward children and people with children would be a good target for computer-related items. The SRDS offers such lists and so do other mailing list sources listed in the appendix.

Get the mail read   Obviously, targeting the audience is a nonissue if you happen to be working with someone who is mailing a bill or information to employees. However, getting that mail opened is an issue, whether it has been sent to people expecting it or not.

A postcard is an effective approach, as it is easily read and doesn't need to be opened. Postcards offer limited space, however, so you may want to design a fold-over postcard, closed at the top with a tab so it can be opened easily and offers more space for your client's message. A business reply card can also be attached as half of a fold-over card to make it easy for clients to respond.

How do you know the mail was opened? The response rate is a key indicator. One way to increase the response rate is to follow up the mailing a day or two after it was received with a phone call, which is why lists with phone numbers sell for more than lists without phone numbers. Of course, you don't want to call people who just received payment notices. But a follow-up call to a sales or employee information piece asking if you can provide any further information can garner twice as many responses. It is also another service you can charge for.

Another proven way to increase the response rate is to make the piece look as personally generated as possible. An effective device is to put a message on the outside of the envelope to entice the customer to view the contents such as "Limited time offer," "Big discounts right away," "What will you do with the money you save?" To increase response further, a handwritten message on the outside of the envelope is universally agreed to increase response. This can be automated with computer-generated handwriting fonts, especially those that slant uphill like those offered by Jet Products of Van Nuys, California. The fonts offered by Jet Products are illustrated in FIG. 6-4.

You can also get special paper, and special software to help you design mailing pieces that have an unusual or unique look from Paper Direct and Quill. Both companies offer paper, envelopes, and other accessories which have been designed by professional graphic artists and printed on color presses so when you put the text on them with a laser printer, they appear to be much more expensive than they are. They are especially good for printing very small quantities at a time and still maintaining a professional look. Software templates for common word processing programs to put the text on the preprinted paper are also available from Paper Direct.

Stamps are universally agreed to be more effective in getting the mail opened than metering, and stamps placed crooked are generally agreed to be the most effective. Bulk mail stamps are available in quantity from your post office as discussed in chapter 2.

Direct mailers, with a keen interest in getting the message inside the envelope read, have gone as far as to study where the reader's eye rests in reading the material inside the envelope. It is universally agreed the reader looks first at the salutation, then at the bottom to see who the letter is from, reads any P.S., then goes up to the top line and might read as much as the first paragraph.

The conclusion is those four parts of the letter need to be as interesting and attention grabbing as possible, and there should always be a P.S. This means you need to be able to say the benefit of the offer to the reader in one or two sentences. For example, if a mailing list service was to send a letter to businesses, the salutation might be "Dear Thrifty Business Owner" if a name wasn't available, and the P.S. could be, "If I can't cut your mailing costs, you

Handwrite Font:
Now is the time for all good men to come to the aid
of their country.

Nicehand Font
Now is the time for all good men to come to the aid
of their country.

Finehand Font
Now is the time for all good men to come to the aid
of their country.

Kent Font:
Now is the time for all good men to come to the aid
of their country.

Armstg Font.
Now is the time for all good men to come to the aid
of their country.

Carbon Font
Now is the time for all xxxx good men to come to the aid
of their country.

6-4
Handwriting fonts tend make a mailing appear more personalized and thereby increase response. These fonts for laser printers are offered by Jet Products of Van Nuys, California.

don't owe me anything" or "Two hundred people a week are moving into Pasadena (or whatever city). Don't you think they should be introduced to your business?"

You can use an attention-grabbing statistic pertaining to the offer, such as how many people are moving into the area. Those figures are usually available at the local Chamber of Commerce.

An interview with Don Hauptman
Freelance direct response copywriter/consultant

Effective copywriting

New York-based copywriter/consultant Don Hauptman has 19 years experience doing direct-mail and mail-order copywriting. In a column in *Advertising Age*, Don's name was cited in a short list of direct marketing "superstars."

Many of Don's clients are information producers who publish specialized newsletters and other subscription services. Often these products sell for hundreds of dollars a year. Don's direct mail letters bear the burden of motivating prospective subscribers to part with their money in return for this kind of high-priced information.

In an interview with Don, I asked him to outline the essentials for writing effective copy. Here are six of his principles:

1. Start with the prospect, not with the product. "People are so bombarded by advertising messages that, in self-defense, they have become hostile and resistant. Avoid superlatives and brag-and-boast language. Wherever possible, incorporate anecdotes, testimonials, success stories, and other believable elements of human interest."

Don explains how he made the principle work with a client:

"A client of mine acquired a newsletter called Cardiac Alert and assigned me to write a direct mail subscription promotion package.

"During our discussions, he mentioned his intense personal interest in the subject, stemming from a family history of heart disease. Sensing an idea, I probed further for the details.

"When the package appeared, it contained a "publisher's letter," a brief note in addition to the main sales letter. The outside of the folded note contained, in simulated handwriting, the 11 words, 'When I was 16, my father died of a heart attack. . . .'

"Inside, the copy I wrote ran as follows:

Dear Reader,
When I was 16 my father died of a single massive heart attack. He was only 46 years old.
The shock of this tragedy had an enormous impact on my life. As I grew older, I found myself increasingly concerned about heart disease. I vowed that I would not follow in my father's footsteps.
Heredity was, of course, beyond my control. But environmental factors were not. I knew there were actions I could take to minimize the chances of falling victim to America's #1 killer.
I began by reading whatever I could find on heart attacks. When Cardiac Alert *first appeared, I became a Charter Subscriber. (I still have the first issue.) I was impressed by the newsletter, and by its excellent research and writing.*
Then came an unusual twist of fate.
As president of Philips Publishing, Inc., I was suddenly presented with the opportunity to become the publisher of Cardiac Alert. *And I did.*
I consider it a privilege to be able to help others protect themselves against this savage disease that killed my father.

I hope you'll read the enclosed letter and decide—as I did years ago—to become a subscriber.

Cordially,

Thomas L. Philips
Publisher

"What makes this short note so powerful?" Don asks. The copy has human interest and strong emotional content. "'Real people' are involved in events that matter—matter to the reader."

2. Do research. "Interview customers, ask questions, listen carefully," Don advises. His favorite question is, "What are the prospect's greatest problems, needs, and concerns right now?" Don told me that when he is on an assignment, he spends half his time in the research stage.

3. Use specifics to add power and credibility. "Cite precise documented figures and facts," Don advises. "Exploit data or opinions from outside, impartial sources. Specific information in your copy will convey credibility and persuasive power."

Don recalls that the following concrete 'success story' helped sell subscriptions to a hotel industry newsletter by serving as an example of the publication's content.

"The Concord Resort in the Catskills invited a bunch of superstar ice-hockey players to stay for a week. The result was that the house was packed with enthusiastic sports fans fulfilling their fantasies, says executive director Gordon Winarick. The athletes socialized and played the game with guests, creating excitement for adults and kids alike. Another plus was that the players served as entertainment for the week. 'We had 250 people we wouldn't have normally,' reports Winarick. That totaled 1500 room-nights that would otherwise have gone unsold."

Note how the hotel executive's citation of specific numbers adds credibility. Copy without specifics, Don notes, is anemic, superficial, and vague.

4. Don't try to change behavior. Suppose you're marketing a mail-order book on diet and health. It can be futile and expensive to try to sell the overweight, out-of-shape person who has never shown any effort to change on your mail-order book on a healthier diet. The best prospect for a health-related book would be a health-related buyer, Don suggests. Such lists are available, such as subscribers to health magazines, Don suggests. These prospects will pull the best response. "Unless you have an unlimited marketing budget, don't try to alter behavior. Instead, 'preach to the converted,'" Don maintains.

5. Fear is a stronger motivator than greed. Laboratory experiments have shown that people are more strongly motivated to hang on to their own $10

than to get $10 from someone else. The need to protect one's self from loss is the psychologically more urgent.

For example, Don once wrote a promotional piece to launch a newsletter about computer security. The sales letter began, "Dear Executive: Right now, the security of your firm's computer system is being compromised." Notice how Don's wording is designed to make the executive frightened over his firm's security.

6. Write with enthusiasm. Don observes too many ads are boring. They display no passion for the subject. Don't let your copy be dull, he advises. After all, if your reader is not enthused, how can you expect him to be motivated enough to reach for his checkbook?

These six principles of Don's give you a good foundation for writing effective copy. If you have a copywriting assignment for a client, couldn't these guidelines help you make that assignment successful?

Use the expert approach

You might be able to help your customer's sales by directing them toward the expert approach in their mailings. This approach is a common one and known especially in the food industry where the best recipes aren't in the cookbooks but on the back of the lasagna noodle box or the cocoa can. For direct mail, a car stereo shop might add tips on the bottom of a postcard on caring for audiotapes or compact discs. An auto body shop might add hints for keeping up your car's finish. An appliance sales outlet could offer suggestions on how to handle the hot water heater when it fails, and so on.

Quill, the catalog marketer of office supplies, and Paper Direct, who markets preprinted paper products to small business, have both taken the expert approach in marketing their lines of paper supplies. The papers, designed to go through laser printers, are designed by professionals and preprinted to offer an upscale look to the small business. Both companies offer tips on how much and what to say and offer hints on effective promotional ideas interspersed between photographs of the special paper products.

Ask for the sale

Both you and your customer have to ask for the sale. A friendly, warm, no-pressure approach usually is the best for everyone, whether you're trying to get the business, or you and your customer are working to attract clients.

The easiest way to close the sale, once you feel your prospect is ready, is to make an assumptive close. Questions like, "When would you like me to have this mailing out?" or "Can I pick up those order forms for data input now or should I come back tomorrow?" are the easy way to ask for the business.

However, with a mailing, asking for the sale needs to be more direct. "Call today," "We have operators standing by" and a phone number, "Take advantage of our low prices today" and a map to the location, or some other way to ask for the sale is needed.

Presort houses are relatively new. They make money by buying expensive barcoding machines and paying people to sit there and input barcodes on individual pieces of mail. The presort house collects mail from a variety of businesses each day after the business has stamped or metered the mail at a pre-agreed upon rate, say $.262 cents each instead of $.29 cents. The presort house then barcodes each piece, sorts the mail, and delivers it the same day to the post office. Because the mail is posted for more than is required to deliver it, the presort house gets a cash refund of the difference between that $.262 cents and the $.233 the post office charges for presorted five-digit first-class mail.

On 1000 pieces of mail, the presort house makes $29. That doesn't sound like much until you calculate a big presort house can process tens of thousands of mail pieces each day.

While it may sound like presort houses will beat out mailing list services, there's still an opportunity for good management of mailings there. Two opportunities exist. One is list cleaning, meaning that barcoding discount won't apply unless the address is a good one. The second is to barcode the first-class mail for the business before it is sent out. The business might not have 500 pieces or it might not have 500 pieces that qualify for the sorting discounts, but if the mail is already barcoded, a business might be able to bargain with the presort house for a lower rate. If you can offer barcoded envelopes or labels to the business using a presort house, they can meter their first-class mail at $.248 or a gross profit for the presort house of say $.015 cents instead of the $.029 cents. Because the presort house doesn't have to barcode the mail, they still make money, and the business you're working for saves money, and you make some too by providing the labels or envelopes.

Now that we've seen why list maintenance is so economical, we can explore the answers to why someone who isn't mailing should start.

Direct marketing is an entire discipline by itself. Some people have devoted their entire lives to doing statistical analysis and study of what works in marketing and what doesn't. You can access their hard work in literally volumes of books and magazines written on the subject, many of which are available at your local library.

Many mailing list services said they subscribe to the popular direct marketing magazines, such as *Advertising Age*, *DM News*, and *Direct Marketing*. Other publications of interest include the *Advertising Mail Marketing Association (AMMA) Bulletin*, *Catalog Age* (whose December issue each year offers valuable and interesting trends and statistics), *Direct Marketing Letter*, *The Guerrilla Marketing Newsletter*, *Mail Order Digest Monthly*, and *Target Marketing*.

Work with presort houses

Direct marketing

The direct marketing magazines are information sources not only on postal issues, but on privacy legislation, taxation issues, and other information you as a mailer should be aware of. The contact information for these publications is listed in appendix B.

Databased marketing

A new buzzword in the direct marketing field, databased marketing is becoming popular because of its effectiveness. But it is more than just mailing to names on a list. A databased marketer uses a computer and database software to track specific information about customers for the purpose of targeting marketing efforts more directly. With rising postage costs and more limited budgets, companies are attempting to track who are the most likely prospects for an offer.

For example, Mollie Neal in the April 1993 issue of *Direct Marketing* talked about how Andersen Windows has used databased marketing to capture 15 percent of the window market, pass three of its largest competitors, and bring sales up to nearly one billion dollars annually. In the article, "Andersen Takes Great `Panes' To Build Relationships," the databased marketing tactics of the company are outlined.

To begin with, Andersen starts with attractive direct response television ads and print ads in specific publications that pull in 300,000 responses a year. Potential customers can respond by either coupon or call an 800 number. Either way information about the prospect's plans to build, remodel, or replace windows are recorded with the standard name, mailing address, and phone number data. Andersen uses the data to determine if the potential customer is an active or an inactive buyer and where they are in the buying cycle.

Prospects are sent a copy of a brochure and *Come Home* magazine, a quarterly publication published by Andersen. *Come Home* deals exclusively in building, remodeling, decorating, and outdoor living as well as new products, answers to reader's questions, definitions of terminology, help on buying furniture, and even help on shopping for a mortgage.

The most serious buyers, determined by the answers to the questions on the coupon or by telephone, are given a full-year subscription to *Come Home*. The company has determined one year is the amount of time it takes the average customer to go through the "buying cycle." The magazine also offers a Project Survey Card where readers are asked to respond to multiple choice questions about their building or remodeling plans. The reward for responding is one of three publications; a "Residential Product Guide," a "Window and Patio Door Installation," or the "Patio Door Guidebook" for free.

All the promotions are designed to get the customer into the retail outlets where the company offers its products. Each issue of *Come Home* is personalized on the address label with an invitation to visit an Andersen dealer and even has the name, address, and phone number of a retailer convenient to the prospect. Prospects are informed in the promotional literature and the magazine that their local dealer will have further helpful information and even videos, available at nominal cost. This also means Andersen has to maintain contact with over 1500 retailers not only with materials, but with local prospect information. Andersen provides directions on various follow-up, depending on where the prospects are in the buying cycle.

After a year, prospect's names are removed from the company's magazine list, while new names are continually being added. In addition, "did you buy" studies are conducted on an annual basis.

While Andersen Windows is a large company, you have the same capability with your personal computer to target and track customers. Admittedly, you'll probably be doing so on a smaller scale, but proportionately the results can be just as effective.

Herman Holtz, in *Databased Marketing*, relates how Jan and Kurt Williams, operators of a Merle Norman Cosmetics and women's clothing store in Albuquerque, New Mexico, successfully applied databased marketing techniques. The Williams' received with the store a list of 800 customers they managed to double in a year and a half. Beginning in 1990, Kurt Williams decided the information in the card file, which included birthdays and purchasing history along with name and address information, should be entered into a database. Then the Williams' decided to try to make use of the information to build business and the most successful scheme has been the birthday club.

They began mailing a "Happy Birthday, thank you for being a customer" at the beginning of each month to the customers with birthdays that month and included a $5 gift certificate. In eight months Kurt mailed 269 letters and 106 certificates were redeemed, a whopping 39 percent response rate, but more importantly, the total sales generated were $2,735.41 with the average sale being $25.81. The profit margin of 45 percent meant those sales brought in $1,230.93. Expenses were $.50 per letter for a total of $134.50 and the certificates redeemed totaled up to $530.00. That means the gross profit was $566.43 and that doesn't count the other increased business from more customers who are reminded to visit the store or the average sales per customer, which is $100. And the Williams' don't even have all the birthdays of all their customers yet.

Baskin Robbins, the 31-flavor ice cream chain has been successfully offering the birthday club to children who visit the store for years. The company advertises to visitors its birthday club in which parents or children fill out a card giving the child's name, address, and birthday. Each year for the child's birthday, a certificate arrives good for a free ice cream cone on the child's birthday. This means the parent will probably have to buy a cone to eat with the child and any siblings will also have to have cones, which are not free. And it has the added advantage of getting the parent in the store near the child's birthday where the decorated ice cream cakes and other novelty party items are openly displayed in a glass freezer.

If your client has customers, they can benefit from effective databased marketing techniques. And you can be the one to deliver the benefits.

Offer a sample

You've talked, you've smiled, you've offered all the benefits and still this customer is hanging on the edge, teetering as to whether or not you'll get this business. What do you do?

Wayne Stoler of Letter Perfect Information Services says he puts the final touch on his sales approach by offering to produce for the demographics on businesses and residences within a 15-mile radius of the customer's own business. If he's dealing with a customer on the phone, he simply faxes the demographics in moments. He uses Zip*Select from Melissa Data, keys in the zip code, enters the number of miles he wants to go for zip code, and lets the computer do the rest. Once the report is printed, he faxes it to the client. He says this approach is a winner just about every time.

Profile

Wayne Stoler
Letter Perfect Information Services, Baltimore, Maryland

Wayne Stoler, who currently holds the title of "World's Fastest Typist," says he's always liked to type, even in high school. Back then he made extra money typing papers and reports for friends. He now owns and operates Letter Perfect Information Services in Baltimore.

In 1984, after graduating from high school, he had the opportunity to buy badly-in-debt Letter Perfect by assuming the debts of the business from a man who was running it out of his basement. At that time it was a typing service, something that was right up Wayne's alley. Most of the work involved merging names and addresses with letters, which led into putting the names and addresses on the envelopes and mailing the pieces.

The niche Wayne found and still works in is the opportunity to offer services to clients with smaller needs. Wayne maintains he can make money handling lists as small as 500 pieces, a job larger mailing services simply wouldn't take.

Letter Perfect offers a variety of services. "We do whatever the client needs," Wayne affirmed. The majority of his business is in mailing services, which includes all the letter shop work to get a mailing out the door. Another large part of his business is in selling mailing lists, which he either compiles in-house or buys at a discount from a large broker, such as American Business Information.

Because he buys such a large volume of names, upwards of two million a year, Wayne can get a discount on his list purchases. This allows him to make a profit on the lists he handles. In addition, he can often get the remainder of the work associated with the mailing of a list as a by-product of brokering the list.

Further, Wayne offers list maintenance services, which constitutes about 10 percent of his business. The remainder of his income is from miscellaneous items, such as subscriptions to a mailing list newsletter he produces as a promotional piece.

Letter Perfect Information Services has grown from a one-man basement operation into a warehouse staffed by a core group of 10 employees. Wayne prefers to hire temporary help from an agency when he needs extra staff rather than keeping on part-time employees. Letter Perfect is expected to break the half-a-million in gross revenue mark in 1993, and Wayne says he expects the business will continue to grow.

By the way, Wayne won his title as the world's fastest typist in the fall of 1991 at the Keytronics World Invitational Type-off held at the computer trade show Comdex in Las Vegas, Nevada. While he normally types 150 to 160 words per minute, he won in the type-off at 140. His prizes included a new Buick, a 386 notebook computer, $13,000 cash, and a variety of software. He says his wife drives the Buick, and sometimes she even lets him ride in it. Wayne doesn't do all the data entry work in his business anymore, but he prefers to keep his typing speed up, just in case.

If you can show prospects what you can do, you can often sell without even trying. A.G. Pitsilos said he got his first client for producing both a newsletter and mailing it by helping a friend do a demonstration of how it could be done. By the time Pitsilos and his friend finished the demonstration, the company officials were asking them if they'd consider putting out the newsletter and handling the list.

A.G. Pitsilos
TechImages, Inc., Bethlehem, Pennsylvania

Profile

A.G. Pitsilos said he didn't start out doing mailing, or even to have his own business at all. Employed by his father, he first got into computers at a local community group where, in doing a haunted house for a fund-raiser, he discovered it was difficult to manage the paperwork and organization. Someone suggested using a computer, and A.G. talked the group into buying an IBM-compatible personal computer (PC), which he immediately learned to use.

The next step was to get a copy of Ventura Publisher and become proficient with it, which A.G. said he did. A friend asked him to help do a presentation to a company interested in doing a newsletter in-house. The presentation went so well, to his surprise, the company asked him to do the newsletter and the distribution. His friend became his partner in the venture.

It was in doing the distribution of the newsletter that A.G. said he first got into mailing. He obtained a bulk mailing permit and the company's client list and went to work. Later, he bought out his partner, and began full-time work doing desktop publishing and even selling desktop publishing equipment.

But it became apparent desktop publishing was more limited than A.G. had anticipated. "You can only make as much money as you can charge an hour, times however many hours you can stand to work," he said. The demand for mailing list services appeared to be much less limited and not as bottlenecked by how many hours he could put in.

So he transitioned to mailing lists, concentrating on cleaning lists and printing labels and not on the manual work of actually folding and stuffing the materials (although he admitted he has done that as well). He says his average job is between 20,000 and 100,000 addresses and the majority of his customers are larger, out-of-town companies. At $.02 per name for list cleaning, A.G. admits he can make $2000 per hour with a fast computer and a big hard disk, processing at the rate of 100,000 names per hour.

He has also obtained work from letter shops who can't handle smaller jobs and have farmed the work out to him or referred customers to him. He's placed an ad in the Yellow Pages Business-to-Business directory, attends local Chamber of Commerce meetings, and uses on-line networking through computer bulletin boards to get customers. He also suggests mailers consider offering services to previous employers. To those new to the mailing list service, he said they should make themselves valuable. That can mean offering extra services, being faster, taking jobs others won't, and developing a reputation for good work.

A.G. says one of the most helpful books for him was *Guerilla Marketing* and he regularly reads *Ad Age* and other advertising and mailing trade journals. While the knowledge he gains from reading helps, he emphasized it is important to have some "staying power" financially. "If you can stay in there, you can often get that one good-sized client that makes all the difference."

You can demonstrate that you know what you're talking about in lots of ways. MapLinx, a Windows-based program from MapLinx Corporation of Plano, Texas, allows you to take a mailing list and show on a map where the names on the list are. You can be as detailed as a single city, a zip code as in FIG. 6-5, or show the entire United States. This technique is not only impressive, it gives you an idea of where the concentration of you prospect's business is.

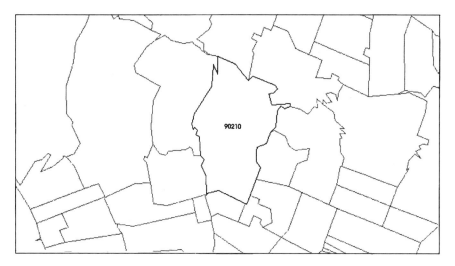

6-5
A customer mailing list displayed in MapLinx for Windows Professional Version is enlarged to show a portion of Southern California, specifically the 90210 zip code area.

Just as a side note, it might make sense for you to target one or two key types of businesses to begin, like all the dry cleaners in your community or all the hotels. Besides gaining knowledge about the business, you can also end up with tools, like lists, you can reuse to increase your profit margins. It's also a more effective use of your time as the scheme you invented for one plumber or restaurant will probably work for others.

If you can pinpoint an area where your customer has a concentration of business, you can use demographic information to find other similar areas where mailing might increase that business. This not only sells your services, it increases your client's customer base as well. The term for this approach is *market mapping*.

Use market mapping to increase business

Many companies used to perform market mapping by putting colored pins in a wall map, but now the computer can perform the task. Based on *geographic information systems* (GIS), software programs initially developed for use with public data, such as Census Bureau information, market mapping is playing an increasing role in many segments of marketing. By taking information from addresses in a database, many mapping programs can produce immediate results, showing where the members of the database are located on an on-screen map that can be printed as well.

Geoffrey Hollander of Mail Pouch, a Port Hueneme, California-based mailing service says he uses this technique. Hollander gets as much information on the list as possible, including carrier route information, even if the list owner isn't mailing by carrier route. He says with some clients he's noticed a high concentration of responses in a certain carrier route. Once you know where your clients are, you can get demographic statistics on the area as well as other similar areas. Hollander suggests to clients they should consider allowing him to get information to target mailings to demographically similar areas.

Demographic information for a residential area would include information broken down into percentages such as the median income of the residents, what percentage own or rent their homes, how many cars the residents own, what type of education they have and so on. This information is usually available in the form of census data collected by the government every 10 years. The Census Catalog & Guide available from the Superintendent of Documents details what census information is available and how to get it. A monthly announcement of what census data is available from the last census, called the *Monthly Product Announcement* is free by request from Customer Services, Bureau of the Census, Washington, D.C. 20233. Demographic information for local markets based on zip code, carrier route, a physical drawing on a map, or so many miles in radius from a certain point is available from companies like Urban Decision Systems of Los Angeles, California. However, your best source for how to go about collecting and using demographic information will be the direct marketing publications listed earlier in this chapter.

But the location of customers can be used for more than just mailing. Companies are using such information to assign territories to their sales force and to plan sales calls. Because most programs can present information right down to the house on the corner, effective mapping techniques can save time and money. Other uses for market mapping are springing up as well.

In "Putting Sales On The Map" an August 1992 article in *Sales & Marketing Management*, author Richard Lewis describes how a medical Wisconsin-based General Electric Medical Systems (GEMS), a manufacturer of diagnostic imaging equipment, broke through a tough market barrier by using mapping software as a sales tool.

GEMS's sales representatives were finding it increasingly difficult to sell the company's diagnostic imaging equipment. They had trouble reaching the hospital administrators who could make a buying decision and instead ending up dealing with people in hospitals' radiology departments who had some influence on purchasing but couldn't "sign on the dotted line." Further complications were added by tight budgets caused by government reductions and government regulations. The company had to find a new approach to break the tough selling climate.

David Wells, the company's program manager for database marketing, opted for mapping software, and a presentation was developed for the sales representatives to use in their presentations. A particular hospital's market area is defined, and demographic, disease, physician, and spreadsheet projections are imported and segmented according to the boundaries of the map. The result is sales representatives can demonstrate a need in the hospital's market for GEMS' diagnostic imaging equipment. Wells was quoted in the article as saying, "If reps can come in with valuable information about the market forces driving the need for diagnostic imaging equipment [as well as] a profile of the hospital's market, hospital administrators have to be interested. We've essentially moved from taking orders to consultative selling. We get lots of reps telling us the hospital administrators went wild over the maps and information."

Market Intelligence Research Corporation, a Mountain View, California-based firm centered on the hi-tech industry, contends the 1991 worldwide GIS market was close to $5 billion, and predicts the market will grow to $21 billion by 1997. The firm predicts the commercial and business portion of the market will grow sevenfold in that seven-year period.

You can take advantage of that growth. Market mapping services require equipment you will already have and expertise in the use of the computer and software. Many mapping software packages are available, including MapLinx from MapLinx Corporation for the IBM and compatible personal computer and Atlas Pro from Strategic Mapping for the Macintosh. Whether it's pinpointing areas to target for mailings, producing maps for a client's sales force, or helping develop a mapping presentation to show a need for a product, your expertise can help clients increase their business.

So, you've seen why management of mailings is important, why direct mailing is effective and desirable, and how you can show customers you're the one who should handle their mailings. You've also gotten some tips on how you can help clients with their mailings, the most important things to look for, and resources for new ideas. I would encourage you to continue investigation into direct marketing approaches via the many books and magazines available on the subject. Your search will be richly rewarded. You'll find the materials mentioned in appendices A & B will offer you a practically endless flow of new ideas which you can use to get and keep customers.

References

Holtz, Herman. 1992. *Databased Marketing.* New York, N.Y.: John Wiley & Sons, Inc.

Lewis, Richard. "Putting Sales On The Map." August 1992. *Sales & Marketing Management*, v144 (n9): p76(5).

Neal, Mollie. "Andersen Takes Great 'Panes' To Build Relationships." April 1993. *Direct Marketing*, v67: p28(4).

Raphel, Murray. "The man with the plan: direct mail programs of Stan Golomb." March 1992. *Direct Marketing*, v54 (n11): p38(2).

Ziglar, Zig. 1984. *Zig Ziglar's Secrets of Closing the Sale.* New York, N.Y.: Berkley Publishing Company.

7 Extra income with related services

"Occasions are rare; and those who know how to seize upon them are rarer."
— Josh Billings

In a big city, you may find plenty of work sticking to just generating labels or cleaning mail lists and not need to seek other related services you can offer. However, if you happen to be in a smaller community, you might find it necessary to offer other services in order to make ends meet. The number of related services for the mailing list service business is one of the best things about this type of business. Most of your clients will probably need one or more of these services, so you might let them know what you can offer.

Instruction in the software you use

One of the services you can offer is to teach courses on how to use the software you use. This will help you to get your name out as someone with expertise in this area, and it can help you get work as well. While it seems that people taking a course in mailing or dBASE or whatever you feel you can teach would want to do the job themselves, they often are either looking for some expertise so they can feel comfortable in choosing someone to hire, or simply decide it's too much trouble to learn. You are the natural choice for someone to hire because they already know you and are convinced you know what you are doing.

Because you use the software daily, you're a natural for answering the sticky questions and providing good practical tips in getting past the rough spots.

Junior colleges and high school-based community adult programs are often on the look-out for part-time instructors on hot topics such as database, word processing, or even mailing. One of the tip-offs that a school is short on teachers for a certain subject is when the catalog says "staff" instead of an instructor's name in a course offering. It never hurts to make a call. Ask to speak to the department head, tell him or her what you have in mind, and ask if you could send along your resume and perhaps a short course outline.

After you send your resume, follow up a week or so later with a phone call to see if there's any further information you can provide.

Word processing & secretarial services

Word processing is a natural service, often that goes right along with a mailing and one for which you already have the equipment. You can get clients from local colleges and local businesses by advertising on bulletin boards on campus, taking out an add in your local newspaper, and sending out fliers.

Because so many companies have the capability to do word processing in-house, you might want to expand into full secretarial services. Those services could include transcription, dictation, photocopying, telephone answering, notary services, repetitive (or mail merged) letters, mailbox rental, shipping services, sending and receiving facsimiles, bookkeeping and billing, and resumes. If you have the capability, you might go the extra mile for clients by also offering pick-up and delivery of their materials.

Also, I've run across many secretarial services that are members of the National Association of Secretarial Services. If you can say you're a member of a similar organization, this can help distinguish your service by making you appear more serious and professional about your services. Again, your public library is the place to find out about these organizations.

Typesetting

If you purchased a laser printer, you may be able to offer typesetting services. A.G. Pitsilos got into the mailing business by starting with a newsletter. You might be able to get into the newsletter business by offering mailing services. It's simply a matter of finding someone who is starting a newsletter to promote their business, such as a real estate agent, or you might have a client whose business lends itself to the expert approach and could benefit from a newsletter.

Microsoft Publisher is an elegant and inexpensive desktop publishing package. The professional products for desktop publishing on the personal computer are PageMaker from Aldus and Ventura Publisher from Ventura Software.

You can get ideas for the types of typesetting services you can offer from the Paper Direct catalog. Paper Direct also offers a PaperKit which contains all of its most recent paper samples for you to show clients. Using your laser printer and preprinted color paper you can offer 3-fold flyers with punch-out rotary cards; eye-catching letterhead and envelopes; printed notices and acrylic stands to stand them in for conferences or meetings; customized certificates; and even colored foil lettering on anything you can print.

Quill is offering a smaller collection of similar papers. You can request a Paper Direct catalog by calling (800) 272-7377 or a Quill catalog at (909) 988-3200. Address and phone information is also in appendix B.

Collection

Debt collection is an art, especially these days with so many having financial problems. It can be quite profitable for you and a service to your clients.

Your best sales pitch in offering debt collection services is how quickly you can respond. The more time that passes on a past due account, the less likely the amount will be collected. After one month, the likelihood of collecting drops to 94 percent, after three months to 74 percent, and after a year, there is only a 27 percent chance of collecting. So, while you can expect to get hardcore cases that your client has given up on, you'll want to shoot for encouraging clients to move on their past due accounts as soon as possible.

Collection services usually charge a percentage (between 10 and 50 percent) that increases based on how overdue the account is. However, some agencies are beginning to charge a $7 to $10 flat rate fee per account, whether they collect or not. If you're doing a client's mailings, there's a good chance you'll already have their mailing list. This means you can easily offer a service to clients to put out a letter to the past due account on your letterhead within 24 hours after receiving the request to do so.

Like Transworld Systems Incorporated (TSI), you may find that flat rate debt collection done quickly is profitable. In the April 15, 1992 Fairfield County Business Journal, an article entitled "TSI is Rewriting the Script on Overdue Debt Collection," by Joan Stableford outlines the company's tactics. TSI says its success is in immediately increasing a client's cash flow by charging less than $10 per account with a recovery average of 56 percent—more than double the national average of 27 percent for all other collection. The company also performs faster, handling delinquent accounts for clients in an average of 35 days, instead of four months which is the national average for collection agencies.

Traditional collection agencies can charge a 20 to 50 percent commission and can legally hold that money for up to 60 days. But TSI has payments sent directly to its clients to immediately increase the creditor's cash flow. This might be a practice you can take advantage of as well.

Good collection almost always means following up with a telephone call. If you have a modem connected to your computer, you can have the computer dialing the calls for you and a script prepared to go from when a caller answers the phone. A polite, firm, and empathetic approach is best and a script will help keep you on track during the call.

One of the prime questions to ask when doing collection calls is why the account hasn't been paid. This practice can result in clearing up misunderstandings, revealing errors in the creditors records, and can help expedite payment.

For example, if the bill is incorrect or the customer has been overbilled, then contacting them repeatedly is not only a waste of your time, it could also alienate the customer. If it is a claim that the customer might plan to cover with insurance, the record on the bill might be improperly recorded so the insurance company won't pay. By asking, you can increase your chances of getting those payments.

A visit to your local library will reveal numerous books and articles on collection practices and techniques. You'll also want to be sure you stay well within the bounds of the legal requirements for what you can and cannot do when collecting. Those legal boundaries vary from state to state, such as whether or not you can call people at their work (probably not) so be sure to find out.

Coordinating with printers

If you've taken a look at the Franklin Estimating Systems book then you know that most of it is for printers. This means that printers often come across people who mail and vice versa. You can offer to coordinate with a printer for a client and have everything delivered to you for mailing. With the Franklin Estimating book and by learning some of the terminology, you can make a pretty fair estimate of what a printing job a client has in mind will cost, adding in something for your efforts as well. Then you handle all the tough stuff and let your client relax. Many printers also accept input from disks created on personal computers, which means you might be able to do the typesetting as well. Some mailing list services have even gone as far as to buy their own printing equipment in order to offer one-stop shopping to their clients.

Profile

Jim and Michelle McCartney
LCS Direct Mail Advertising & Printing, Ft. Lauderdale, Florida

Jim and Michelle McCartney, owners of LCS Direct Mail Advertising & Printing in Ft. Lauderdale, are former members of the corporate world. Jim was an executive for the publisher Harlequin, and Michelle worked in public relations. The couple decided to go into semi-retirement in Florida to live on a boat.

But after a while, they decided to do something to bring in an income. The business the two decided to start was doing database research work for legal firms. They bought a computer, back then a Tandy from Radio Shack, and started with some word processing programs.

They did a mailing to all the local law offices they could find, and Jim went away on a trip, leaving Michelle to learn word processing. When he came back, Jim was greeted at the airport by Michelle who informed him they had their first client.

As they laughingly recount now, their first client was a dress shop and the work was computerizing customer lists for mailing. A printer referred Michelle to the dress shop, who was having their sales clerks hand address advertising postcards during the day. The process was a slow one, and the dress shop couldn't get their sales information out on time, so they were delighted to hire someone who could computerize the process.

Because they had a client, Jim and Michelle abandoned the legal research idea and went into mailing list services. They said they finally did get a call from a legal firm, but the call was six months later and it was too late.

The dress shop stayed as a client and grew from one store to five stores. Other clients came on board as well. The McCartney's took out a Yellow Pages ad, although they indicate they still get most of their customers by word of mouth. The ad said, "No job too big or too small."

And the jobs got bigger. When that happened, they enlisted the aid of relatives—Michelle's parents, an aunt, and an uncle—to help out. The extra "staff" helped them land a big account.

They were approached by *Newsweek* Magazine's Latin American division about mailings; this was a referral from American Express, who was already a client. However, they heard *Newsweek*, like other large companies, was concerned about a small company being able to handle its jobs. When the *Newsweek* representative came by to see the facilities, the whole family was hard at work.

They got the *Newsweek* account, but a couple of years later the magazine's representative told Michelle that an older women present that first day looked a lot like Michelle and asked who that was. Michelle answered that the woman was her mother. The *Newsweek* representative laughingly told them it wasn't the size of the operation, but it was quality that she was looking for. Seven years later, the McCartney's still have the *Newsweek* account.

Jim and Michelle added printing to their business when they discovered there was a market for it, and now offer a complete one-stop service to companies. The printing makes up about 10 percent of the total business they do, most of which is letter shop work.

As part of their fulfillment services, LCS has mailed unusual items such as Nerf balls and gum drops. In a self-promotion campaign, they've also mailed rubbery men, the kind that when thrown at a glass window, work their way down. Included with the rubber men is promotional literature that says, "We bend over backward for you."

The couple has three children who have been involved in the business, too, although now they've all grown up and graduated from college. None of the kids are interested in taking the business over eventually, so Jim and Michelle say their plans are to convert the business to an employee-owned operation.

Their plan is to allocate a percentage of profits to the employees and then require the profits be used to purchase business equity. As they buy up equity, eventually the employees will acquire LCS. The McCartney's stress they believe the employees who end up in control of the business will be much more effective in running it. Part of Jim and Michelle's motivation is self-interest, as well, as they hope the business will be able to contribute to their retirement.

Jim says he feels like one of the important skills to have is to be able to repair the business equipment himself to save money. He also feels workman's compensation insurance is important, even for home-based businesses and even though the expense can make business owners think twice. "If something happens when you're working at home, your property insurance company is likely to say, 'We didn't insure you for a business' and there you'll be."

Being in Florida, there are special quirks to the region that LCS can help clients with. For example, South Florida has a 2 percent-per-month address change rate, higher than the national average. So in a year, as much as 24 percent of a list for the area is not deliverable. This is further complicated by the "snowbirds" or people from the northern states that only are at their Florida addresses during the winter months. But the McCartney's track the fluctuations in the population and use the information to help clients get the most for their mailings.

Jim and Michelle say one of the things they've tried to do is serve the client's need, whatever that need was. Michelle said, "People would call us up and say, 'Do you do . . .' and we would say yes, even if it meant doing it by hand. We often did hand work until we could afford the machine we needed for the task." Their business, that started with a Sears Portable typewriter and a Tandy TRS-80, has grown to a company with more than $250,000 worth of equipment!

The most interesting mailing Jim and Michelle remember was mailing wanted posters for a couple whose son had been murdered. LCS did a direct mail campaign to people who lived in a certain neighborhood who might have seen a particular make and model of automobile at a convenience store with a composite drawing of the suspect. The police did get more clues based on that mailing, although a conviction in the case was never made.

LCS also offers list brokering and offers a free software diskette written by a young programmer for them in the database language Clipper. The program is "idiot proof" according to Jim, and it can print labels and reports (including a summary of zip codes), do zip selects, and import any ASCII file. The user has a list from which to pick the printer to send the program's output to. With a large order the program is free, otherwise the McCartneys charge an additional $25.

The McCartneys emphasized there is a lot to be said for people who stay small and don't get too big. "The danger is you can end up working more yourself and paying your employees time and a half. You can actually make less money per hour for your efforts." Jim and Michelle suggest the way to stay small is to limit the amount of work taken on and avoid the heavy machinery, such as mailing equipment that costs $40,000.

The McCartneys claim trends in the mailing list service are moving toward a stronger reaction to privacy issues and more concern about conservation. The high cost of postage is also forcing mailers to try to mail smarter by being more selective and they believe there is more interest in the new worksharing postal discounts.

As a final note, Jim has traveled all over the world and says despite the shortcomings, he insists the U.S. mailing system is by far the fastest with the lowest cost. He has visited sites in other countries and recalls how he has actually seen foreign postal workers without any automated equipment, hand-sorting and canceling mail. Both Jim and Michelle say we in the U.S. have a lot to be proud of.

Telemarketing

There's no reason, if you have a phone, that you can't offer to follow up yourself or hire someone to follow up on a mailing. This doesn't mean you have to do the telemarketing yourself. You could hire telemarketing services and tack on a percentage for yourself, just as you might coordinate a package deal with a printer.

The reason you might consider coordinating the telemarketing instead of doing it yourself is telemarketing people are set up to handle the job. They know the questions to ask and they handle hiring the help. However, they might also get requests for mailing list services, and if they know about you, they might be able to make referrals to you as well. It's not hard to find telemarketing firms. You can find them in the telephone book and you can find them through their advertisements for employees in neighborhood newspapers. Or you could just ask the next telemarketer who calls you who they work for.

Inventory

This may surprise you, but since you're in the business of printing labels anyway, you might be able to help businesses keep up their inventory. Bear Rock Labeler from Bear Rock Technologies prints not only POSTNET barcodes, but it will also print Universal Product barcodes and other types of barcodes. Small businesses with a lot of inventory, such as car stereo shops or video stores need a way to keep track of their inventory and adding a barcode reader to a PC is one way to do that. A barcode reader is a wand that generates a laser beam and when it is passed over a barcode it inputs characters into the computer just as though they were typed in on the keyboard (FIG. 7-1).

7-1
You can gain extra income producing labels with barcodes for small businesses with inventory to track. The barcode can be read into the computer with hand-held wands like this one.

Bear Rock Labeler will generate unique numbers in succession and translate those numbers into a barcode that can be printed on a label. That means a unique number and barcode can be printed on labels. You can even make several copies of the same barcoded unique number which can then be placed on the product, on the box, and on the shelf where the product is kept. It might be useful to a business to have the labels preprinted so as inventory comes in it can be labeled, then scanned into a program designed to track inventory. When that inventory is sold or rented, it can be quickly scanned to take it out of stock.

Also, people who make food items are required to label those food items with the ingredients and their contact information. Small candy producers, or restaurants offering vending machine food items need labels for those items. You can generate those labels and even barcode them as well.

Label generation

Custom labels with graphics or company logos for files, raffles, conferences, price tags, product labels, and all the various needs that come up in the course of business are another avenue for you. You have the labels. You can add an optical scanner to your computer and scan a company's custom artwork for printing on a variety of labels (FIG. 7-2). This is especially useful for rush jobs, as you can generate hundreds or thousands of labels in a day, and small quantities of labels larger printers won't touch. The Bear Rock Labeler and MyAdvancedLabelDesigner from MySoftware are both geared toward this type of activity.

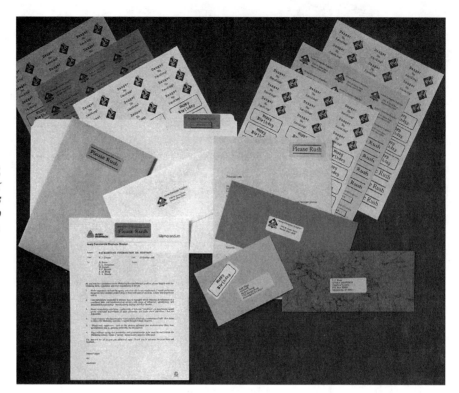

7-2
Producing short runs or custom labels for various business needs can help you gain extra income.

Starting your own mail-order business

Some of the business owners I talked with learned so much about marketing and mail order that they've decided to take their expertise and equipment and start their own mail order business.

Mail order is an exciting and fast growing field with a variety of possibilities. Some of the mail-order pioneers include Sears and Roebuck and Montgomery Ward. While the benefits of shopping at home are obvious when you consider the busy lives most people lead, businesses are increasingly using direct mail shopping as well.

Take the success story of Jack Miller who started an office supply company from the back of his father's chicken store in Chicago in 1956. Miller decided to send out a mailing to the 153 customers he had done business with on the telephone featuring five price-cut specials. The postcard was a success and Miller continued the effort which has grown into the Quill Corporation.

Leon L. Bean, who started the famous L.L. Bean clothing catalog was quoted by the Direct Marketing Association as having said: "Sell good merchandise at a reasonable profit, treat your customers like human beings, and they'll always come back for more."

Catalog Age magazine is dedicated to offering help and research to catalog advertisers. Its December issue is loaded with facts and figures on the trends in the catalog industry.

If you want to get an idea of what's out there so you can plan your approach, for $3 each there are three catalogs for catalogs. The Direct Marketing Association offers the *Great Catalog Guide* featuring over 50 catalogs with descriptions and contact numbers. Send check or money order for $3 to Great Catalog Guide, Direct Marketing Association, 11 West 42nd Street, P.O. Box 3861, New York, NY, 10163-3861. Catalog Revue has a 52-page catalog of catalogs with over 175 catalog listings. It is also $3 and is available by writing 144 S. First Street Department 5DMR-006, P.O. Box 4013, Burbank, CA 91503. A collection of 140 international catalogs is available by sending a $3 check or money order to International Catalogue Collection, 144 S. First Street Department 5DMI-007, P.O. Box 4013, Burbank, CA 91503. Mail-order how-to books abound. Your local library probably has an entire collection.

You might want to branch into providing delivery services. Who knows which way to send a package is the least expensive? There are software programs on the market, listed by *Mailer's Review* in the magazine's disk of software for mailers, whose sole purpose is to compare the various delivery services, such as United Parcel Service (UPS), Roadway Package Service (RPS), Federal Express, and the USPS for the lowest cost on a particular package delivery. Contact *Mailer's Review* magazine for details on the diskette.

Package shipping services

If you're interested in offering package delivery services, some software vendors specialize in software geared toward automating the paperwork requirements of delivery companies such as United Parcel Service (UPS) or Federal Express. QUICKUP from Arrakis Publishing is one such package geared toward UPS services. Also, UPS will pickup at your home or place of business for a standard rate of just a few dollars per week and Federal Express will also pick up packages for per-package charge.

These are just a few of the opportunities available for you as you pursue the mailing list service business. You can find other ideas and help in magazines such as *Home/Office Computing*, available in most bookstores.

Conclusion

Because you already have a computer, you might consider getting a modem to investigate some of the electronic bulletin board services that offer forums for people working at home. Those forums not only offer support and networking, but they often have case histories and help on starting and maintaining a variety of businesses from home. The Working from Home Forum on CompuServe, maintained by Paul and Sarah Edwards, is such a resource. The Home Office/Small Business Round Table on the bulletin board service GEnie offers similar services and also allows you to list your company in The Business Resource Directory, a searchable reference tool for people looking for services. CompuServe starter kits are available at most software stores and information on GEnie can be obtained at (800) 638-9636. You can expect to pay a minimum of $10 to $15 a month for these services and significantly more if you become an active subscriber.

I think there's nothing like mail. Rare indeed is the day I don't get any. But I'm always disappointed when it happens.

And now you have the know-how to be on your way, starting your own home-based mailing service business. This is exciting because you can realize your own potential and be assured you'll be helping other businesses and individuals boost their bottom line. Congratulations!

Now, let's make sure other people don't have any disappointing no-mail days, shall we?

Reference   Stableford, Joan. "TSI is Rewriting the Script on Overdue Debt Collection." April 15, 1991. *Fairfield County Business Journal*, v22 n13 p11(1).

Suppliers

Friden Neopost (formerly Friden Alcatel)
30955 Huntwood Ave.
Hayward, CA 94544-7084
(800) 624-7892
(800) 827-4543 in California
Friden Neopost offers postage meters and other mailing equipment.

GBR Systems Corporation
4100 Corporate Sq., Ste. 113
Naples, FL 33942-4704
(813) 643-0530
GBR Systems offers folding machines and other equipment for mailing.

International Mailing Systems
Hasler Mailing Machines
19 Forest Pky.
Shelton, CT 06484-6122
(203) 926-1087
International Mailing Systems manufactures mailing equipment.

Martin Yale Industries
500 N. Spaulding Ave.
Chicago, IL 60624-1512
(312) 826-4444
Martin Yale Industries offers folding machines and other equipment for mailing.

Postage meters

Pitney Bowes
One Elmcroft Rd.
Stamford, CT 06926-0700
(800) 672-6937
Pitney Bowes rents postage meters and offers equipment for mailing.

Postalia
1423 Centre Circle Dr.
Downers Grove, IL 60515-1087
(708) 629-9100
Postalia offers equipment for mailing, including postage machines.

Equipment sales

Dispensa-Matic Label Dispensers
725 N. 23rd St.
St. Louis, MO 63103-1500
(800) 325-7303

Metalproducts Engineering
3864 Santa Fe Ave.
Los Angeles, CA 90058
(213) 581-8121
(800) 824-0222
Metalproducts Engineering offers the MP 4000 Postage Scale for $3.75 +
$1.00 postage & handling. California residents must add $0.31 each sales tax.

Software vendors

Alpha Software
One North Ave.
Burlington, MA 01803
(617) 229-2924
(617) 272-4876 (fax)
Alpha Four develops the Alpha Four database application package.

American Business Information
5711 86th Circle
P.O. Box 27347
Omaha, NE 68127
(402) 593-4565
American Business Information supplies lists on CD-ROM.

Arrakis Publishing
Box One Hundred
Crystal River, FL 32623
Arrakis offers UPS Manifest System software QUICKUP.

Digital Directory Assistance
(617) 639-2900

Digital Directory Assistance offers White Pages and Yellow Pages phone book listings on CD-ROM.

Borland International
1800 Green Hills Rd.
P.O. Box 660001
Scotts Valley, CA 95067-0001
(408) 438-5300
Developers of database application product dBASE IV.

Business Computer Center
813 Bedford Ct.
Libertyville, IL 60048-3001
(800) 453-3130
The Business Computer Center offers software products for mailing including list management software Mail Manager 2000, ZCR 2000 for list cleaning.

FDC, Inc.
Attn: Mike Talbot
9900 Bren Rd. E., Ste. 201
Minnetonka, MN 55343-4411
(612) 936-5400
FDC is a licensee of the USPS NAIC for change-of-address information.

Fairhaven Software
3 Cabot Place
P.O. Box 57
Stoughton, MA 02072
(617) 341-1990
Producers of database software product Nutshell Plus.

Franklin Estimating Systems
P.O. Box 16690
Salt Lake City, UT 84116-9970
(800) 346-7363
355-5954 (Utah residents only)
(801) 322-5822 (fax)
(801) 355-5980 (bbs)
Franklin offers an estimating catalog for use in determining labor and materials costs for mailing services and printing.

Group 1 Software
6404 Ivy Ln., Ste. 500
Greenbelt, MD 20770-1400
(800) 368-5806 product information
(301) 982-4069 (fax)
Group 1 Software has ArcList, AccuMail for list cleaning and list management.

Jet Products
Attn: Gene Mallory
5656 Buffalo Ave.
Van Nuys, CA 91401-4505
(800) 678-5277
Jet Products offers handwriting fonts and Jet Reply, a software package for generating business reply mail.

Lorton Data
43 Main St. SE, Ste. 408
Minneapolis, MN 55414-1029
(612) 623-3130
Lorton Data is the licensee for FDC, Inc., who is a licensee of the USPS NAIC for change-of-address info.

Lotus Development
Word Processing Division
1000 Abernathy Rd. NE
Atlanta, GA 02142
(800) 668-1509
(404) 698-7656 (fax)
Lotus produces Ami Pro for Windows.

Software for Mailing and Shipping Directory
Mailer's Review
7850 SE Stark
Portland, OR 97215-2380
(503) 257-0764
(503) 257-7935 (fax)
Mailer's Review produces a directory of vendors on disk called the *Software for Mailing And Shipping Directory*.

MapLinx Corporation
5068 W. Plano Pky.
Plano, TX 75093
(214) 231-1400
(214) 733-8193 (fax)
MapLinx Corporation offers market mapping software MapLinx for Windows.

McDermott Consulting
15065 Lebanon Rd.
Old Hickory, TN 37138-1809
McDermott Consulting offers PC DMM, an electronic version of the Direct Mail Manual.

Melissa Data Corporation
32122 Paseo Adelanto
San Juan Capistrano, CA 92675-3600

(800) 443-8834
Melissa Data offers a variety of software for mailers and has a catalog of products for mailing. Some of the company's own products include ZIPHONE*1, ZIPHONE*2, ZIPHONE*3, ZIP*Data*Jr, ZIP*Data, and ZIP*Select.

Microsoft
One Microsoft Way
Redmond, WA 98052-6399
(800) 426-9400
Developers of database applications Access for Windows, FoxPro for Windows, FoxPro for DOS. Also developers of Microsoft Windows, Microsoft Word for Windows, and Microsoft Word for DOS.

Peoplesmith Software
18 Damon Rd.
P.O. Box 384
North Scituate, MA 02060
(617) 545-7300
Peoplesmith Software specializes in software for troublesome database problems and produces DynaKey, DataLift, Right Fielder, Personator, and GenderBase.

PostSaver Systems
2731 S. Adams Rd., Ste. 102
Rochester Hills, MI 48309-3103
PostSaver Systems are producers of Bar_Lite barcoding software, PostSaver list management software, dB_Mailer barcoding and zip code sorting software.

PSI Associates
247 High St.
Palo Alto, CA 94301-1041
(415) 321-2640
(415) 321-0356 (fax)
PSI produces Envelope Manager and DAZzle, both of which allow you to use your modem to look up zip+4 Codes.

RAM Solutions
P.O. Box 28450
Tempe, Arizona 85285-8450
(602) 759-5520
RAM Solutions distributes PostMark, a software package for printing Business Reply Mail pieces on laser printers.

Scriptomatic
10 Clipper Rd.
W. Conshohocken, PA 19428-2721
(215) 825-6205

(215) 825-1397 (fax)
Scriptomatic offers BarRight barcoding software for 9-pin dot matrix printers.

Symantec
3040 Oakmead Village Dr.
Santa Clara, CA 95051
(408) 252-3570
(408) 255-3344 (fax)
Producers of Q&A database application software.

Window Book
P.O. Box 390697
Cambridge, MA 02139-0008
(800) 370-2410
Window Book offers an on-disk version of the Direct Mail Manual called *The DMM Easy Reference.*

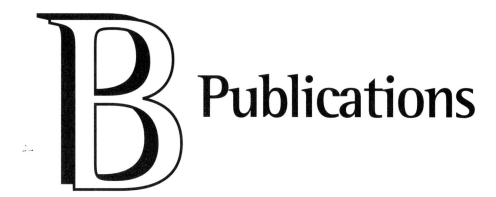

Publications

Magazines

Advertising Age
Crain Communications
740 Rush St.
Chicago, IL 60611-2590
Advertising Age looks at issues involving advertising and the effective use of advertising.

Catalog Age
Catalog Age Publishing
P.O. Box 4006
New Canaan, CT 06840-1406
Catalog Age focuses on direct marketing via catalogs and publishes market survey information each year in its December issue.

Direct Marketing
Hoke Communications
224 Seventh St.
Garden City, New York 11530
(516) 746-6700
Direct Marketing is a publication geared toward direct marketers, but deals with USPS issues and mailing issues as well.

Memo to Mailers
U.S. Postal Service
P.O. Box 999
Springfield, VA 22150-0999
Memo to Mailers is a free publication geared toward mailers and published by the USPS.

Mast Magazine
RB Publishing
2701 E. Washington Ave.
Madison, WI 53704-5002
(608) 241-8777
Mast publishes the "Power Guide Listing" of equipment manufacturers,
software publishers, and service providers.

Mailing and Shipping Technology
RB Publishing
2701 E. Washington Ave.
Madison, WI 53704-5002
(800) 536-1992
Mailing and Shipping Technology will mail you a free sample issue if you call
or write to request one.

Mailer's Review
7850 SE Stark
Portland, OR 97215-2380
(503) 257-0764
(503) 257-7935 (fax)
Mailer's Review is a magazine geared toward the mailing industry and offers
articles, reviews, and USPS news.

Mail: The Journal of Communication Distribution
(607) 746-7600
(607) 746-2750 (fax)
Mail is geared toward information about the mailing industry. Call to request
free sample copy.

Postal Bulletin
Available from Superintendent of Documents
Biweekly
List ID POB
File Code 2E
S/N 739-001-00000-5
$63 a year

Target Marketing
Who's Mailing What
401 N. Broad St.
Philadelphia, PA 19108
(215) 238-5300
Published by the North American Publishing, Co., it deals with marketing
and mailing issues.

The Complete Direct Mail List Handbook
By Ed Burnett
Prentice Hall, Englewood Cliffs, New Jersey, 1988
ISBN 0-13-159278-5

Domestic Mail Manual
Available from Superintendent of Documents quarterly
List ID DOM
File Code 2S
S/N 739-003-00000-8
$36 a year
See the Superintendent of Documents order form, FIG. B-1, on the next page.

Guerrilla Marketing Excellence, The 50 Golden Rules for Small Business Success by Jay Conrad Levinson
Houghton Mifflin Company, Boston, MA 1993
ISBN 0-395-60844-9

How to Find, Capture, and Keep Customers
Golomb Group Productions
7664 Plaza Ct.
Willowbrook, IL 60521
(708) 887-7339
(708) 887-7347 (fax)
Focuses on marketing techniques for small businesses.

International Mail Manual
Available from the U.S. Superintendent of Documents semiannually
List ID IMM
File Code 2S
S/N 739-004-00000-4
$17 a year
See the Superintendent of Documents order form, FIG. B-1, on the next page.

Standard Industrial Classification (SIC) Manual
National Technical Information Service
5285 Port Royal Rd.
Springfield, VA 22161
Order Number: PB 87-100012

Standard Rate & Data Service
3004 Glenview Rd.
Wilmette, IL 60091
(800) 323-4601
(708) 441-2264 (fax)
The rate guide for mailing list rental for the entire industry, *Standard Rate & Data Service* publishes several directories of mailing lists for rent.

Subject Bibliography

ORDER FORM

S169

Please type or print

ORDER BY PHONE: (202) 783-3238
8 a.m.–4 p.m.eastern time

To fax your orders (202) 512–2250
(24 hours a day, 7 days a week)

Customer's Name and Address Ship To: (If other than address at left)	Ship To: (If other than address at left)
ZIP ZIP	ZIP

B-1

You can use this form, phone in, or fax your orders for books and materials printed by the government, including special information for mailers offered by the USPS. For a catalog of what materials are available, write to Free Catalog, P.O. Box 37000, Washington, DC 20013-7000.

( )
Customer's Daytime Telephone Number

Your order number _____

Date _____

May we make your name/address available to other mailers? **YES NO** ☐ ☐

Publications

Qty.	Stock Number	Title	Price Each	Total Price
			Total for Publications	

Subscriptions

Qty.	(List ID)	Title	Price Each	Total Price
			Total for Subscriptions	
			Total Cost of Order	

NOTE: Prices include regular domestic postage and handling and are subject to change. International customers please add 25%.

Please Choose Method of Payment:

☐ Check Payable to the Superintendent of Documents
☐ GPO Deposit Account ☐☐☐☐☐☐☐–☐
☐ VISA or MasterCard Account
☐☐☐☐☐☐☐☐☐☐☐☐☐☐☐☐☐☐☐☐
☐☐☐☐ (Credit card expiration date)

_____
(Authorizing Signature)

Thank you for your order!

MAIL ORDER TO:
Superintendent of Documents
P.O. Box 371954
Pittsburgh, PA 15250-7954

Zig Ziglar's Secrets of Closing the Sale
By Zig Ziglar
Berkley Books, New York, NY 1982
ISBN 0-425-08102-8

Catalog Revue
144 S. First St., Dept. 5DMR-006
P.O. Box 4013
Burbank, CA 91503
Catalog Review offers a catalog of over 175 catalog listings for $3.

U.S. Government Periodicals and Subscription Services Catalog
Free Catalog
P.O. Box 37000
Washington, DC 20013-7000
The U.S. Government Periodicals and Subscription Services Catalog is
published quarterly and available without charge upon request.

Great Catalog Guide.
Direct Marketing Association
11 W. 42nd St.
P.O. Box 3861
New York, NY, 10163-3861
The Great Catalog Guide is a listing of 50 other catalogs available for $3.

International Catalog Collection
144 S. First St., Dept. 5DMI-007
P.O. Box 4013
Burbank, CA 91503
The International Catalog Collection offers a catalog of 140 international
catalogs for $3.

Paper Direct, Inc.
205 Chubb Ave.
P.O. Box 618
Lyndhurst, NJ 07071-0618
(800) 272-7277
(201) 507-0817 (fax)
Paper Direct offers a free catalog featuring its preprinted paper designs.

Quill
P.O. Box 50-050
Ontario, Canada 91761-1050
(909) 988-3200
(708) 634-5708 (fax)
Quill offers a free catalog featuring office supplies and preprinted business
paper and envelopes.

C United States Postal Service information

USPS addresses   Address Change Services
National Address Information Center
U.S. Postal Service
6060 Primacy Pky., Ste. 101
Memphis, TN 38188-0002
(800) 238-3150
Listing of all CASS-certified software manufacturers, including
mainframe software.

Assistant General Counsel
General Administrative Law Division
U.S. Postal Service
475 L'Enfant Plaza SW
Washington, DC 20260-1113

Business Requirements Division
Office of Classification and Rates Administration
U.S. Postal Service
475 L'Enfant Plaza SW
Washington, DC 20260-5365

Citizens Stamp Advisory Committee
Stamp Market Development Branch
U.S. Postal Service
475 L'Enfant Plaza SW
Washington, DC 20260-6753

Consumer Advocate
U.S. Postal Service
475 L'Enfant Plaza SW
Washington, DC 20260-2200

Consumer Protection Division
LAW Department
U.S. Postal Service
475 L'Enfant Plaza SW
Washington, DC 20260-1144

Contracts Branch
National Inventory Control Center
U.S. Postal Service
500 SW Montara Pky.
Topeka, KS 66624-9402
(For die hub requests)

CRIS Customer Fulfillment Requests
Address Information Center
U.S. Postal Service
6060 Primacy Pky., Ste. 101
Memphis, TN 38188-0008

Delivery Management Division
U.S. Postal Service
475 L'Enfant Plaza SW
Washington, DC 20260-7151

Director
Office of Classification and Rates Administration
U.S. Postal Service
475 L'Enfant Plaza SW
Washington, DC 20260-5903

Director
Office of Transportation and International Services
U.S. Postal Service
475 L'Enfant Plaza SW
Washington, DC 20260-7130

Director
Postal Data Center
P.O. Box 80143
St. Louis, MO 63180-9143

Engineering and Development Center
U.S. Postal Service
8403 Lee Hwy.
Merrifield, VA 22082-8101

General Manager
Customer and Field Support Division
Office of Classification and Rates Administration
U.S. Postal Service
475 L'Enfant Plaza SW
Washington, DC 20260-5904

General Manager
Stamp Manufacturing Division
U.S. Postal Service
475 L'Enfant Plaza SW
Washington, DC 20260-6751

Label Printing Center
U.S. Postal Service
500 SW Montara Pky.
Topeka, KS 66624-9502

LAW Department
U.S. Postal Service
475 L'Enfant Plaza SW
Washington, DC 20260-1100

Manager
Claims and Inquiry Branch
Postal Data Center
P.O. Box 14677
St. Louis, MO 63180-9000

Mail Equipment Shops
U.S. Postal Service
2135 Fifth St. NE
Washington, DC 20260-6224

Materiel Distribution Center
U.S. Postal Service
VA Supply Depot
152 Hwy. 206 S.
Somerville, NJ 08877-0001

Materiel Distribution Center
U.S. Postal Service
500 SW Montara Pky.
Topeka, KS 66624-0001

Money Order Branch
Postal Data Center
P.O. Box 82453
St. Louis, MO 63182-9453

MPQC Training Program
National Address Information Center
U.S. Postal Service
6060 Primacy Pky., Ste. 101
Memphis, TN 38188-0001
(800) 331-5746 ext. 640

NSCM Program Manager
U.S. Postal Service
475 L'Enfant Plaza SW
Washington, DC 20260-6757

Office of Licensing
Philatelic and Retail Services Department
U.S. Postal Service
475 L'Enfant Plaza SW
Washington, DC 20260-6700

Official and International Mail Accounting Division (OIMAD)
U.S. Postal Service
475 L'Enfant Plaza SW
Washington, DC 20260-5230

Office of Licensing
Philatelic and Retail Services Department
U.S. Postal Service
475 L'Enfant Plaza SW
Washington, DC 20260-6700

Parts Section
Materiel Distribution Center
U.S. Postal Service
500 SW Montara Pky.
Topeka, KS 66624-0001

Philatelic Marketing Division
Office of Stamps and Philatelic Marketing
U.S. Postal Service
475 L'Enfant Plaza SW
Washington, DC 20260-6755

Philatelic and Retail Services Department
U.S. Postal Service
475 L'Enfant Plaza SW
Washington, DC 20260-6700

Philatelic Sales Division
U.S. Postal Service
8300 NE Underground Dr. Pillar 210
Kansas City, MO 64144-9998

Private Express Liaison Office
Advertising and Account Services Department
U.S. Postal Service
475 L'Enfant Plaza SW
Washington, DC 20260-6332

Procurement Division
Office of Contracts and Property Law
Law Department
U.S. Postal Service
475 L'Enfant Plaza SW
Washington, DC 20260-1122

Recorder
Judicial Office Department
U.S. Postal Service
475 L'Enfant Plaza SW
Washington, DC 20260-6100

Regional Chief Postal Inspector
MOSC Central Region
Main Post Office Bldg. Rm. 712
433 W. Van Buren St.
Chicago, IL 60607-5401

Regional Chief Postal Inspector
MOSC Eastern Region
1 Bala Cynwyd Plaza, Ste. E300
Bala Cynwyd, PA 19004-9000

Regional Chief Postal Inspector
MOSC Northeast Region
Gateway 2 Center, 8th Fl. S.
Commerce & McCarter Highway
Newark, NJ 07175-0001

Regional Chief Postal Inspector
MOSC Southern Region
1407 Union Ave., 10th Fl.
Memphis, TN 38161-0001

Regional Chief Postal Inspector
MOSC Western Region
850 Cherry Ave., 5th Fl.
San Bruno, CA 94098-0100

Superintendent of Government Mails
Washington DC Post Office
900 Brentwood Rd. NE
Washington, DC 20066-9704

Stamped Envelope Unit
U.S. Postal Service
P.O. Box 500
Williamsburg, PA 16693-0500

Superintendent of Documents
P.O. Box 371954
Pittsburgh, PA 15250-7954
(202) 783-3238 (Order by phone, via MasterCard or Visa)
(202) 512-2233 (fax order line)
The U.S. Government Periodicals and Subscription Services Catalog lists the
publications and information available from this office.

D Postal Business Centers

Albany, NY	(518) 869-6526	Long Island, NY	(516) 582-7516
Anchorage, AK	(907) 564-2824	Los Angeles, CA	(213) 586-1843
Atlanta, GA	(404) 717-3440	Louisville, KY	(502) 454-1784
Austin, TX	(512) 929-1465	Manchester, NH	(603) 644-3874
Birmingham, AL	(204) 521-0456	Memphis, TN	(901) 576-2035
Boston, MA	(617) 338-9725	Miami, FL	(305) 470-0803
Chicago, IL	(312) 286-3538	Milwaukee, WI	(414) 287-2528
Dallas, TX	(214) 393-6701	Nashville, TN	(615) 885-9375
Denver, CO	(303) 297-6186	New Brunswick, NJ	(908) 777-0565
Des Moines, IA	(515) 283-7642	New Orleans, LA	(504) 589-1368
Detroit, MI	(313) 961-6574	New York City, NY	(212) 425-2081
Grand Rapids, MI	(616) 776-6144	Newark, NJ	(201) 731-4863
Greensboro, NC	(919) 665-9740	North Suburban IL	(708) 260-5511
Hartford, CT	(203) 525-1490	Northern VA	(703) 207-6800
Honolulu, HI	(808) 423-3925	Oakland, CA	(510) 251-3157
Houston, TX	(713) 226-3349	Oklahoma City, OK	(405) 278-6119
Indianapolis, IN	(317) 464-6270	Omaha, NE	(402) 573-1332
Jackson, MS	(601) 360-2700	Orlando, FL	(407) 826-5695
Jacksonville, FL	(904) 359-2725	Phoenix, AZ	(602) 225-3933
Kansas City, MO	(816) 374-9513	Pittsburgh, PA	(412) 359-7601
Little Rock, AR	(501) 374-9163	Portland, OR	(503) 294-2306
Long Beach, CA	(310) 983-3068	Providence, RI	(401) 276-5038

Queens, NY	(718) 321-5704	Seattle, WA	(206) 442-6006
Richmond, VA	(804) 775-6224	South Suburban, IL	(708) 563-5256
Rochester, NY	(716) 272-7220	Springfield, MA	(413) 731-0306
Sacramento, CA	(916) 923-4357	St. Louis, MO	(314) 534-2678
Salt Lake City, UT	(801) 974-2503	Tampa, FL	(813) 877-0791
San Antonio, TX	(512) 493-0788	Tucson, AZ	(602) 325-9815
San Diego, CA	(619) 574-5241	Twin Cities	(612) 349-4703
San Francisco, CA	(415) 550-6570	Van Nuys, CA	(818) 787-8948
San Jose, CA	(408) 723-6155	Westchester, NY	(914) 345-1237
Santa Ana, CA	(714) 662-6213	Wichita, KS	(316) 946-4615

E Professional organizations & conferences

Direct Marketing Association Headquarters
11 W. 42nd St.
New York, NY 10036-8096
(212) 768-7277
(212) 768-4546 (fax)
The Direct Marketing Association also maintains the consumer services such as the Mail Preference Service and the Telephone Preference Service.

MailCom Conference
P.O. Box 8477
Philadelphia, PA 19101
(607) 746-3450
(607) 746-2750 (fax)
Call for schedule. Sponsored by The Mail Systems Management Association and *Mail: The Journal of Communication Distribution.*

National Postal Form
Non-profit, educational organization that sponsors tradeshows for the mail industry, among other things.
Contact: Communications Department
United States Postal Service
475 L'Enfant Plaza SW
Washington, DC 20260-3100
(202) 268-2341

National Postal Forums
Location and Date:

Minneapolis Convention Center, Minneapolis	September 26–29, 1993
San Francisco Marriott	May 22–25, 1994
Sheraton Washington Hotel, Washington, DC	September 25–28, 1994
Opryland Hotel, Nashville, TN	May 7–10, 1995
Philadelphia Convention Center	August 27–30, 1995
Anaheim, CA	April 21–24, 1996
Sheraton Washington Hotel	August 25–28, 1996

Postal abbreviations

Mail processing abbreviations

Abbreviation	Meaning	Abbreviation	Meaning
3C	Third Class	FCM	First Class Mail
ASF	Auxiliary Service Facility	FLTS	Flats
BMC	Bulk Mail Center	GD	General Delivery Unit
CR	Carrier Route	HC	Highway Contract Route
CR RTS	Carrier Routes	LTRS	Letters
CRIS	Carrier Route Information System	MXD	Mixed
		PO BOX SECT	Post Office Box Section
DDU	Destination Delivery Unit	RR	Rural Route
DG	Digit	SCF	Sectional Center Facility
DIS	Distribution		

State name abbreviations

Abbreviation	State name	Abbreviation	State name
AL	Alabama	GA	Georgia
AK	Alaska	GU	Guam
AS	American Samoa	HI	Hawaii
AZ	Arizona	ID	Idaho
AR	Arkansas	IL	Illinois
CA	California	IN	Indiana
CO	Colorado	IA	Iowa
CT	Connecticut	KS	Kansas
DE	Delaware	KY	Kentucky
DC	District of Columbia	LA	Louisiana
FM	Federal States of Micronesia	ME	Maine
FL	Florida	MH	Marshall Islands

Abbreviation	State name	Abbreviation	State name
MD	Maryland	OR	Oregon
MA	Massachusetts	PW	Belau, formerly Palau
MI	Michigan	PA	Pennsylvania
MN	Minnesota	PR	Puerto Rico
MS	Mississippi	RI	Rhode Island
MO	Missouri	SC	South Carolina
MT	Montana	SD	South Dakota
NE	Nebraska	TN	Tennessee
NV	Nevada	TX	Texas
NH	New Hampshire	UT	Utah
NJ	New Jersey	VT	Vermont
NM	New Mexico	VA	Virginia
NY	New York	VI	Virgin Islands
NC	North Carolina	WA	Washington
ND	North Dakota	WV	West Virginia
MP	Northern Mariana Islands	WI	Wisconsin
OH	Ohio	WY	Wyoming
OK	Oklahoma		

Regional abbreviations

Abbreviation	Description	Abbreviation	Description
CR	Central Region	NE	Northeast Region
ER	Eastern Region	SR	Southern Region
NATL	All Regions	WR	Western Region

Directional abbreviations

N	North	NE	Northeast
E	East	SE	Southeast
S	South	SW	Southwest
W	West	NW	Northwest

Secondary address unit indicators

Abbreviation	Meaning	Abbreviation	Meaning
APT	Apartment	FL	Floor
BLDG	Building	RM	Room
DEPT	Department	STE	Suite

USPS street suffixes

Suffix	USPS abbreviation	Suffix	USPS abbreviation
ALLEE	ALY	ANNX	ANX
ALLEY	ALY	ANX	ANX
ALLY	ALY	ARC	ARC
ALY	ALY	ARCADE	ARC
ANEX	ANX	AV	AVE
ANNEX	ANX		

Suffix	USPS abbreviation	Suffix	USPS abbreviation
AVE	AVE	CAUSWAY	CSWY
AVEN	AVE	CEN	CTR
AVENU	AVE	CENT	CTR
AVENUE	AVE	CENTER	CTR
AVN	AVE	CENTERS	CTR
BAYOO	BYU	CENTR	CTR
BAYOU	BYU	CIR	CIR
BCH	BCH	CIRC	CIR
BEACH	BCH	CIRCL	CIR
BEND	BND	CIRCLE	CIR
BG	BG	CLB	CLB
BLF	BLF	CLF	CLFS
BLUF	BLF	CLFS	CLFS
BLUFF	BLF	CLIFF	CLFS
BLUFFS	BLF	CLIFFS	CLFS
BLVD	BLVD	CLUB	CLB
BND	BND	CMP	CP
BOT	BTM	CNTER	CTR
BOTTM	BTM	CNTR	CTR
BOTTOM	BTM	CNYN	CYN
BOUL	BLVD	COR	COR
BOULEVARD	BLVD	CORNER	COR
BOULV	BLVD	CORNERS	CORS
BR	BR	CORS	CORS
BRANCH	BR	COURSE	CRSE
BRDGE	BRG	COURT	CTWY
BRG	BRG	COURTS	CTS
BRIDGE	BRG	COVE	CV
BRK	BRK	COVES	CV
BRNCH	BR	CP	CP
BROOK	BRK	CRCL	CIR
BROOKS	BRK	CRCLE	CIR
BTM	BTM	CRE	CRE
BURG	BG	CRECENT	CRES
BURGS	BG	CREEK	CRK
BYP	BYP	CRES	CRES
BYPA	BYP	CRESCENT	CRES
BYPAS	BYP	CRESENT	CRES
BYPASS	BYP	CRK	CRK
BYPS	BYP	CROSSING	XING
BYU	BYU	CRSCNT	CRES
CAMP	CP	CRSE	CRES
CANYN	CYN	CRSENT	CRES
CANYON	CYN	CRSNT	CRES
CAPE	CPE	CRSSNG	XING
CAUSEWAY	CSWY	CSWY	CSWY

Suffix	USPS abbreviation	Suffix	USPS abbreviation
CT	CT	FORDS	FRD
CTR	CTR	FOREST	FRST
CTS	CTS	FORESTS	FRST
CV	CV	FORG	FRG
CYN	CYN	FORGE	FRG
DALE	DL	FORGES	FRG
DAM	DM	FORK	FRK
DIV	DV	FORKS	FRKS
DIVIDE	DV	FORT	FT
DL	DL	FRD	FRD
DM	DM	FREEWAY	FWY
DR	DR	FREEWY	FWY
DRIV	DR	FRG	FRG
DRIVE	DR	FRK	FRK
DRIVES	DR	FRKS	FRKS
DRV	DR	FRRY	FRY
DV	DR	FRST	FRST
EST	EST	FRT	FRT
ESTATE	EST	FRWAY	FWY
ESTATES	EST	FRWY	FWY
ESTS	EST	FRY	FRY
EXP	EXPY	FT	FT
EXPR	EXPY	FWY	FWY
EXPRESS	EXPY	GARDEN	GDNS
EXPRESSWAY	EXPY	GARDENS	GDNS
EXPW	EXPY	GARDN	GDNS
EXPY	EXPY	GATEWAY	GTWY
EXT	EXT	GATWAY	GTWY
EXTENSION	EXT	GDN	GDNS
EXTN	EXT	GDNS	GDNS
EXTNSN	EXT	GLEN	GLN
EXTS	EXT	GLENS	GLN
FALL	FALL	GLN	GLN
FALLS	FSL	GRDEN	GDNS
FERRY	FRY	GRDNS	GDNS
FIELD	FLD	GREEN	GRN
FIELDS	FLDS	GREENS	GRN
FL	FL	GRN	GRN
FLAT	FLAT	GROV	GRV
FLATS	FLT	GROVE	GRV
FLD	FLD	GROVES	GRV
FLDS	FLDS	GRV	GRV
FLS	FLS	GTWAY	GTWY
FLT	FLT	GTWY	GTWY
FLTS	FLT	HARB	HBR
FORD	FRD	HARBOR	HBR

Suffix	USPS abbreviation	Suffix	USPS abbreviation
HARBORS	HBR	KNOL	KNLS
HARBR	HBR	KNOLL	KNLS
HAVEN	HVN	KNOLLS	KNLS
HAVN	HVN	KY	KY
HBR	HBR	KYS	KY
HEIGHT	HTS	LAKE	LK
HEIGHTS	HTS	LAKES	LK
HIGHWAY	HWY	LANDING	LNDG
HIGHWY	HWY	LANE	LN
HILL	HL	LANES	LN
HILLS	HLS	LCK	LCKS
HIWAY	HWY	LCKS	LCKS
HIWY	HWY	LDG	LDG
HL	HL	LDGE	LDGE
HLLW	HOLW	LF	LF
HLS	HLS	LGT	LGT
HOLLOW	HOLW	LIGHT	LGT
HOLW	HOLW	LIGHTS	LGT
HOLWS	HOLW	LK	LK
HRBOR	HBRW	LKS	LK
HT	HTS	LN	LN
HTS	HTS	LNDG	LNDG
HVN	HVN	LNDNG	LNDG
HWAY	HWY	LOAF	LF
HWY	HWY	LOCK	LCKS
INLET	INLT	LOCKS	LCKS
INLT	INLT	LODG	LDG
IS	IS	LODGE	LDG
ISLAND	IS	LOOP	LOOP
ISLANDS	ISS	LOOPS	LOOP
ISLANDS	ISS	MALL	MALL
ISLE	ISLE	MANOR	MNR
ISLES	ISLE	MANORS	MNR
ISLND	IS	MDW	MDWS
ISS	ISS	MDWS	MDWS
JCT	JCT	MEADOW	MDWS
JCTION	JCT	MEADOWS	MDWS
JCTN	JCT	MEDOWS	MDWS
JCTNS	JCT	MILL	ML
JCTS	JCT	MILLS	MLS
JUNCTION	JCT	MISSION	MSN
JUNCTN	JCT	MISSN	MSN
KEY	KY	ML	ML
KEYS	KY	MLS	MLS
KNL	KNLS	MNR	MNR
KNLS	KNLS	MNRS	MNR

Suffix	USPS abbreviation		Suffix	USPS abbreviation
MNT	MT		PORT	PRT
MNTAIN	MTN		PORTS	PRT
MNTN	MTN		PR	PR
MNTNS	MTN		PRAIRIE	PR
MOUNT	MT		PRK	PARK
MOUNTAIN	MTN		PRR	PR
MOUNTIN	MTN		PRT	PRT
MSN	MSN		PRTS	PRT
MSSN	MSN		PT	PT
MT	MT		PTS	PT
MTIN	MT		RAD	RADL
MTN	MTN		RADIAL	RADL
NCK	NCK		RADIEL	RADL
NECK	NCK		RADL	RADL
ORCH	ORCH		RANCH	RNCH
ORCHARD	ORCH		RANCHES	RNCH
ORCHRD	ORCH		RAPID	RPDS
OVAL	OVAL		RAPIDS	RPDS
OVL	OVAL		RD	RD
PARK	PARK		RDG	RDG
PARKS	PARK		RDGE	RDG
PARKWAY	PKY		RDS	RD
PARKWY	PKY		REST	RST
PASS	PASS		RIDGE	RDG
PATH	PATH		RIDGES	RDG
PATHS	PATH		RIV	RIV
PIKE	PIKE		RIVER	RIV
PIKES	PIKE		RIVR	RIV
PINE	PNES		RNCH	RNCH
PINES	PNES		RNCHS	RNCH
PKWAY	PKY		ROAD	RD
PKWY	PKY		ROADS	RD
PKWYS	PKY		ROW	ROW
PKY	PKY		RPD	RPDS
PL	PL		RST	RST
PLACE	PL		RUN	RUN
PLAIN	PLN		RVR	RIV
PLAINES	PLNS		SHL	SHL
PLAZA	PLZ		SHLS	SHLS
PLN	PLN		SHOAL	SHL
PLNS	PLNS		SHOALS	SHLS
PLZ	PLZ		SHOAR	SHR
PLZA	PLZ		SHOARS	SHRS
PNES	PNES		SHORE	SHR
POINT	PT		SHORES	SHRS
POINTS	PT		SHR	SHR

Suffix	USPS abbreviation	Suffix	USPS abbreviation
SHRS	SHRS	TRACKS	TRAK
SMT	SMT	TRAFFICWAY	TRFY
SPG	SPG	TRAIL	TRL
SPGS	SPGS	TRAILER	TRLR
SPRING	SPG	TRCE	TRCE
SPRINGS	SPGS	TRK	TRAK
SPRNG	SPG	TRKS	TRAK
SPRNGS	SPGS	TRL	TRL
SPUR	SPUR	TRLR	TRLR
SPURS	SPUR	TRLRS	TRLR
SQ	SQ	TRLS	TRL
SQR	SQ	TRNPK	TPKE
SQRE	SQ	TUNEL	TUNL
SQU	SQ	TUNL	TUNL
SQUARE	SQ	TUNLS	TUNL
SQUARES	SQ	TUNNEL	TUNL
ST	ST	TURNPIKE	TPKE
STA	STA	TURNPK	TPKE
STATION	STA	UN	UN
STATN	STA	UNION	UN
STN	STA	UNIONS	UN
STR	ST	VALLEY	VLY
STR	ST	VALLEYS	VLY
STRA	STRA	VALLY	VLY
STRAV	STRA	VDCT	VIA
STRAVE	STRA	VIA	VIA
STRAVENUE	STRA	VIADCT	VIA
STRAVN	STRA	VIADUCT	VIA
STREAM	STRM	VIEW	VW
STREET	ST	VIEWS	VW
STREETS	ST	VILL	VLG
STREME	STRM	VILLAG	VLG
STRM	STRM	VILLAGE	VLG
STRT	ST	VILLG	VLG
STRVN	STRA	VIS	VIS
STRVNUE	STRA	VIST	VIS
SUMIT	SMT	VISTA	VIS
SUMITT	SMT	VL	VL
TER	TER	VLG	VLG
TERR	TER	VLGS	VLG
TERRACE	TER	VLLY	VLG
TPK	TPKE	VLLY	VLY
TPKE	TPKE	VLY	VLY
TRACE	TRCE	VLYS	VLY
TRACES	TRCE	VST	VIS
TRACK	TRAK	VSTA	VIS

Suffix	USPS abbreviation	Suffix	USPS abbreviation
VW	VW	WELL	WLS
VWS	VW	WELLS	WLS
WALK	WALK	WLS	WLS
WALKS	WALK	WY	WY
WAY	WAY	XING	XING
WAYS	WAY		

Standard Industrial Classification (SIC) codes

These codes were originally devised by the government to classify businesses. The SIC codes also allow mailers to retrieve information on businesses by the category of business. The SIC code is a four-digit code. The first two digits indicate the major group. Subgroups within the major groups are indicated by the first three digits. The four-digit code indicates a single industry, such as 8111 is the SIC code for attorneys.

The information here was in use by the Department of Commerce as of June 1992. This is not a complete listing of the SIC codes, but it is often enough for you to deal with a list broker. A complete list fills an entire book by itself. That book is the *Standard Industrial Classification Manual*, available from the National Technical Information Service, 5285 Port Royal Rd., Springfield, VA 22161. When ordering, ask for number PB 87-100012. Call 703-487-4600.

A	**Agriculture, Forestry, and Fishing**
01	Agriculture Production Crops
011	Cash Grains
013	Field Crops, Except Cash Grains
016	Vegetables and Melons
017	Fruits and Tree Nuts
018	Horticultural Specialties
019	General Farms, Primarily Crop
02	Agricultural Production Livestock
021	Livestock, Except Dairy and Poultry
024	Dairy Farms
025	Poultry and Eggs
027	Animal Specialties
029	General Farms, Primarily Animal

07		Agricultural Services
	071	Soil Preparation Services
	072	Crop Services
	074	Veterinary Services
	075	Animal Services, Except Veterinary
	076	Farm Labor and Management Services
	078	Landscape and Horticultural Services
08		Forestry
	081	Timber Tracts
	083	Forest Products
	085	Forestry Services
09		Fishing, Hunting, and Trapping
	091	Commercial Fishing
	092	Fish Hatcheries and Preserves
	097	Hunting, Trapping, Game Propagation

B **Mining**

10		Metal Mining
	101	Iron Ores
	102	Copper Ores
	103	Lead and Zinc Ores
	104	Gold and Silver Ores
	106	Ferroalloy Ores, Except Vanadium
	108	Metal Mining Services
	109	Miscellaneous Metal Ores
12		Coal Mining
	122	Bituminous Coal and Lignite Mining
	123	Anthracite Mining
	124	Coal Mining Services
13		Oil and Gas Extraction
	131	Crude Petroleum and Natural Gas
	132	Natural Gas Liquids
	138	Oil and Gas Field Services
14		Nonmetallic Minerals, Except Fuels
	141	Dimension Stone
	142	Crushed and Broken Stone
	144	Sand and Gravel
	145	Clay, Ceramic, & Refractory Minerals
	147	Chemical and Fertilizer Minerals
	148	Nonmetallic Minerals Services
	149	Miscellaneous Nonmetallic Minerals

C **Construction**

15		General Building Contractors
	152	Residential Building Construction
	153	Operative Builders
	154	Nonresidential Building Construction

G   **Retail Trade**

561	Men's & Boys' Clothing Stores
562	Women's Clothing Stores
563	Women's Accessory & Specialty Stores
564	Children's and Infants' Wear Stores
565	Family Clothing Stores
566	Shoe Stores
569	Misc. Apparel & Accessory Stores
57	Furniture and Home Furnishings Stores
571	Furniture and Home Furnishings Stores
572	Household Appliance Stores
573	Radio, Television, & Computer Stores
58	Eating and Drinking Places
581	Eating and Drinking Places
59	Miscellaneous Retail
591	Drug Stores and Proprietary Stores
592	Liquor Stores
593	Used Merchandise Stores
594	Miscellaneous Shopping Goods Stores
596	Nonstore Retailers
598	Fuel Dealers
599	Retail Stores

H	**Finance, Insurance, and Real Estate**
60	Depository Institutions
601	Central Reserve Depository
602	Commercial Banks
603	Savings Institutions
606	Credit Unions
608	Foreign Bank & Branches + Agencies
609	Functions Closely Related to Banking
61	Nondepository Institutions
611	Federal & Fed.-Sponsored Credit
614	Personal Credit Institutions
615	Business Credit Institutions
616	Mortgage Bankers and Brokers
62	Security and Commodity Brokers
621	Security Brokers and Dealers
622	Commodity Contracts Brokers, Dealers
623	Security and Commodity Exchanges
628	Security and Commodity Services
63	Insurance Companies
631	Life Insurance
632	Medical Service and Health Insurance
633	Fire, Marine, and Casualty Insurance
635	Surety Insurance
636	Title Insurance

H Direct Marketing Association Guidelines

Reprinted with permission from the Direct Marketing Association from *The Direct Marketing Association's Ethical Business Practices, Mailing List Practices, and the Fair Information Practices Checklist.*

Mail list practices

I. General

All involved in the transfer, rental, sale, or exchange of mailing lists—owners, managers compilers, brokers, and users, and their suppliers and agents—should follow these guidelines.

Accuracy in Description of Lists: Article #1

All concerned should fairly, objectively, and accurately describe each list, particularly with respect to its content, age of names, selections offered, quantity, source, and owner.

Advertising Claims: Article #2

Before and at the time of distributing a list data card or promoting or advertising a list as available for rental, those who promote the list should be prepared to substantiate any claims they make and should avoid any untrue, misleading, deceptive, or fraudulent statements and any references that disparage competitors or those on the list.

Screening of Offers/List Usage: Article #3

All involved should establish and agree upon the exact nature of a list's intended usage prior to the transfer or permission to use the list. Samples of all intended mailings should be reviewed by all involved in the rental process, and only approved material should be used in the mailing, and on an agreed-upon date. Lists should not be transferred or used for an offer that is believed to be in violation of any of the DMA *Guidelines for Ethical Business Practices*.

Protection of Lists: Article #4

All those involved with a list transaction should be responsible for the proper use of list data and should take appropriate measures to assure against unauthorized access, alteration, or dissemination of list data. Those who have access to such data should agree in advance to use those data only in an authorized manner.

One-Time Usage: Article #5

Unless agreement to the contrary is first obtained from the list owner, a mailing list transaction permits the use of a list for one time only. Except for respondents to its own mailing, a list user and its agents may not transfer names or information to its own customer files or recontact names derived from a rented or exchanged list, or provide the names for another to make such contact, without prior authorization.

DMA Mail Preference Service/Name Removal Options: Article #6

Consumers who provide data that may be rented, sold, or exchanged for direct marketing purposes should be periodically informed of the potential for the rental, sale, or exchange of such data. Marketers should offer a means by which a consumer's name may be deleted or suppressed upon request.

List compilers should suppress names from lists when requested by the individual.

For each list that is to be rented, sold or exchanged, the DMA Mail Preference Service name-removal list and, when applicable, the Telephone Preference Service name-removal list should be used. Names found on such suppression lists should not be transferred except for suppression purposes.

All persons involved in the rental, sale, or exchange of lists and data should take reasonable steps to ensure that industry members follow these guidelines.

Purposes of Lists/List Data: Article #7

Lists should consist only of those data that are appropriate for marketing purposes. Direct marketers should transfer, rent, sell, or exchange lists only for those purposes.

List Data/Privacy: Article #8

Direct marketers should be sensitive to the issue of consumer privacy and should limit the combination, collection, rental, sale, exchange, and use of consumer data to only those data that are appropriate for direct marketing purposes.

Information and selection criteria that may be considered to be personal and intimate in nature by all reasonable standards should not provide the basis for lists to be made available for rental, sale, or exchange when there is a reasonable expectation by the consumer that the information would be kept confidential.

Any advertising or promotion for lists being offered for rental, sale, or exchange should reflect the fact that a list is an aggregate collection of marketing data. Such promotions should also reflect a sensitivity for the consumers on those lists.

Laws, Codes, Regulations, and Guidelines: Article #9
Direct marketers should operate in accordance with all applicable laws, codes, and regulations and with DMA's various guidelines as published from time to time.

II. Considerations for mailing list transactions
Mailing list transactions are controlled by the legal principles affecting contracts. As such, mutual understanding, good faith, clear communication, defined terms and a meeting of the minds are imperative. To that end, a list of factors to be considered when entering into a mailing list transaction has been developed to assist contracting parties in developing a clear understanding of their respective rights and obligations as well as to help avoid the problems that typically ensue as a result of misunderstanding.

The list of factors that follows is not intended to be exhaustive, nor is it intended to dictate the terms of any agreement. Rather, it is presented to raise pertinent questions so that they may be addressed properly and adequately by the parties. The list of factors may be modified from time to time as trends develop in the industry or as technology or list usage changes.

1. Identification of All Parties to the Transaction
   - Has each party to the transaction been identified by proper name and address?
   - Are there other parties involved besides the list owner and list user (e.g., list broker, list manager, list compiler, or service bureau)?
     ○ Have these other parties been properly identified?
     ○ Is the scope of authority of these third parties understood?
     ○ Should each of these third parties agree to be bound by the list agreement?
2. What Is Being Transferred?
   - Is the agreement intended to be comprehensive?
     ○ Is any unspecified activity prohibited unless permitted?
     ○ Is any unspecified activity permitted unless prohibited?
   - Is the transaction an outright sale or assignment of the list?
   - Is the transaction an exchange or trade for the use of another list?
   - Is the transaction a rental or one-time permission to use?
   - May the user add information to the rented list before using it (e.g., telephone numbers)?

- Does adding information to the rented list change its nature?
- Who owns the enhanced list after information has been added to it?
3. What Constitutes Use?
    - May the user merge-purge the list with other rented lists?
    - Is the user permitted to add names that appear on more than one owner's list to its own list?
    - May the user code or tag its own file with information derived from a rented list when the rented list contains names that already appear on the user's list?
    - May the user impose its own "qualifications" on a list, return the names that do not "qualify," and receive a refund?
        - ○ Does it matter what the qualifier is (e.g., names on more than one list, a particular carrier route, certain demographics)?
        - ○ Is it all right if the list owner "qualifies" the list prior to rental?
    - May the user send "address correction requested" mail and retain results?
4. What Constitutes One-Time Use?
    - May the rented list be used a second time in a different medium (e.g., telephone)?
    - May the user mail to a name on a list one time for each rented list the name appears on?
        - ○ Does it matter whether each list owner was paid for the name?
        - ○ Does it matter whether multiple mailings to the same name are related (e.g., part of a series of mailings)?
        - ○ Does it matter what the time period is between mailings?
    - May the list user or its service bureau retain names that appear on one or more rented lists for comparison with future rentals?
    - May the list user do so to suppress names from future mailings to the same rented list?
    - May the user do so for non-list specific data?
    - Are there any additional purposes for which the rented list may be retained?
5. The Method of and Basis for Payment
    - How many names are being rented?
    - What are the allowances, if any, for duplicates, undeliverables, etc.?
    - Is there a special request or selection to be satisfied?
    - What is the price (e.g., dollars per thousand names)?
    - Has sales tax, if any, been accounted for?
    - Is there a broker or manager involved?
        - ○ To whom is payment sent?
        - ○ Are commissions spelled out?
    - Is there a net name agreement?
        - ○ Are the terms clear?
        - ○ Is there a provision for verification?
        - ○ Have duplicates and multibuyers been removed or accounted for?
    - Is there a reuse discount?
    - Have the payment terms been clearly set forth and agreed upon?

6. What is to be Received, Where and When?
   - What is the format of the rental (e.g., tapes, labels)?
   - How much information will physically appear on tapes or labels (e.g., name and address, address only, with zip + 4)?
   - Where and when is the list to be shipped?
     - Who is at risk for failure to satisfy this provision?
     - Upon whom does loss fall if damaged in transit?
     - Upon whom does loss fall if mailing dates cannot be kept?
   - Are there any guarantees on deliverability?
7. Approval of the Mailing and Date
   - Does the list owner have the right to approve the mailing?
   - Must each phase of a staged or sequenced mailing (e.g., catalog followed by gift certificate followed by personalized letter) be approved?
   - Has the mailing date been approved?
   - Must the list user notify the list owner if the date is to be changed?
8. Impact on Others
   - Does the user have the right to prohibit the rental of a list competitive mailing for a specified time period before and after the user's mailing date?
   - Do the parties employ a name-removal option, or DMA's Mail Preference Service or, where applicable, Telephone Preference Service for the protection of those on the list?
   - Is the list being used only for a marketing purpose?
   - Has the list been seeded?
   - May the user refer to the source of the list in any promotion?
   - Is it clear that the user becomes an owner of all respondents?

III. Suggestions for advertising acceptance

When a decision is made to make your list available in the List Rental marketplace, you are accepting the responsibility for the advertising your customer will see. Most list owners who rent their list to others understand they are "licensing" their most valuable asset for monetary consideration. Protecting the value of that asset is what these guidelines are all about.

As a list professional, the establishment of an adherence to strict ad acceptance standards not only protects your relationship with your customers, it can save your firm countless dollars. Frequently, companies that defraud consumers also defraud their suppliers.

A typical question asked by many list professionals involves the legal liabilities involved in denying a company access to a mailing list. A mailing list transaction is a matter of contract. Generally speaking, one is free to decide with whom one wants to conduct business. Thus, if one exercises his own independent judgment, he is free to deal or not to deal with whomever he chooses without incurring legal liability.

These recommendations do not deal with the legalities of advertising procedures but rather with their ethics. Nor do they deal with the do's and don'ts of technical copywriting. They do deal with DMA's desire to promote more honesty in mail-order advertising, more credibility in the eyes of consumers, and consequently, generate more business for direct marketing professionals.

While each advertisement must be evaluated on an individual basis, there are warning signs that may signal a fraudulent promotion. If the initial order is large, was "too easy to get," and/or was not preceded by a test, the list professional should carefully evaluate the offer by following these suggestions:

1. If the offer is unclear to you, it will be equally unclear to the recipient. If you have read the copy twice, and you still don't know the exact nature of what is being offered, insist on clarification of the copy. The mere act of requesting additional information may deter some unscrupulous advertisers.

2. Make yourself the surrogate reader. Are the copy claims outlandish or are they too strong to be believable? Be particularly wary of ads that claim to cure physical ills such as arthritis, obesity, sexual impotence, cancer, or hair loss.

3. Taste is a subjective matter, and each list professional must decide what is in good or bad taste for his audience. However, as a representative of the list owner, or as the list owner, you have a responsibility to ask for a new illustration or change of copy before you approve copy for a mailing.

4. The list professional should know the street address and telephone number of every advertiser. In many cities, post office box numbers must be accompanied by a street address. Be aware that mail receiving agencies are sometimes used by fraudulent advertisers to appear legitimate. The list broker should become acquainted with such addresses. Finally, if the company is very small, know the address and telephone number of the principal.

5. Be extremely careful of advertisements with no address which require the use of toll free number and charge card to order merchandise. This method of payment is often an attempt to avoid use of the mails to circumvent the jurisdiction of the United States Postal Service.

6. Another warning sign aimed directly at the list professional is payment for advertising with insufficient funds or account closed check. This disregard for ethical business practice may signal that the promoter has a similar outlook regarding responsibility to maintain truth in advertising.

7. Deceptive marketers may lull list owners into a false sense of security by placing several small orders, mailing the approved piece, and then asking for a large order for a mailing that may not meet your company's guidelines. The use of seeds or decoy names to confirm the list was mailed to the appropriate piece may be helpful in detecting such misuse.

8. When in doubt, list professionals should ask for a sample of the merchandise. Be careful that the sample is an actual production sample and not a handmade mockup. If the advertiser cannot submit the sample before the closing date, you should consider declining the order.

If you have suspicions regarding the offer, you may want to verify past performance of the company with such agencies as the Better Business Bureau, local consumer agencies and the United States Postal Inspection Service. These agencies can be a source of information and may aid in the decision of whether to accept a list order. These agencies may also be helpful if your company has been defrauded by a deceptive advertiser.

In addition to the consumer agencies which can provide list professionals with information on the history, business practices and general reputation of a firm submitting questionable advertising, DMA may be able to provide assistance in evaluating ad copy by providing you with a copy of *DMA Guidelines for Ethical Business Practice*.

Lists   I. Direct marketers should subscribe to DMA's Mail Preference Service and Telephone Preference Service

A primary focus of the DMA guidelines pertaining to privacy is on marketers' data gathering and list rental practices. The guidelines also discuss allowing consumers the opportunity to opt out of having their names rented or exchanged.

That's why in 1971 DMA's Mail Preference Service (MPS) name removal file was established in answer to increased consumer and regulatory concerns regarding personal privacy. A companion service, the Telephone Preference Service (TPS), was established in January, 1985, as an answer to increased consumer complaints and regulatory concerns regarding the usage of the telephone to market goods.

In 1977, the Presidentially appointed Privacy Protection Study Commission recognized MPS as a legitimate and effective alternative to legislation. The Commission encouraged direct marketers to give people on lists an opportunity to indicate they do not wish their names made available to outside sources for marketing purposes. DMA supported this effort in its "Freedom To Mail" campaign.

Direct marketers have long utilized in-house name removal options, or suppression files, so that consumers could enjoy the convenience of shopping by mail, while at the same time controlling access to their names for promotional use. Telephone marketers also use in-house suppression.

Your company's opt out program is important to good customer relations. The following questions should prove helpful in evaluating your policies.

A. 1. Does your company offer your customers name removal options?
2. Are they effectively communicated?

B. 1. Does your company see to it that MPS names are removed prior to list rentals or exchanges?
2. If not, does your company's service bureau subscribe to MPS directly?

C. 1. Does your company see to it that TPS names are removed prior to calling?
2. If not, does your company's service bureau subscribe to TPS directly?

II. Direct marketers should employ security measures

A. 1. Is there someone in your company responsible for list security? Who?

B. 1. Are your lists physically secure?
2. Are there sufficient restrictions on your employees to protect against unauthorized access?
3. Does your company instruct your employees that customer data are confidential? Are employees aware of personal or civil liability for misuse?
4. Are there security measures in place that would prevent remote access to your list via computer?

C. 1. Does your company see to it that security measures are in place during the transfer of lists?
2. Is your company satisfied that the recipient of your lists employs sufficient safeguards?
3. Are there measures in place that assure the secure and timely return or destruction of your lists?

D. 1. Does your company employ a monitoring system to track list usage?

List security practices

III. Data should be collected by fair and lawful means

A. 1. Is there someone responsible for keeping up to date on current fair trade and credit reporting laws and regulations? Who?

B. Regarding the sources of information used to create your lists:
1. Where was the information derived: a) internally, b) from public sources, c) purchased or rented from an outside source?

IV. Customer marketing data should be collected and used for marketing purposes only

A. 1. Is your company collecting only those marketing data that are pertinent and necessary for marketing purposes?
2. In using data, are you sensitive to a consumer's reasonable expectation that some information may be considered confidential and should not be used for marketing purposes?

B. 1. Does your company contribute customer data to a cooperative database? Are you satisfied about the database's security provisions to prevent misuse or unauthorized usage?

V. Customer data should be accurate

A. 1. Does your company have the means to update its customer data?

2. Are customer data reviewed and revised by your company on a regular basis?

3. Are customer inquiries regarding data accuracy answered promptly and to the customer's satisfaction?

Ethical business practices

The terms of the offer

Honesty: Article #1

All offers should be clear, honest, and complete so that the consumer may know the exact nature of what is being offered, the price, the terms of payment (including all extra charges), and the commitment involved in the placing of an order. Before publication of an offer, direct marketers should be prepared to substantiate any claims or offers made. Advertisements or specific claims which are untrue, misleading, deceptive, fraudulent, or unjustly disparaging of competitors should not be used.

Clarity: Article #2

A simple statement of all the essential points of the offer should be clearly displayed in the promotional material. When an offer illustrates goods that are not included or that cost extra, these facts should be made clear.

Print Size: Article #3

Print which by its small size, placement, or other visual characteristics is likely to substantially affect the legibility of the offer or exceptions to it should not be used.

Actual Conditions: Article #4

All descriptions and promises should be in accordance with actual conditions, situations, and circumstances existing at the time of the promotion. Claims regarding any limitations (such as time or quantity) should be legitimate.

Disparagement: Article #5

Disparagement of any person or group on grounds of race, color, religion, national origin, sex, marital status, or age is unacceptable.

Standards: Article #6

Solicitations should not contain vulgar, immoral, profane, or offensive matter nor promote the sale of pornographic material or other matter not acceptable for advertising on moral grounds.

Advertising to Children: Article #7

Offers suitable for adults only should not be made to children.

Photographs and Art Work: Article #8

Photographs, illustrations, artwork, and the situations they represent should be accurate portrayals and current reproductions of the products, services, or other subjects in all particulars.

Sponsor and Intent: Article #9

All direct marketing contacts should disclose the name of the sponsor and each purpose of the contact. No one should make offers or solicitations in the guise of research or a survey when the real intent is to sell products or services or to raise funds.

Identity of Seller: Article #10

Every offer and shipment should sufficiently identify the name and street address of the direct marketer so that the consumer may contact the individual or company by mail or phone.

Solicitation in the Guise of an Invoice: Article #11

Offers that are likely to be mistaken for bills or invoices should not be used.

Postage and Handling Charges: Article #12

Postage or shipping charges, or handling charges, if any, should reflect as accurately as practicable actual costs incurred.

Special offers

Use of the Word "Free" and other Similar Representations: Article #13

A product or service which is offered without cost or obligation to the recipient may be unqualifiedly described as "free."

If a product or service is offered as "free," for a nominal cost, or at greatly reduced price, and/or if the offer requires the recipient to purchase some other product or service, all terms and conditions should be clearly and conspicuously disclosed, in close conjunction with the use of the term "free" or other similar phrase.

When the term "free" is used or other similar representations are made (for example, 2-for-1, half-price or 1-cent offers), the product or service required to be purchased should not have been increased in price or decreased in quality or quantity.

Negative Option Selling: Article #14

All direct marketers should comply with the FTC regulation governing Negative Option Plans. Some of the major requirements of this regulation are as follows:

Offers which require the consumer to return a notice sent by the seller before each periodic shipment to avoid receiving merchandise should contain all important conditions of the plan including:

A. A full description of the obligation to purchase a minimum number of items and all the charges involved, and

B. The procedures by which the consumer will receive the announcements of selections, and a statement of their frequency, as well as how to reject unwanted items, and how to cancel after completing the obligation.

The consumer should be given advance notice of the periodic selection so that the consumer may have a minimum of ten days to exercise a timely choice.

Because of the nature of this kind of offer, special attention should be given to the clarity, completeness, and prominent placement of the terms of the initial offering.

Sweepstakes

Sweepstakes, as defined here, are promotional devices by which items of value (prizes) are awarded to participants by chance without the promoter's requiring them to render something of value to be eligible to participate (consideration). The coexistence of all three elements—prize, chance, and consideration—in the same promotion constitutes a lottery. It is illegal for any private enterprise to run a lottery.

When skill replaces chance, the promotion becomes a skill contest. When gifts (premiums or other items of value) are given to all participants independent of the element of chance, the promotion is not a sweepstakes and should not be held out as such.

Violations of the anti-lottery laws are policed and enforced at the federal level by the United States Postal Service, the Federal Communications Commission (when broadcast advertising is involved), and the Federal Trade Commission. Because sweepstakes are also regulated on a state-by-state basis, and the laws and definitions may vary by state, it is recommended that an attorney familiar with and experienced in the laws of sweepstakes be consulted before a sponsor conducts its promotion.

While this section of the Guidelines may focus on the promotional aspects of running a sweepstakes, it is equally important that the operation and administration of the sweepstakes be conducted in compliance with the ethical standards set forth in other sections as well.

Use of the Term "Sweepstakes": Article #15
Only those promotional devices which satisfy the definition stated above should be called or held out to be a sweepstakes.

No-Purchase Option: Article #16
The no-purchase option as well as the method for entering without ordering should be clearly disclosed. Response devices used only for entering the sweepstakes should be as visible as those utilized for ordering the product or service.

Prizes: Article #17

Sweepstakes prizes should be advertised in a manner that is clear, honest, and complete so that the consumer may know the exact nature of what is being offered.

Photographs, illustrations, artwork, and the situations they represent should be accurate portrayals of the prizes listed in the promotion.

No award should be held forth directly or by implication as having substantial monetary value if it is of nominal worth. The value of a prize given should be stated at regular retail value, whether actual cost to the sponsor is greater or less.

Prizes should be delivered without cost to the participant. If there are certain conditions under which a prize or prizes will not be awarded, this fact should be disclosed in a manner that is easy to find and understand.

Premium: Article #18

If a premium, gift, or item of value is offered by virtue of a participant's merely entering a sweepstakes, without any selection process taking place, it should be clear that everyone will receive it.

Chances of Winning: Article #19

No sweepstakes promotion, or any of its parts, should state or imply that a recipient has won a prize when this is not the case.

Winners should be selected in a manner that ensures fair application of the laws of chance.

Disclosure of Rules: Article #20

All terms and conditions of the sweepstakes, including entry procedures and rules, should be easy to find, read, and understand.

The following should be set forth clearly in the rules:

A. No purchase of the advertised product or service is required in order to win a prize.

B. Procedures for entry.

C. If applicable, disclosure that a facsimile of the entry blank or promotional device may be used to enter the sweepstakes.

D. The termination date for eligibility in the sweepstakes. The termination date should specify whether it is a date of mailing or receipt of entry deadline.

E. The number, retail value, and complete description of all prizes offered, and whether cash may be awarded instead of merchandise. If a cash prize is to be awarded by installment payments, that fact should be clearly disclosed, along with the nature and timing of the payments.

F. The approximate odds of winning a prize or a statement that such odds depend on number of entrants.

G. The method by which winners will be selected.

H. The geographic area covered by the sweepstakes and those areas in which the offer is void.

I. All eligibility requirements, if any.

J. Approximate dates when winners will be selected and notified.

K. Publicity rights are the use of winner's name.

L. Taxes are the responsibility of the winner.

M. Provision of a mailing address to allow consumers to submit a self-addressed, stamped envelope to receive a list of winners of prizes over $25.00 in value.

Price Comparisons: Article #21

Price comparisons may be made two ways:

A. Between one's price and a former, future, or suggested price.

B. Between one's price and the price of a competitor's comparable product.

In all price comparisons, the compared price against which the comparison is made should be fair and accurate.

In each case of comparison to a former, suggested, or competitor's comparable product price, substantial sales should have been made at that price in the recent past.

For comparisons with a future price, there should be a reasonable expectation that the new price will be charged in the foreseeable future.

Guarantees: Article #22

If a product or service is offered with a "guarantee," or a "warranty," either the terms and conditions should be set forth in full in the promotion, or the promotion should state how the consumer may obtain a copy. The guarantee should clearly state the name and address of the guarantor and the duration of the guarantee.

Any requests for repair, replacement, or refund under the terms of a "guarantee" or "warranty" should be honored promptly. In an unqualified offer of refund, repair, or replacement, the customer's preference shall prevail.

Special claims

Use of Test or Survey Data: Article #23

All test or survey data referred to in advertising should be competent and reliable as to source and methodology, and should support the specific claim for which it is cited. Advertising claims should not distort the test or survey results nor take them out of context.

Testimonials and Endorsements: Article #24
Testimonials and endorsements should be used only if they are:

A. Authorized by the person quoted,

B. Genuine and related to the experience of the person giving them, and

C. Not taken out of context so as to distort the endorser's opinion or experience with the product.

The product

Product Safety: Article #25
Products should be safe in normal use and free of defects likely to cause injury. To that end, they should meet or exceed the current, recognized health and safety norms, and should be adequately tested, when applicable. Information provided with the product should include proper directions for its use and full instructions covering assembly and safety warnings, whenever necessary.

Product Distribution Safety: Article #26
Products should be distributed only in a manner that will provide reasonable safeguards against possibilities of injury.

Product Availability: Article #27
Direct marketers should offer merchandise only when it is on hand or when there is a reasonable expectation of its receipt.

Direct marketers should not engage in dry testing unless that special nature of the offer is disclosed in the promotion.

Fulfillment

Unordered Merchandise: Article #28
Merchandise should not be shipped without having first received the customer's permission. The exceptions are samples or gifts clearly marked as such, and merchandise mailed by a charitable organization soliciting contributions, as long as all items are sent with a clear and conspicuous statement informing the recipient of an unqualified right to treat the product as a gift and to do with it as the recipient sees fit, at no cost or obligation to the recipient.

Shipments: Article #29
Direct marketers are reminded that they should abide by the FTC regulation regarding the prompt shipment of prepaid merchandise, the Mail-Order Merchandise (Thirty-Day) Rule.

Beyond this regulation, direct marketers are urged to ship all orders as soon as possible.

Credit and debt collection

Equal Credit Opportunity: Article #30

A creditor should not discriminate on the basis of race, color, religion, national origin, sex, marital status, or age. If an individual is rejected for credit, the creditor should be prepared to give reasons why.

Debt Collection: Article #31

Unfair, misleading, deceptive or abusive methods should not be used for collecting money. The direct marketer should take reasonable steps to assure that those collecting on the direct marketer's behalf comply with this guideline.

Use of mailing lists

List Rental Practices: Article #32

Consumers who provide data that may be rented, sold or exchanged for direct marketing purposes periodically should be informed of the potential for the rental, sale, or exchange of such data. Marketers should offer an opportunity to have a consumer's name deleted or suppressed upon request.

List compilers should suppress names from lists when requested by the individual.

For each list that is to be rented, sold or exchanged, the DMA Mail Preference Service name-removal list and, when applicable, the DMA Telephone Preference Service name-removal list should be used. Names found on such suppression lists should not be rented, sold, or exchanged, except for suppression purposes.

All persons involved in the rental, sale, or exchange of lists and data should take reasonable steps to ensure that industry members follow these guidelines.

Personal Information: Article #33

Direct marketers should be sensitive to the issue of consumer privacy and should omit the combination, collection, rental, sale, exchange and use of consumer data to only those data which are appropriate for direct marketing purposes.

Information and selection criteria that may be considered to be personal and intimate in nature by all reasonable standards should not provide the basis for lists made available for rental, sale, or exchange when there is a reasonable expectation by the consumer that the information will be kept confidential.

Any advertising or promotion for lists being offered for rental, sale, or exchange should reflect the fact that a list is an aggregate collection of marketing data. Such promotions should also reflect a sensitivity for the consumers on those lists.

List Usage Agreements: Article #34

List owners, brokers, compilers, and users should make every attempt to establish the exact nature of the list's intended usage prior to the sale or rental of the list. Owners, brokers, and compilers should not permit the sale or rental of their lists for an offer that is in violation of any of the Ethical Guidelines of DMA. Promotions should be directed to those segments of the public most likely to be interested in their causes or to have a use for their products or services.

List Abuse: Article #35

No list or list data should be used in violation of the lawful rights of the list owner nor the agreement between the parties; any such misuse should be brought to the attention of the lawful owner.

Telephone marketing

(See also Article #9 and #29)

Reasonable Hours: Article #36

All telephone contacts should be made during reasonable hours.

Taping of Conversations: Article #37

Taping of telephone conversations made for telephone marketing purposes should not be conducted without legal notice to or consent of all parties, or the use of a beeping device.

Telephone Name Removal/Restricted Contacts: Article #38

Telephone marketers should remove the name of any customer from their telephone lists when requested by the individual. Marketers should use the DMA Telephone Preference Service name-removal list and, when applicable, the Mail Preference Service name-removal list. Names found on such suppression lists should not be rented, sold, or exchanged, except for suppression purposes.

A telephone marketer should not knowingly call anyone who has an unlisted or unpublished telephone number, except in instances where the number was provided by the customer to that marketer.

Random dialing techniques, whether manual or automated, in which identification of those parties to be called is left to chance should not be used in sales and marketing solicitations.

Sequential dialing techniques, whether a manual or automated process, in which selection of those parties to be called is based on the location of their telephone numbers in a sequence of telephone numbers should not be used.

Disclosure and Tactics: Article #39

All telephone solicitations should disclose to the buyer, during the conversation, the cost of the merchandise, all terms conditions and the payment plan, and whether there will be postage and handling charges. At no time should "high pressure" tactics be utilized.

Use of Automatic Electronic Equipment: Article #40
No telephone marketer should solicit sales using automatic electronic dialing equipment unless the telephone immediately disconnects when the called person hangs up.

Fund-raising
(See also Article #28)

Commission Prohibition/Authenticity of Organization: Article #41
Fund-raisers should make no percentage of commission arrangements whereby any person or firm assisting or participating in a fund-raising activity is paid a fee proportionate to the funds raised, nor should they solicit for non-functioning organizations.

Laws, Codes, and Regulations: Article #42
Direct marketers should operate in accordance with the Better Business Bureau's Code of Advertising and be cognizant of and adhere to laws and regulations of the United States Postal Service, the Federal Trade Commission, the Federal Reserve Board, and other applicable federal, state, and local laws governing advertising, marketing practices, and the transaction of business by mail, telephone, and the print and broadcast media.

Glossary

9-track tape   A format for data transfer used in the mainframe computing world and widely used by corporations and government.

ACS (Address Correction Service)   A service offered by the USPS so list owners can find out the correct addresses of the members of their list.

Advanced POSTNET   An 11-digit POSTNET barcode which includes the zip+4 and the last two digits of the street address. See also *zip+4*. This is the only type of barcode currently accepted for automation discounts.

ASCII (American Standard Code for Information Interchange)
Pronounced "ask-ee," this is a table that translates characters displayed on the screen or in print to their numeric representation for use by the computer.

barcode sorter (BCS)   A piece of equipment used by the USPS to automate the processing of mail. The barcode sorter reads the barcode printed on mail and sorts it accordingly.

BRM (Business Reply Mail)   A recipient-paid reply mail format.

BRMAS (Business Reply Mail Accounting System)   A type of business reply mail permit offered to heavy users of business reply mail.

byte   A basic measure of space on a computer, either on disk or in memory. One byte is composed of eight bits and is the amount of memory required to represent a single character.

CANDVS (Customer Advance Notification Distribution Verification Service)   If you deal with carrier route presort "dated mailings," the USPS can verify the carrier distribution to the recipients of your mailings. Basically, your only requirement is to provide advance notice of planned mailings.

continuation   Mailing to the remainder of a list once you have tested a portion of the list.

CRM (Courtesy Reply Mail)   A sender paid reply mail format.

database A database is a system that organizes information to serve a particular purpose.

DMA The Direct Marketing Association.

DOS (Disk Operating System) The software that controls the hardware on the computer such as the hard disk and is used by all applications software to perform tasks such as writing information on the hard disk.

DMM (Domestic Mail Manual) The bible of the USPS in which all the regulations for mailing are explained.

EBCDIC (Extended Binary Coded Decimal Interchange Code) Pronounced "ebb-sa-dik," this table is used for the basic representation of characters on mini- and mainframe computers.

FCM First-Class Mail.

field Used to store the attribute of an entity within a table and might also be called a column.

FIM (Facing Identification Mark) The mark used to orient the envelope for processing by USPS automated equipment.

fonts Styles and sizes of lettering used in typesetting.

formatting The addition of characters, usually outside those on the computer keyboard, to indicate special functions to the printer and to the program.

franking The practice of sending mail without charge, usually used by the government.

gigabyte A measure of space, either on the disk or in memory. A gigabyte is 1,073,741,824 bytes, although most people just round to 1 billion bytes.

GUI (Graphical User Interface) A user interface, such as Microsoft Windows, that uses a mouse to point and click graphical representations of commands rather than the remember-and-type approach found in the DOS command line.

index Used in a relational database to organize the information in a table so that information within the table can be found quickly.

Indicia An imprint that can be printed on mail by a postal permit holder instead of placing stamps or metering the mail.

kerning The process in typesetting of moving individual letters closer together for appearance's sake.

key field A field within a relational database table that is used to build an index and identify the rows within the database. When a key uniquely identifies the row, such as a social security number, it is called the primary key.

megabyte   A measure of space, either on the disk or in memory. A megabyte is 1,048,576 bytes, although it is often rounded to 1 million bytes.

megahertz   A measurement of speed.

memory   Memory generally refers to the computer's working memory, called random access memory (RAM), though portions of the computer's hard disk can also be set aside for use as memory.

MPS (Mail Preference Service)   A service offered by the Direct Marketing Association to consumers who do not wish to have their names on mailing lists. See also *TPS*.

NCOA (National Change of Address)   A central pool of all the change of address information offered to the USPS by moving customers is maintained. Mailers may have their mailing list compared to the NCOA in order to update their lists.

NDI (National Deliverability Index)   NDI is a rating based on the number of undeliverable addresses in the list. See also *nixies*.

nixies   Undeliverable mail returned by the post office.

non-proportional   A type of font that has the same amount of space between each character instead of spacing characters in a more eye-pleasing manner.

parse   The practice of looking for character strings inside a field in a table.

PC (personal computer)   While the desktop computers used by individuals all qualify as personal computers, the PC, sometimes called the IBM or IBM-compatible personal computer, is characterized by using the operating system DOS. Hence it is sometimes called the DOS-based PC.

PCC (Postal Customer Councils)   Customer support groups made up of postal employees and mailers.

POSTNET   This is a barcode containing the zip or zip+4 code.

query   A request to a database to find and return a group of records that all meet a set of criteria defined in the query.

RAM (Random Access Memory)   See *memory*.

record   The space allocated within a relational database table to store all of the attributes about one entity.

relational database   A database that organizes information into tables so that every entity is stored in a separate table. Information in the tables can be tied together, or related, based only on the values within the tables, creating a relational database.

residual mail   Non-qualifying pieces (residual mail) are pieces of mail included in a presort mailing that do not meet the standards to qualify for a postage discount.

sans-serif   A font used in typesetting. See also *font*.

SIC Codes   Standard Industrial Classification codes used by the government to classify businesses.

SIMM (Single In-line Memory Modules)   A card with memory for installation in PCs.

slush code   An error code generated during an attempt to look up a zip+4 code for an address which corresponds to a list of explanations as to why the zip+4 look-up was not successful for that address.

SMP   Sample mailing piece.

SQL (Structured Query Language)   A language recognized by many databases that is used to perform operations with the database such as adding, updating, deleting, and selecting records.

table   The space within a relational database that is used to store all of the information about a single entity.

TPS (Telephone Preference Service)   A service offered by the Direct Marketing Association to consumers who do not wish to have their phone numbers distributed. See also *MPS*.

truncate   The practice of some computer programs to cut off the remaining portion of a field when the field is longer than the program is prepared to handle.

USPS   United States Postal Service.

wide area barcoding   A POSTNET barcode can be placed above or below an address instead of just at the bottom right hand side of an envelope.

WYSIWYG (what-you-see-is-what-you-get)   The practice of showing on the computer screen what will actually print on the paper is WYSIWYG (pronounced "whiz-ee-wig").

zip code (Zoning Improvement Plan Code)   A 5-digit numeric code identifying the delivery area.

zip+4   A 9-digit address code in the format xxxxx-xxxx that identifies each delivery address.

Index

*Boldface page numbers refer to art

***Boldface** page numbers refer to art

*****Boldface** page numbers refer to art

M

Macintosh computers, 83

magazines, 175-176

Mail Manager 2000, 107

mail merge (*see* merge operations)

Mail Order Digest Monthly, 149

Mail Order Moonlighting, 65

Mail Piece Quality Control (MPQC) course, 34

Mail Pouch, 58-60, 155

Mail Preference Service (MPS), 138

mail-order business of your own, 166-167

MailCom Conference, 188

Mailer's Guide, 46

Mailer's Review, 95, 109, 167

mailing list compilation and use (*see also* databases), 57-58, 107-109

  abuses to mailing lists, 79-81

  backup copies, 81

  buying, questions to ask, 63-65

  change-of-address, 135, **136**

  cleaning the list, 58, 78-79, 103-104

  compiled lists, 62-63

  data entry, 57, 98-**100**

  database design (*see* databases)

  designing a list, 57

  encrypting mailing list data, 80

  exporting data, 100

  form letters, 101

  importing data, 100

  merge operations, 58, 79, 101, 128-131, **129-130**

  ownership rights, 77-78

  per/M abbreviation, 77

  postage cost reduction, 134-135

  purge operations, 58, 79, 101, 128-131, **129-130**

  reformatting software, 102

  renting lists, 63-65, 70-71

  reports from list data, 57

  response lists, 62-63

  seeding or salting a list, 79

  soft costs reduction, 135-136

  sorting the list, 57, 102

  Standard Industrial Classification (SIC) codes, 78

  stolen lists, 79-81

  testing lists, 78-79

mailing service (*see also* letter shop), 66

MailMiser Plus, 107

maintaining mailing lists (*see* mailing lists)

MapLinx, 154-**155**, 157

mapping, market mapping, 155-157

Market Intelligence Research Corp., 157

marketing (*see also* advertising; designing mailing pieces that sell), 65-66

  asking for the sale, 148

  break-even point analysis, 139-**140**

  buying a customer, 140-141

  copywriting tips and techniques, 145-148

  customers, client's customer base, 142-143

  databased marketing, 131, 150-152

  direct mail advantages, 136-139

  direct marketing, 149-150

  "expert approach," 148

  getting mail read, 143-145

  "handwritten" fonts, 144-**145**

  Letter Perfect Information Services and Wayne Stoler, 152-153

  mapping, market mapping, 155-157

  Market Intelligence Research Corp., 157

  net profit per order, 139

  postage cost-reduction to business, 134-135

  presort houses, 149

  rating customers, **141**-142

  regional demographics, 154-157

  samples offers, 36, 152

  soft cost-reduction to business, 135-136

  statistics used in mailing, 145

  targeting an audience, 142

  TechImages Inc. and A.G. Pitsilos, 153-154

  twelve tactics for successful direct mail campaign, 139

  why customers should hire you, 139

Marketing Dimensions, 131-133

McCartney, Jim, 30, 161-164

McCartney, Michelle, 161-164

Melissa Software, 95-96

Melissa, Ray, 95-96

memory capacity, computers, 85

merge operations, 58, 79, 101, 128-131, **129-130**

Metalproducts Engineering, 73

Microsoft, 133

Miller, Jack, 166

modems, 88

monitors, computer, 84

Montgomery Ward, 166

Monthly Product Announcement, 156

mouse, 97

multimedia PC (MPC), 88-89

MyAdvancedLabelDesigner, 165

MyInvoices, 110

MySoftware, 110, 165

N

Nation's Business, 7

National Address Information Center (NAIC), 45, 103, 104

National Five-Digit Zip Code and Post Office Directory, 46

National Postal Forum, 188

Neal, Mollie, 150

need for mail list services, 1-4, 134

*****Boldface** page numbers refer to art

About the Author

As Los Angeles Bureau Chief for the award-winning Newsbytes News Network, Linda Rohrbough reports daily on computer news events in Southern California and around the world. When she isn't reporting, Linda is writing articles or helping small business owners with, you guessed it, computers. She teaches university courses on computer use and has also hosted a late-night, computer-oriented radio show.

In April 1993, Linda received the computer industry's highest honor, the Computer Press Association Best Online Publication Award, for her work with Newsbytes News Network.

Linda lives in Van Nuys, California, with her husband Mark and her two daughters, Jessica and Margaret.